THE LANGUAGE OF PAINTING

THE LANGUAGE OF PAINTING

BY

CHARLES JOHNSON, M.A.

Official Lecturer, National Gallery, London

CAMBRIDGE
AT THE UNIVERSITY PRESS
1949

PUBLISHED BY
THE SYNDICS OF THE CAMBRIDGE UNIVERSITY PRESS
London Office: Bentley House, N.W.1
American Branch: New York
Agents for Canada, India, and Pakistan: Macmillan

Printed in Great Britain at the University Press, Cambridge
(Brooke Crutchley, University Printer)

PREFACE

As this book was begun a number of years ago and has gradually developed from the study of paintings and the practice of defining their character, it is not possible to name everyone to whom it is indebted. Some of those to whom it owes most are no longer alive. Others have unconsciously contributed to it in casual conversations, now perhaps remembered only for the ideas that sprang from them. But there are four whom I wish here to thank individually: Sir Kenneth Clark, whose constructive criticism led to important changes in the first four chapters; Miss S. M. M. Furness, who, after careful reading, suggested many valuable improvements, especially in the two chapters on light (XIX and XX); Mr F. I. G. Rawlins, who explained to me the scientific causes of colour, but is by no means responsible for my aesthetic speculations on that subject; and Mr H. Ruhemann, on whose patient expositions concerning details of technique the practical portions of Chapters XXIV and XXV are mainly based.

C. W. H. J.

ABBREVIATIONS

B.M.	British Museum, London, W.C.1
Courtauld Institute	Courtauld Institute of Art, 20 Portman Square, London, W.1
Louvre	Le Musée du Louvre, Paris
N.G.	National Gallery, Trafalgar Square, London, W.C.2
N.P.G.	National Portrait Gallery, St Martin's Place, London, W.C.2
Prado	Museo del Prado, Madrid
T.G.	Tate Gallery, Millbank, London, S.W.1
Uffizi	Uffizi Gallery, Florence
V. and A.	Victoria and Albert Museum, London, S.W.7
Wallace	Wallace Collection, Manchester Square, London, W.1

When only a town is mentioned the reference is to the principal museum or gallery in that town.

Note: In the text, figures etc. in parentheses following the title of a picture refer to the catalogue number and, when not preceded by the name of any gallery, to the catalogue number of the National Gallery, London.

The dates of the births and deaths of painters are given in the Index.

The dates on the illustrations at the end of the book refer to the dates or probable approximate dates at which the pictures were painted.

CONTENTS

LIST OF PLATES

CHAPTER I

INTRODUCTION

PAINTING is one means of expressing emotions and ideas. It may thus be called a language, as in the title of this book, which is concerned both with what painting expresses and with how it is expressed. The book's aim is: first, to consider what constitutes a good picture, and secondly to analyse the methods of attaining pictorial coherence. Most of the examples are from the National Gallery, which represents European painting fairly comprehensively from about 1250 to about 1890; but I also discuss some problems peculiar to the twentieth century.

The book is based on lectures given to audiences, who knew something about painting and wanted to know more. It concerns the painter's temperament, manner of seeing and manner of giving his vision clarity. In such an account some clumsiness is inevitable. Thus I define, as though it had been conscious, much in the painter's methods that was in fact instinctive; but if, by this means, the reader is led to absorb the elements of a design without conscious analysis, the book will have served its main purpose.

Painting has recently become, more than ever before, the subject of conflicting theories. We prefer generalizing about pictures to painting them; and those who do paint them are often hindered by too strict an adherence to one or the other of the many 'isms'.

Writers on aesthetics tend to sum up what they regard as the only merits of every type of picture in a single word or phrase, such as 'architectonic value' or 'significant form'. Such phrases are apt either to narrow the field of appreciation, or else to claim a preciseness of meaning more pretended than real. If a single term for pictorial merit *must* be used, I should prefer the old word 'beauty', just because it is as indefinable as other fundamental abstractions such as 'goodness'. In distinction from 'prettiness', the superficially pleasing, 'beauty' should imply what is finally satisfying. The beauty of a painting and that of a sunset are not identical, but are sufficiently analogous to justify the use of the same word. Beauty in this broad sense is applicable to widely differing artistic achievements.

This book aims at a balanced standard and at giving equal importance to the leading aspects of painting. These aspects may conveniently be divided into three: (i) the expression of emotion; (ii) vision; (iii) obedience to material conditions.

The three aspects must co-operate. Material and vision must not be forgotten in the mere heat of emotional impulse; feeling and quality of paint must not be disregarded merely in order to record something seen; and the expression of an emotion aroused through the eyes must not be sacrificed to pigment however delightful to the senses, or to a scheme of decoration however appropriate to its destined setting.

The word 'emotion', being another fundamental term, is indefinable. To be an artist means not merely to experience, but to *express* emotion, that is to communicate it in comprehensible form. The artist under discussion, the painter, expresses his emotion by means of what he sees and by means of paint, brushes, canvas, etc. In turn these limiting conditions, vision and the use of materials, determine both what emotions he expresses and his method of expressing them. Vision and what it involves is the topic of Chapter III. The use of materials is discussed in detail in Chapters XXIV and XXV and more generally in Chapter IV, which also deals with the question of the picture's destination.

Artistic creation, then, depends first upon emotional impulse; but this impulse demands for its expression the co-operation of the intellect also. A work of art can be born only out of the union of emotion with intellect. In particular cases the emotional aspect of its origin may be more conspicuous than the intellectual aspect and vice versa. But without emotion art is lifeless; without intellect it is shapeless. Van Gogh may seem actuated by warm impulse alone; but in his greatest works, such as the *Sunflowers* (T.G. 3863) there is a reason, albeit an instinctive reason, for every stroke of his palette knife. Conversely Piero della Francesca or, in his later paintings, Nicolas Poussin may at first seem governed exclusively by their intellectual force; but more intimate insight will reveal the deep feelings which this force controls and expresses. Experience, moreover, proves that some of the deepest feelings in painting, as in other arts, can be expressed only by the use of the severest intellectual control (see also p. 161).

When the painter's emotions are fully expressed, he and the man who looks at his picture are potentially *en rapport*. The spectator is then in a position to experience some of the painter's emotions, but not all. Some belong to the artist only as creator; others to the spectator as recipient; but completeness of expression takes place only when those emotions that the painter wishes to express have been fully communicated.

Since the artist's emotions are affected by his personality and environment, knowledge of all these matters is relevant to appreciation. It is impossible fully to appreciate a picture in terms of 'pure aesthetics', regardless of its place in history. Painting is the outcome of an attitude towards life, and the understanding of it demands the study of contemporary events and ideas; but these matters are dealt with only incidentally in this book, which is intended as a supplement to historical and biographical reading.

It may seem a platitude, but it needs to be reiterated, that painting expresses emotion through its appeal to the eye. However profound the emotion may be that the painter desires to express, unless its origin is visual or has directly inspired a visual image, his attempt to express it pictorially will be worthless. Further, it is the special province of painting to express such emotions as can be expressed only by visual means.

This is by no means a plea for literal representation. Every good picture has some likeness and some unlikeness to natural appearances. There is nothing contradictory about this, since two things can be like in one respect, and unlike in another—like for instance in colour and unlike in shape. According to the artist's preference the likeness will vary in kind and in degree; some pictures will resemble appearances more closely than others; but none can be mere mirrors and none can be creations independent of visual experience. What kind of resemblance to appearance is desirable and why, and what kind is undesirable, is discussed in Chapter VI and, in more detail, in Chapters VII, VIII, XVI and XIX. Chapters IX and X are concerned with distortion and abstraction, that is with non-representation.

Since the language of painting is addressed to the eye, the writer on painting is at best an imperfect interpreter, a clumsy translator from the visual into the verbal. He can analyse the *means of expression* and such analysis is the main topic of this book. But the *emotion itself* he must leave to the painter's own visual eloquence. He can only hint vaguely at its general character, gay or grave, agitated or calm. For pictures, like music, express clearly perceptible, but verbally indefinable, blends of feeling.

In Chapters XII, XIII and XIV I attempt this impossible feat by means of what might be called emotional descriptions, as distinct from the analytical descriptions of Chapters XXVI and XXVII. In Chapters II, III, IX and X, I touch upon another problem, more fully discussed in the last three chapters, the question of what emotions are worth expressing. Here aesthetics border on ethics. Some emotions are more worth expressing than others. Sincerity in experiencing them and skill in expressing them are not enough. Originality, in the sense of presenting an experience in a new light, is desirable; but the experience is more worth communi-cating the more widely it is capable of being shared. The conscious cult of originality and self-expression is non-productive. Great artists do not set out to express themselves. An inner urge drives them to do so, as it were incidentally, in the course of pursuing their conscious aims.

So far I have said nothing about 'design', a word which I use in an unusually wide sense. Without attempting a single definition, some of the senses in which I use it are indicated here, others in Chapter v, and particular methods of design in Chapters xv, xvii, xviii, xx, xxii and xxiii.

I regard design as the principal, though not the only means of pictorial expression. Full expression demands complete clarity. The proper use of materials is another such means; and attention to one set of material conditions, viz. the destination of the picture, is one of the aspects of design.

Secondly, design includes the idea of *intention* or purpose. It implies that the painter does what he means to do and leaves nothing to accident. In the design his intentions, conscious, partly conscious or wholly instinctive, are fully carried out.

Thirdly, I use it to cover all methods of giving a picture unity and coherence. By means of design the parts are related to the whole. It might almost be regarded as synonymous with arrangement, except that arrangement suggests too con-sciously calculated a process. The conception of creating *order* from chaos is included in this conception of design.

In my phraseology *pattern* and *composition* are subdivisions of design. The word 'pattern' is often used in a narrower sense to mean the *repetition* of flat shapes. For this I use the plural form 'patterns'. By the singular form 'pattern' I mean something wider than this, namely the design of the picture regarded as something flat, the relation of lines, tones and colours and of areas (full or empty) upon the picture plane itself, i.e. the *picture area*, which coincides with the normally vertical plane of the canvas or panel, etc. By composition I mean the design as conceived in *three dimensions*, the grouping and spacing of volumes (full or empty) in relation to each other and to the ground plane, within what I call the *picture-volume*. Composition is impossible without the realistic power of representing solid objects as existing in space, whereas in theory at least pattern might be purely non-representational. The picture-area exists and is a conditioning factor in all pictures. The picture-volume does not exist, but is merely something represented in pictures of one particular type.

Another aspect of design is implied by my use of the word 'decoration'. By decoration, as applied to a picture, I mean its relation to its architectural setting. All the above definitions include the word 'relation'. Indeed, the relation of one thing to another is necessarily involved in all aspects of design.

The sense in which I use the word 'design' almost coincides with that in which other writers use the word 'form'. 'Form' might seem to be a better word, as being applicable to other types of art, architecture, sculpture, pottery, etc. Also in the case of a picture, the word 'form' would mean, not merely the organization of shapes upon its surface, but also—as the word 'design' does not—the texture of that surface. On the other hand 'design' has the advantage over 'form' in implying the picture's human origin and purpose. Also, in discussing how objects are represented in pictures, I use the word 'form' for the solid shapes of the said objects. In analysing the picture, therefore, I prefer to keep to the word 'design'.

Many particular methods of designing pictures can be analysed, but must never be regarded as rules or laws. Their rightness for the purpose in hand is an instinctive matter for the eye to decide. As Roger Fry wrote in a lecture on 'Sensibility', a work of art 'will perpetually approximate to a law and perpetually vary from it'. According to academic rules the design of a picture may be perfect; but if it carries no conviction, as something in the fullest sense of the word *seen*, the result is valueless. And, since the vision of the mind's eye is partly the result of the normal vision of the bodily eye (however legitimately distorted for emotional or other reasons), a book about painting cannot altogether ignore the world of actuality and of appearances, or 'Nature' as I call it and as Ruskin did. Thus Chapter XIX on the 'Rendering of Light' deals with actual appearances as well as with ways of representing them, and Chapter XXI with the optics of 'Colour' in preparation for the two chapters on its use in pictures. In this book a chapter on some branch of representation usually precedes a chapter on the allied branch of design. For instance 'Perspective' is treated before 'Design in three Dimensions'.

The purpose of painting is not mere representation; but good painting does depend upon the knowledge of appearances. The creation of a masterpiece, even a masterpiece of 'Abstract Art', is not the arbitrary putting together of shapes and colours never seen before, but the *invention*, that is the discovery and selection, in some cases the rearrangement or even conscious distortion, of such natural appearances as suit the painter's purpose. Invention in its original Latin sense means *discovery*, and is therefore the process leading from vision to design.

This leads to the old question of the connexion between beauty and truth. To regard imitation of appearance as the only criterion of painting is to cut oneself off from enjoying some of the best pictures, ancient and modern. Yet a connexion between beauty and truth certainly exists.

The statement that 'Beauty is truth, truth beauty' belongs to poetry, not to reasoned argument. 'Beauty is truth enjoyed' has been suggested as a substitute. The merit of a work of art depends, not on the truth of the artist's statement, but on his enjoyment of that truth. Enjoyment, however, is only one of the emotions. Great art includes the expression of the tragic and the painful by means of contrast, harshness, discord and even, in one sense of the word, ugliness. For ugliness is an ambiguous term. In one of its senses ugliness is indispensable to expression, a subdivision of beauty. In its other sense it is the contrary of beauty and incompatible with artistic merit. Among the many causes of ugliness in the bad sense are lack of emotion, failure to express emotion and failure to extract order from chaos (see also Chapters IX, X, XXIX and XXX).

This leads to a further amendment: 'Beauty is truth emotionally experienced.' But since expression is also a requisite, even this is not enough. I suggest: 'The merit of a work of art depends on truth emotionally experienced and expressed in language inspired by the medium.'

This formula, although not completely comprehensive, has two advantages. It denies the notion that beauty can be created independently of truth and implies that artistic creation is an act of *invention* or *discovery*. It also denies the notion that the representation of appearances in itself constitutes a work of art. The aim of painting is not representation, but the satisfaction of the intellect and emotions through the eye. Realistic representation is merely a means towards that end, though, in its widest application, an indispensable means. It is a power that can be wielded for good or ill. The moment it becomes an end in itself the picture has ceased to be a work of art.

CHAPTER II

PAINTERS AND THE PUBLIC

PEOPLE visit galleries, exhibitions and collections of pictures for a great variety of reasons. There is the professional artist or art historian. There is the casual visitor, who drops in from having nothing better to do. Then there are those who return again and again to see old favourites and utter the formula: 'I don't know anything about pictures, but I know what I like.' This phrase is laughed at, but deserves more respect than the timid ejaculation: 'This is considered a good picture.' Compared with such an admission of taste at second-hand, the most obstinate prejudice is worthy of respect. For prejudice is at least alive. The most stimulating critics, such as Ruskin and Fry, have often been the most prejudiced.

Yet there are dangers in trusting too much to first impressions. With pictures, as with acquaintances, those who never alter their likes and dislikes may easily be missing opportunities. The greatest masterpieces, to be fully appreciated, must be looked at hundreds of times; and only the greatest can stand this test. In fact repeated study of masterpieces is the only valid ground for authority on matters of taste.

Lovers of painting acquire the habit of actively perceiving and passively absorbing. The rate of absorption varies greatly; it depends partly on the picture itself, its subtlety or obviousness, but more on the aptitude and training of the spectator.

The first habit to acquire is that of completely concentrating on one picture at a time and mentally isolating it from its surroundings. The untrained rush from picture to picture and confuse the impression of what is before them with what they have just seen and what they are about to see. Beginners do well to go slow at first. Attending lectures in galleries has the advantage of tying the visitor down to the contemplation of twelve pictures only (or in extreme cases three) per hour.

This slowness is only a means towards an end. The student will learn to dismiss bad art quickly; to a good painting he will return again and again; but whether each gaze be prolonged or brief will depend on his temperament and the particular purpose of his study. One day he may consciously and actively examine the design or the technique of a picture; another day he may subconsciously and passively drink in what it has to express.

There are similar active and passive ways of appreciating music. Subject to some simple logical precautions, music and painting may be profitably compared. Of course they are not identical. Similarity is one thing; identity another. Nor do such words as 'rhythm, colour, and tone' mean the same thing when applied to the two arts. There are numerous respects, too obvious to need defining, in which the two arts differ. But there are also some in which they are alike: they both derive from, and consequently appeal to, emotional experience through the senses; and they both involve alternations between the expected and the unexpected, between repetition and contrast; pattern is analogous to melody and composition to harmony (see also pp. 23, 72, 75 and 76).

A comparison between the *appreciation* of the two arts is also possible within similar limits. Since music takes place in time and painting in space, there can be no analogy between the *rates* of their absorption. But the *spirit* in which they may be absorbed has points of similarity. Apart from more consciously analytical methods, much enjoyment may be gained from listening to music alertly and from gazing at pictures intently, while receptively and passively absorbing what each art has to say.

So long as moods are not mistaken for judgements, there are sometimes advantages in indulging in a mood. Just as one day Brahms's music meets an emotional need and another day nothing later than Bach will satisfy, so, apart from their relative merits, there may be an urge one day to inhale excitement from Rubens and another day to absorb contentment from Raphael.

Moreover, music and painting—and indeed all the arts—are subject to the same test of being heard or seen in repetition. What is shallow will quickly pall if heard or seen too often. The greatest music requires to be heard, just as the greatest painting requires to be seen, many times. It is true that even the greatest examples of both arts, too often repeated, may temporarily lose their meaning; but after a requisite interval the enjoyment of them will return.

To know what will last requires experience. But even trained opinions should never be swallowed uncritically. Everyone must reserve a right to his own preferences. Whatever the stage of his knowledge, he will still feel more affection for one painter, one nationality, one period than for another. But his range of enjoyment will be wider if he can admire one picture without liking it, and like another, while recognizing its weaknesses.

It is by no means easy to discriminate between the good and the bad in contemporary art. This raises the question of the reasons for which pictures are painted. The primary reason is the painter's creative impulse. But in addition, economic factors affect him. If patrons will buy, painters will produce. Demand creates supply; supply but rarely creates demand.

The buyer pays to have a picture painted for a number of different reasons: he may wish by its means to inculcate a religious or political creed; he may wish to increase his worldly prestige; he may have a personal liking for the painter as a man; or he may value a picture for itself, for its intrinsic beauty, either in connexion with, or apart from, its place on his wall; lastly, he may be actuated by fashion, snobbery or commercial speculation. With the buyer's unworthy motives the painter should have no concern; but he should consult his legitimate demands.

In his sixth discourse Reynolds says: 'It is by being conversant with the inventions of others that we learn how to invent.' This does not mean that each new masterpiece should be a *pastiche* of earlier masterpieces, but merely that a painter's originality is helped by a knowledge of his predecessor's work. Even deliberate imitation may be educative at first. Raphael trained himself by slavish repetitions of Perugino, and even Cézanne by closely imitating Daumier, Courbet and Pissarro. Real originality is often most apparent when the debt to previous art is greatest. Likenesses merely emphasize differences.

The disappearance in modern times of regular patronage tempts a painter either to become a recluse, working only for his own enjoyment, or to go to the other extreme of painting solely to catch the public eye. This means striving by some fashionable insincerity, sentimental, melodramatic, superficially dexterous or merely loud and violent, to arouse an emotion unfelt by the artist. Compared with this the work of the recluse is preferable because it is at least sincere. But the recluse too has his foibles. No doubt he is right in desiring the public to be more patient and sympathetic, in desiring it not to condemn as obscure all unfamiliar forms of expression. But the painter on his side should express something bigger than private idiosyncrasies and with as much clarity as is consistent with sincerity.

It is sometimes thought that painters of genius have always met with neglect; but in fact this has become frequent only since the early nineteenth century. Until then most great painters were admired during their lifetime; recognized, if not always promptly paid, by kings, cardinals, merchants and bankers; and not a few, such as Titian and Rubens, were prosperous and widely renowned long before they died. In the seventeenth century (especially in Holland), taste became less cultivated and more capricious than before; but Rembrandt was the most fashionable portrait painter of Amsterdam, until exceptional circumstances brought about his bankruptcy; his final poverty was shared by most Dutch painters who lived through the English wars of the 1660's.

In the eighteenth century more adaptability to fashion was necessary to success. Yet Watteau's poverty would have ceased if he had lived longer; Wilson could have prevented his, if he had kept up portraiture as a profession and landscape merely as a hobby. It was only after the French Revolution and still more after the Industrial Revolution that the position of a painter of genius and small means became precarious. Corot attained wealth by virtually deserting his own standards. Turner in his final phase was despised by his previous admirers; Constable received little honour in his own country; Cézanne was mistaken for an incompetent impressionist.

Yet these painters were expressing experiences that a more patient public might have shared, not bypaths of emotion peculiar to themselves. But the ultimate recognition of their works as masterpieces arose from their lasting appeal to a wide public.

Few critics are able to judge their contemporaries in perspective, shrewd enough to see through what is shoddy or unprejudiced enough to bring hidden worth to light. One hindrance is the vast amount of mediocre work that has to be examined before the discovery of a single masterpiece. Another is the difficulty of escaping from the influence of fashion either to follow it or to react from it. Sheer proximity is a third obstacle. While painters are still engaged on a picture, they usually alternate between exaggerated notions of its merits and of its defects; if they ever judge their own work justly, it is only after the lapse of three-quarters of a lifetime. Critics, who lose more by lack of insight into the painter's mind than they gain by detachment from it, often take even longer to reach an objective estimate.

These difficulties are no excuse for ignoring contemporary art. We should try to understand new themes and new modes of expression. But in spite of every effort to be fair, the fact remains: we can be much more certain about the precise merit of works of the past than of the ultimate position of a painter of to-day. Even regarding the past, fashions in taste alter. Piero della Francesca and El Greco, both beloved of the twentieth century, were little esteemed in the nineteenth. We now feel that nothing could alter their position. Is this confidence justified? Can we prophesy? Probably not, if the question concerns this or that aim in painting. No one can tell what will be the fashionable mood in 1979. But the future judgement not upon a painter's *aim*, but upon his achievement of that aim, will probably confirm a reputation once established. Thus now or in 1979, a student of pictures might take no pleasure in the style, say, of Correggio, but could not deny his power in achieving what he sought to achieve.

All great painters put fidelity to their inner vision first and public recognition second. Yet they know that their vision has value for the public. They crave for legitimate admiration as every artist must. They paint, as Reynolds would have said, not for their own age but for posterity. They seek, that is, to satisfy, not merely to excite, contemporary taste. Originality such as theirs, not sought for its own sake, but based on conviction, comes ultimately to lead taste as distinct from being led by it. If the vision is of a kind to be shared, the public will in the end be capable of sharing it (see also pp. 170-2).

Can the gap in time between the creation of an original masterpiece and its recognition be avoided? On the one hand the painter can help by cultivating clarity of statement. On the other hand the public can help by patient sympathy, open-mindedness, and avoidance alike of hasty acceptance and hasty condemnation. The aims of the artist must first be fathomed; then the work of art must be judged partly from the merits of the aims themselves, and partly from the artist's success or failure in carrying them out.

CHAPTER III

VISION AND INSPIRATION

MANY pictures fail because vision has not been the painter's inspiration. He has had some sermon to preach, some theory of aesthetics to demonstrate, some technical trick to display and these ulterior motives have prevented him from seeing his subject with his mind's eye.

This is why most propagandist art is bad, though not to be condemned merely for being propagandist. There are rare cases, especially in Goya's and Daumier's work, in which propaganda instead of hindering vision, has helped the artist to see.

The relation of his vision to the world of appearances varies with the temperament of the artist. If the relation is close, it is convenient to call his art visual, and, if not so close, to call it visionary. But, in any case, the painter feels and even reasons in terms of what he sees. This consideration removes much of the difficulty of deciding how far a given painter's aims were conscious or unconscious. No doubt there are different degrees of consciousness of aim according to the temperament of the particular painter. Raphael seems to have been conscious and deliberate, Giorgione to have been comparatively instinctive. The greatness of each depended on his eye. Since a painter's reasoning power is concerned with what he sees, it has nothing to do with his skill in using words. Whether he has verbal skill or not is an accident, independent of the merit of his art. Delacroix, whose emotions when painting were not always under sufficient intellectual control, could speak and write eloquently about painting. Turner, whose work proves the consummate power of his brain, was a confused talker and writer, who uttered only one profound dictum upon art—and that scarcely explicit: 'Well, painting is a rum thing!'

The power of seeing decides both the emotional and the intellectual elements in painting. What he sees (whether outside him or in visions) gives the artist his primary impulse. His prevision of what the picture will ultimately look like also determines the reasoned and formal qualities of his work. With this purpose always in view he creates order out of chaos. The work of the greatest artists has a completeness and rightness, satisfying to the reason through its appeal to the eye.

How this organic completeness is reached will vary in different cases. Inspiration, the emotion inciting the artist to create, may come to him suddenly or gradually.

Its force may at first be too disturbing for immediate and clear expression. The moment of greatest heat may not coincide in time with the act of communication; for this act requires a clear head. The head must be clear, but not cold. In giving his emotion expression the artist must remember completely what the emotion was, in all its intensity. Any failure to do so will result in dullness or confusion or both. At the same time the memory of the emotion may become clearer during the process of painting the picture.

Some painters (Tintoretto in one of his moods was one of them) seem to have seen their works complete in their mind's eye before their brush touched the canvas. Others achieved completeness more gradually. Titian was always plunging into difficulties and then extricating himself from them. For instance in *Bacchus and Ariadne* [(35),[1] Pl. 36] among other changes he altered Bacchus's right foot three times. But its final position has the air of utter spontaneity. Similarly Beethoven thought of an air, hammered at it, altered it again and again, until the final tune he decided upon seems as if it must have come straight out of his head. If genius consists in taking infinite pains, it also consists in appearing to take no pains at all.

Titian's alterations of *Bacchus and Ariadne* were inspired. There is another type of alteration which is the reverse of inspired. In old fashioned art-schools students, finding the foreground of their compositions empty, were recommended to fill it with an Oriental jar. Such alterations of course are useless. They prove that the student never saw anything in his mind's eye at all, but merely composed according to one rule, and then by another rule got out of a difficulty. Great painters never compose by rule. Writers on art, explaining their works afterwards, may talk as if they did—but the artist himself is governed, not by rule, but by vision. Each alteration he makes is not an afterthought or an addition, but in some mystical sense an uncovering or clarification of the vision that first came to him.

This distinction may seem fanciful. 'Surely' it will be said, 'the mere fact that Titian altered his pictures proves that his vision was not complete in the first instance. I can see no difference between his alterations and the introduction of the jar, except the difference between skill and the lack of it. How can you prove the existence of what you call inspiration?'

To this I can only reply that it cannot be proved any more than a religious conviction can be proved. The difference is a difference of spirit. In the one case

[1] Figures etc. in parentheses indicate the owner or the catalogue number of the National Gallery, London.

the student says: 'How can I get myself out of this muddle?' In the other the master says: 'I thought I had put down what I saw; but I have not yet got it quite right; let me feel back to my vision and realize it more completely.' Then, in searching to recover his vision, he sees that this figure is not part of it and must be eliminated or that object, which he had overlooked, *is* part of it and must be included. What an artist sees with the mind's eye will probably be an unconscious selection, rearrangement or distortion of what he has seen in other pictures or in Nature or in both (see Chapter VI); it will also depend on his knowledge of his medium and of where the picture is to be placed (see Chapter IV); but in any case there is an essential relation between *inspiration* (the often painful excitement that drives a man to paint) and *vision* in the completest sense of the word, not merely optical perception, but the deeply felt and intelligent comprehension and co-ordination of what is before the mind's eye.

This insistence upon vision implies that a picture must be more than a mere decoration. It excludes one type of art, which I do not condemn, but which I refuse to describe as pictorial. There exist paintings consisting of flat squares or rectangles of different colours, e.g. a large blue square beside a small yellow square and a middle-sized red square. The result may be pleasing to the eye and a highly suitable decoration to the right type of room; but such objects express no visual experience.

A picture, in whatever degree it be realistic or non-realistic, should, I believe, satisfy the eye not only by its own content, but also by its derivation from the artist's visual experience, and its appeal to the visual experience of the spectator. It should record and call forth an image, often perhaps beheld before, or a combination of images each in themselves familiar, but never before presented with so fresh and compelling an air of discovery. This alone can hold the spectator's ever returning attention and feed the requirements of his imagination.

CHAPTER IV

DECORATIVE AND TECHNICAL LIMITATIONS

Two other considerations essential to a masterpiece have now to be considered: the decorative purpose of the picture and the limitations imposed by the medium. The desire to paint springs from a wish, not only to express what one has seen, but also to beautify a certain space on wall, panel or canvas, and to bring out to the full the qualities of which the pigment, medium and brush are capable.

Foreknowledge of the destination of a picture will profoundly affect the painter's first mental image of his work. He will welcome the limitation that forces him to visualize beforehand the shapes and colours suitable to the particular setting. Painters commissioned to decorate churches had many advantages. So much space was allotted to a fresco or series of frescoes; architectural divisions helped to determine the shape, size and position of each design. The problem of filling spaces of an awkward shape was a stimulus to invention. With altarpieces on panel or canvas the artist might be given a freer hand; but architectural conditions were still a factor in determining shapes suitable to the setting and colours appropriate to the lighting. The happiest inventions often arose out of these limitations. Painting has always thriven as the servant of architecture.

A painter is fortunate who is commissioned to decorate a particular space, whether in a church, castle, town-hall or private house. He is almost as fortunate, if he can foresee within a little a purchaser for his picture and the type of room in which it will hang. In the seventeenth century the Dutch painters of *genre* pictures could do so. They were supplying a known demand and could guess something about the future setting of their work, the kind of light it would be placed in and the kind of room it would decorate. This applies to Vermeer's *Lady Standing at the Virginals* [(1383), Pl. 64].

The painter, who designs without knowledge of his picture's future, is handicapped, but may have compensating advantages. Some have even preferred the liberty that it gives to design their work independently of any known destination. Rembrandt for instance, in such portraits as that of *Himself at 34* [(672), Pl. 60], seems to have begun by carefully rendering some detail (in this case his right eye), from which he worked outwards with increasing breadth and to have decided at last on the shape of the frame. Velazquez also worked from his subject outwards, and, refusing to imprison his vision in a predetermined frame, even sewed additional strips of canvas in the course of completing a design. Similarly Rubens appears to have begun his landscapes by painting some portion as the nucleus of interest, to which he made additions, sometimes nearly a decade later; thus the distant views in the *Landscape with a Shepherd* (2924) and the *Watering Place* (4805) are almost identical and belong to about 1616, but the foreground and right-hand portion of the *Watering Place* is in the style of the middle 1620's.

Several nineteenth-century painters designed on a similar principle, which might be called *decorative impressionism* (in distinction from optical impressionism). Partly Hokusai's woodcuts and partly perhaps the results of the camera suggested to them the decorative possibilities of unexpected juxtapositions of foreground and background. Degas in *La Plage* [(T.G. 3247), Pl. 76] seems to have been struck first by the quaint natural pattern made by the bathing dress in relation to the near and far figures, and to have developed the shape of his picture from this effect. Renoir in *Les Parapluies* [(3268), Pl. 80] may have had a similar initial impression of umbrellas and ladies in stiff dresses, although differences of technique and of the fashions of the clothes both prove that the picture was partly painted in 1879 and partly in about 1883. Such methods of design gave scope for originality; but whereas the earlier artist adapted his picture to its destination, the onus now fell on the owner to adapt the room to fit the picture.

The question of brushes, paints and media (the subject of Chapters XXIV and XXV) is even more important. Painting in its purely physical aspect consists in using a brush (large or small, soft or stiff) dipping it in paint (of one consistency or another) mingled with a medium (liquid or viscous) and applying the same to a surface (smooth or rough).

Now there are some effects that the brush will produce with ease, and others only attained at the cost of labour unjustified by the result. Shapely, lightly applied brush-strokes are a pleasure to the eye. Correspondingly, paint applied in a heavy, or in a fussily meticulous, manner results in a loss of vitality. The painter should give such life to his execution as is reconcilable with fidelity to his vision, and steer clear between the superficially fluent and the mechanically laboured manner. The painting of trees in three landscapes illustrates this: Hobbema in *Brederode Castle* (831) has attempted so much accuracy in the foliage that the brush strokes lack freshness; conversely, Gainsborough in *The Market Cart* (80) has sacrificed accuracy to fluency of brushwork; the happy mean between these extremes is attained by the combination of accuracy with ease in the bare trees of Turner's *Frosty Morning* [(492), Pl. 72].

Display of brush-work is not a necessary characteristic of good painting. Its suitability or otherwise depends on the purpose in view. Van Eyck deliberately concealed his brush-strokes, in order to produce a smooth, minute finish. But the joy of wielding the brush is one reason for wanting to paint and a legitimate one, provided dexterity is subservient to other purposes. Technical and manual skill in painting resembles verbal skill in speech or writing. It should not be an end in itself, but a means towards the end of attaining expression.

Similarly, economy of manual labour is a virtue, if its purpose be the breadth of treatment necessary to large decorative paintings. When Veronese painted the *Family of Darius before Alexander* [(294), Pls. 45–7] he might have taken as his motto: 'Never use two brush-strokes where one will produce a better effect at a distance.' But if it becomes an excuse for avoiding mental labour, it ceases to be a virtue.

The problem of pigments and media resembles the problem of brush-work. The quality of paint and the way in which it is applied can give the eye a sensuous pleasure, comparable with what the ear receives from the *timbre* of a musical instrument. Tempera has a semi-opaque charm of its own. Fresco and water-colour have their special clean, liquid transparency. Oil has a variety of possibilities from the thinnest glaze in the shadows to the thickest applications of paint in the lights; and this thick paint, known as 'impasto', can itself greatly vary in thickness and richness according to the amount of white mixed with it (see pp. 141 and 145).

How far it is desirable to indulge in these qualities must often remain a matter of taste. Their use, like that of free brush-work, should be reconciled with fidelity to vision. In Wilson's *On The Wye* (1064) the hill on the right in strong sunshine is rendered with such reckless delight in the buttery paint, that delicacy of structure is sacrificed. An admirer would call it 'painterlike' and an adverse critic 'painty'. At the other extreme Turner has been accused of making his medium his slave, of caring nothing about his paint as such, so long as he could force it to do his bidding and produce the effect desired. In fact he seldom deserves this charge; but other artists, such as Leslie, *have* been guilty of ignoring the peculiar beauties of their medium. To steer between this Scylla and this Charybdis is hard; but it can be done. Chardin in *The Lesson* [(4077), Pl. 67] has neither treated paint as his slave, nor himself as the slave of paint, but has used the varied textures of his paint to express the varied textures represented.

The ground to which the paint is applied needs similar consideration. A smooth ground can contribute to the beauty of a smoothly finished painting; whereas a coarse canvas with a pronounced grain, by breaking up the edges of the contours, can help the effect of atmosphere and of texture. These technicalities and many more have to be reconciled by the artist with his other aims, so that the limitations of the medium are turned into advantages.

I once heard Eric Gill point out that the ideal statue of a king ought to be not only a king, but a stone king. In fact the representation of regal power should be equalled by the expressive use of the material. A similar ideal might be upheld in painting. A picture should be the expression of a vision in terms of paint. There should be a balance between fidelity to the vision and fidelity to the material means of its expression (see p. 2). These considerations, though they do not help to define in one phrase what good painting is, do at least determine what it is not.

Just as I argued that a painting of flat coloured squares may be a decoration, but, because devoid of vision, is not a picture, I now maintain that a surface, to which buttons or pieces of tweed are attached, may—I say it unwillingly—express emotion, but is also, because not painted, not a picture. I confine the word 'picture' to surfaces expressive of visual experience by means of *paint*. Strictly this would exclude the raised gesso ornaments in Pisanello's SS. *Anthony and George* (776) and more emphatically the carved wood in Crivelli's 'Demidoff Altarpiece' (788) (see also p. 138).

Mosaic also, in spite of its similar results and of its important influence on painting, comes strictly outside the definition of what makes a picture.

Limits as broad as these are peculiarly needed by the painter. The sculptor and the architect need self-inflicted limitations less. The sculptor, especially the carver in stone or wood, is necessarily limited by the nature of his material; and the architect, though he has scope to be expressional also, by the functional purpose of what he builds. Except as the subordinate of the architect, the painter is comparatively free, and his very freedom is a danger. For him then decorative and technical limitations provide a salutary safeguard.

CHAPTER V

DESIGN

THE first aim of design is unity, coherence, consistency (see p. 4). Disunion, incoherence and inconsistency mean failure in design. Coherence of this kind can seldom be proved, though its existence can be unquestionably felt. In this respect the creation of a masterpiece approaches the ideal of natural creation. We can feel without proving it that the parts of a good design, however diverse, are necessary to the coherence of the whole, just as the leaves, fruit, twigs, branches and trunk are each necessary to a particular tree. Ruskin aptly speaks of *helpfulness* in this connexion. Each part of the picture in relation to the other parts must help to contribute to the whole. It has been said: 'Tout ce qui n'est pas nécessaire est nuisible.' The design, that is to say, will be imperfect if we can merely say: 'This or that object does no harm.' Of a perfect design we are able to assert: 'Without this figure or without that building the picture would fall to pieces.'

In his 'Science of Picture Making' Sir Charles Holmes makes an antithesis between *Unity* and *Infinity*. Some of the greatest European pictures, while preserving unity in being comprehensible as a whole, also express something of the infinity of Nature.

In many of the finest Chinese landscapes the picture is not a single entity to be comprehended in one gaze, but a continuous scroll of changing effects to be studied consecutively.

What unity such landscapes have depends upon consistency of mood and method and is comparable with that of a piece of music in several movements.

In European painting this method of design is rare and only occurs occasionally on friezes. In Italy, though the series of frescoes on walls and the series of panels on altarpieces are intended to be seen continuously, the self-contained unity of each picture is more important than its relation to the next; but, within the unity of the single picture, sensations of infinity can be awakened especially by the use to which European painters have put perspective. Immense distances can be represented as existing between foreground and background and series of objects can be placed within the picture-volume at organized distances from the spectator.

In Claude's *Embarkation of S. Ursula* [(30), see Pl. 56] this has been reconciled with the orthodox conception of design as a self-contained unity. The treatment of

Rubens's *Château de Steen* [(66), Pl. 54] is different. Compactness is sacrificed to the expression of an infinity, of which the landscape in the picture is a mere fragment (see also p. 75). But, if there is not compactness, there is completeness; Claude's landscape expresses infinity within its own unity; Rubens's expresses unity within an infinity including it.

In another respect a picture's unity can be of two kinds, divisible or indivisible. The designs of many paintings (especially of the fifteenth century) form complete unities as a whole and also contain within themselves smaller designs equally unified—so that a photograph of a skilfully selected detail is complete on its own account. Uccello's *Rout of San Romano* [(583), Pls. 16 and 17] is an example. On the other hand many designs invented after 1500 cannot be so split up. Any detail, however well chosen, of Titian's *Bacchus and Ariadne* [(35), Pl. 36] is incomplete in itself; it is only the design as a whole that is so unified that every figure and every detail contributes to it indispensably (cf. also p. 88).

Unity is essential to design; infinity is less essential, but, when reconciled with unity, when in fact *concentrated*, can immensely contribute to the satisfaction given. Infinity can be expressed by other means than those described above, even by something that at first appears to be complexity; but the complexity must always be reduced to order.

This leads to the question of the need or otherwise for *mystery* in a work of art. Unity and coherence are closely to be associated with clarity, since clarity is a means of attaining unity and vice versa. Mystery is closely allied to infinity; but, while infinity can be reconciled with unity, mystery and clarity would at first sight seem to be irreconcilable. The answer to this puzzle depends upon the important distinction between mystery inherent in the *emotion expressed* and mystery inherent in the *means* of expressing it. An emotion that the greatest art often expresses is that of awe in the face of what is unintelligible, an emotion justly to be described as mystery. Such mystery is perfectly compatible with clarity in the means of expression. The means of expression, the language, must always be clear and intelligible; and, in the case of painting, such effects as mists or blurred contours should always have a purpose, and should never be an excuse for confusion, failure of vision, or incompetence of visual utterance.

A painting ceases to be a work of art when it fails to bring order out of chaos. Here another analogy between works of human and of natural creation is appropriate. Nature, as philosophers have pointed out, produces infinite variety within recurrent uniformity. For the likeness of one object to another in one respect and their unlikeness in another respect (used in Chapter I when comparing pictures with natural appearances) applies equally to the comparison of natural appearances with each other.

It also holds of the comparison between two or more parts of the same picture. The design of every picture contains elements both of resemblance and of contrast, or, in other words, of repetition and variety (see p. 8). Mere repetition produces monotony. Mere contrast produces confusion. Good design requires some of each.

These principles are bound up with the need that a work of art should alternately soothe and stimulate. The recipient is now given what he expects and is soothed; if nothing but this went on, he would be lulled into stupor. He is next given something that he did not expect and is stimulated; if nothing but this went on, he would be worn out by mental strain. Satisfaction demands the alternation and interplay of both.

This is implied by another antithesis made by Holmes, between vitality and repose. Too much vitality involves restlessness; too much repose involves tameness. Something of each is required for perfection: a quietness which is not languor and a latent energy kept under control. Repose is overstressed in Puvis de Chavanne's *Summer* (3422). Vitality is excessive in Caravaggio's *Christ at Emmaus* [(172), Pl. 52]. In Raphael's *School of Philosophers* [(Stanza della Segnatura, Vatican), Pl. 35] repose preponderates, but vitality is not absent. In Tintoretto's *S. George* [(16), Pl. 42] vitality preponderates, but repose is not ignored. Each quality has equal importance in Veronese's *Unfaithfulness* [(1318), Pl. 49]. Vitality is attained, among other means, by the unlikeness of one part of the picture to another; and repose by the likeness of the parts. Vitality is the result of *contrast*; repose of *restraint*. All good design demands contrast; and equally all good design demands that the contrast be under some restraint. If the vitality of a design depends upon a contrast of light and shade, the contrast should not be too violent. The same applies to contrasts of lines, or shapes (areas or volumes), of colours, of brush-work and of qualities of paint.

One means of producing vitality is the representation of movement (discussed in Chapter IX). To counterbalance movement, the need for repose demands that moving objects should be contrasted with objects *not* in motion (see pp. 78–80).

A picture should possess a life of its own. The need for repose, or at least for restraint, is already implied by the contention that design means, among other things, purpose and order. Order includes two more allied principles, *balance* and *proportion*.

Balance is a subtler quality than symmetry. Symmetry means repetition, approximate or complete, of the two halves of a picture. Balance, which is a free, almost irregular extension of the concept of symmetry, implies, unlike symmetry, the element of risk. Here again the forms of Nature supply analogic examples. A tree is never exactly symmetrical: but, throughout the volume it occupies in space, the growth in one position is balanced by the growth in another.

A similar 'precarious balance' occurs in painting in certain types of three-dimensional composition (see p. 97); but this is only a special application of a general principle governing all designs, whether patterns upon the picture-area or compositions within the picture-volume. In one part of a two-dimensional design, a line, an accent of red, or an area of dark must have its equivalent echo in some other part. In three-dimensional design a heavy object in the left fore-ground must be echoed by one represented as of equal weight, say, in the right middle-distance. In all cases the expectation of the echo must be satisfied, but both the degree of its resemblance to what is echoed and its exact position may awaken surprise. Whereas mere symmetry involves dull security, balance implies that a threatened instability has been overcome.

The balance of a picture can be of two kinds, static and dynamic. Piero della Francesca's *Baptism of Christ* [(665), Pl. 20] is a static example; each form, balanced against some other form, has its own independent equilibrium. Rubens's *Peace and War* (46) is dynamic; taken separately almost every figure is unbalanced, and only by its being contrasted with the compensating pose of some equally insecure figure is total stability restored.

Design then has a geometrical, or semi-geometrical, basis. This leads to the question of *proportion*, a quality nearly as important to pictures as to architecture. Some of the finest architecture depends on exact mathematical proportion. A room measures exactly two cubes; the height of a façade, in one case equals, in another is two-thirds of, its width. Such methods hardly apply to the works of the more impetuous painters; but more deliberate designers, such as Vermeer, clearly calculated to a nicety the proportion of height to width of the rectangular and other shapes represented in relation to the proportions of the picture-area containing them.

In three-dimensional design the question becomes more complex, since the proportions of the inward depths represented have to be considered in relation to those of the picture's actual height and width. The greatest masters of this art, such as Raphael, Poussin and Cézanne, paid as much attention to problems of proportion as the most scientific of architects.

CHAPTER VI

REALISM

THE word realism is often used, as opposed to 'romanticism', 'idealism' or 'escapism', to mean the description of things unpleasant and painful. These questions affect painting as much as other arts (see Chapters XXIX and XXX). Here, however, I am using 'realism' simply to mean 'realistic representation', i.e. the likeness of a picture to natural appearances.

The problem of realism in this sense still arouses antagonism. One man insists that a picture must 'look real', another that the imitation of appearances is irrelevant, or even detrimental, to its merit. The first may concede a preference for the representation of objects in themselves attractive or arousing higher emotions. A picture of a sunset, he will say, is better than a picture of a biscuit tin. The other may be induced to allow that some great painters have depended for inspiration on having objects in front of them. But neither concession brings them much nearer together. They both cling to a half-truth.

One argument against realism is based on analogy with music. Music, it is pointed out, does not depend on imitation. We do not exclaim at a concert: 'What is all this about? It does not remind me of a cuckoo or a nightingale or even an electric drill.' Instead, we listen and drink in all the sound we can. Why should there not be an art appealing to the eye without imitating recognizable appearances, just as music appeals to the ear without imitating recognizable sounds?

One might answer that in theory there is no reason against such an art, but that in practice it does not yet exist, that designs in painting have so far been limited as much by the world of appearance, as designs in architecture should be by their practical function. This, however, is shirking the challenge. The fair reply is as follows. Musicians do not in practice shut themselves up from the world of sound and evolve music from their inner consciousness. Their ears are sensitive to all that they hear, and what they have heard plays a part, unconsciously perhaps, in the inspiration of their compositions. So the great painter does not shut himself up in his studio, like a monk in his cell, and create from sheer creative ability. He absorbs as many effects of natural appearance as he can, and out of them creates his masterpiece. This holds good even if the masterpiece resembles appearances only remotely, even if it is purely 'abstract'. It must still depend on the vision of the mind's eye, which in turn depends on the vision of the bodily eye (see p. 3).

On the other hand realism has been abused in so many ways as almost to justify the contempt poured upon it. The worst of these is illusionism, the aim at deceiving the eye. One of the most offensive illusions is that of over-projection, by means of which the object represented appears nearer to the spectator than the surface on which it is painted. This is common in advertisements, but not unknown in allegedly serious portraiture. Akin to it is the over-realistic imitation of textures. I remember a picture of a girl seated on the ledge of some oak panelling, which at a distance looked so real, that one had to study it close to make sure than an actual piece of varnished oak had not been inserted in the canvas.

Another illusion is that of light within a picture. I once saw some paintings of moonlight on snow, which appeared to receive light from some unaccountable source. All subtler truths were sacrificed to the one cheap effect. Less extreme examples of a comparable aim occur in certain of Turner's earliest oils, where the contrast of tone (i.e. of degrees of light and shade apart from colour, see p. 92) are so great as to involve a considerable sacrifice of colour, in attempting the normally impossible feat of rivalling the tonal contrasts of Nature (see also Chapter XIX).

Illusions in painting may have their place in the world; but that place is Maskelyne and Devant's or Madame Tussaud's, not a picture gallery or home.

The difference between illusionism and legitimate realism is fundamental. Michelangelo convinces us in his *Entombment* [(790), Pl. 31] that he has grasped the figures in the solid, so that we *voluntarily* submit ourselves to his statement and to belief in their solidity. But we are not really deceived. He has *not forced* us into thinking that what is actually a flat painted panel includes sculptured projections. When Rembrandt in the *Portrait of Himself when Old* [(221), see Pl. 61] imitates the texture of old fur, we do not expect to find a portion of the canvas cut out and some fur substituted for it. When Vermeer paints the *Lady Standing at the Virginals* [(1383), Pl. 64] we may say: 'It looks as if the actual sun was shining in the picture'; but we do not look to see if some electric light is hidden round the edges of the frame. As before, our illusion, if illusion it be, is voluntary.

The illusionist and the legitimate realist differ fundamentally in spirit. The illusionist says: 'See how cleverly I have made one thing appear another.' The realist says: 'Come and enjoy Nature with me. By means of what is only a picture, I may be able to remind you of beauties you have not fully perceived.'

Realism in painting can be misused in other ways, for example, by the mechanical unenjoyed and indiscriminate copying of detail. Minuteness of detail, when enjoyed can be delightful. Van Eyck, by introducing into *Jan Arnolfini and his Wife* [(186), Pls. 10 and 11] a rosary hanging by a nail which casts its shadow on the wall, inspires the exclamation: 'Lucky man! How he enjoyed his work and how essential to the whole is every part of his design!' But Mabuse, by loading the *Adoration of the Magi* (2790) with small, hard, glittering objects, provokes the comment: 'Poor man! How hard he worked! And was the labour worth it in the end?' Also Van Eyck relates everything to the lighting, and, unlike Mabuse, relieves the eye by areas free of detail.

Undigested detail is a fault of many other painters, especially of the seventeenth-century Dutch and nineteenth-century English. Apart from the lack of zest such pictures betray, they frequently also err in two other essentials. The accuracy itself is often not more than a pretence, a trick of using small brush-strokes without observing closely, of displaying the industry of the hand without the control of the eye and brain. Secondly, the mere conglomeration of detail, unless it be related to some comprehensive system of line, tone, mass or colour, may destroy the unity of the design. For all its appeal to the ultra-naïve and the ultra-sophisticated, Frith's *Derby Day* [(615), see Pl. 74] fails in this essential respect.

Conversely, just as a picture can be too crowded, so it can be too empty. The parts cannot be related to the whole, if there is nothing to relate. Much nineteenth-century impressionistic work errs in this way. Boudin, in the *Harbour of Trouville* (2078), has recorded appearances merely for the sake of recording them; and though the effects recorded are true, they are too accidental and fragmentary, too disorganized to form a design.

The representation of movement (see above) is another realistic gift that can be abused (see pp. 78–80). G. D. Tiepolo's *Procession of the Trojan Horse* (3319) has this fault; Rubens's *Rape of the Sabine Women* [(38), Pl. 53] is saved from it by the steadying lines of the architecture.

So much for the ways in which realism can hinder. I must now briefly enumerate some of the ways in which it can help. The question of line may be taken first. In the '*Wilton Diptych*' [(4451), see Pl. 6] the care with which the wings of real birds have been studied has inspired bold and subtle curves, essential to the decorative *ensemble*, such as mere geometry would never have suggested; and in the companion panel even the conventionalized patterns on the robes of the king and his patron saints are derived ultimately from natural forms.

The power to realize solidity profoundly affects and alters the quality of line. This is often what is meant by speaking of *drawing*, as weak or strong. In Ambrogio Lorenzetti's *Heads of Four Nuns* [(1147), Pl. 4] the forms are seen in the flat so that the outlines, sensitive though they are, lack the boldness of those in Spinello Aretino's *Two Apostles* [(276), Pl. 5], where gravity is understood and the curve of the cloak follows the form of the underlying shoulder.

Movement too, even when unaccompanied by solidity, can help to unify design. This is seen in the spontaneous inward rush of the soldiers in Ugolino's *Betrayal of Christ* (1188), by which the eye is led to the principal figure. In more realistic works, such as Titian's *Assumption of the Virgin* (Frari Church, Venice), the design cannot be considered apart from the movements of the figures.

The same connexion between representation and design applies to the problem of space. Command of perspective, aerial and linear, does not automatically result in spatial design. Memling's *Virgin and Child in a Garden* (686) represents space, but could never be called a design in three dimensions. On the other hand, three-dimensional design in its fullest sense can hardly exist without the command of perspective. Without this knowledge Perugino could never have evolved the grand architectural scheme of *Christ giving Keys to Peter* [(Sistine Chapel, Vatican), Pl. 34].

Command of realism can always enrich a design, while ignorance of truth must limit, and may impoverish it. This strikingly applies to *chiaroscuro*, the accentuated treatment of *tone*, i.e. of gradations of light and shade for decorative or dramatic purposes. Wilkie, when he painted *Blind Man's Buff* (921), had not sufficiently studied real effects of lighting to make his stagey treatment of it acceptable. On the other hand Rembrandt in the *Woman Taken in Adultery* [(45), Pl. 58] was able to focus stronger or weaker light on different groups according to their importance, and to give unity to a complex scheme, because he had studied sunshine of varying intensity, transparent shadow and golden reflected light, intently, passionately and often (see also p. 111).

The same is true of colour. Occasionally a fine colour scheme is evolved with little apparent attention to truth, as in Tura's *Madonna and Child Enthroned* (772). But much more often, especially since the Renaissance, the greatest colourists have been observers of colour in relation to light. Raphael and Poussin, who were apt to think first of line, mass and space and to add colour last as something extra, have left fewer masterpieces of colour than the Venetians, Rubens and Chardin, who invariably sought for subtleties of colour in the world around them.

The above arguments bear out the contention that pictures should resemble appearances in *some* respects and differ from them in *others*. In practice they are bound to do both; for the most realistic picture must rely on the painter's memory. We speak of his copying what is in front of him, as though he could both look and paint at the same moment. Actually this is impossible. Looking may precede painting by seconds, hours, months or years. The difference is one of degree, not of kind. The man who 'paints what is in front of him', and the man who records years afterwards what he has seen, differ only in whether they have looked once or repeatedly at what they are recording and in the length of time elapsing between the vision and its realization in paint. Both depend on memory and even the best memory is always partly inaccurate.

CHAPTER VII

THE STRUCTURAL IDEAL

THE concession that realism can help design by no means solves the whole problem. Whistler said that to tell an artist to copy Nature is like telling a musician to sit on the piano. Of all the phenomena before him the painter must select what suits his purpose and reject the irrelevant.

Many painters fail because they forget that 'Art is recollected emotion'. The would-be artist may delight in what he sees before him and wish to paint it, but, by the time he has got down to his task, may forget what has attracted him to his subject and industriously copy all that is before him merely because it is there. If he can recollect the reason for his choice, his work stands more chance of success. To attempt realism of every conceivable kind is impossible. Whatever aspect of his subject attracted him, whether natural linear pattern, balance of form, an effect of light or a relation of colours, to that aspect he must cling tenaciously, and that aspect he must stress at all costs.

There are two main contrasted ways of being realistic in painting, which may be described as the Structural and the Impressionist Ideals. They are seldom combined and are in their extreme forms incompatible; but they are not of necessity mutually exclusive. In some of the greatest masterpieces the two ideals have been reconciled.

Three other realistic or semi-realistic ideals (which may or may not be combined with each other or with the Structural Ideal or Impressionism) may first be considered: viz. *flat-pattern realism*, the representation of *texture* and the representation of *movement*.

Flat-pattern realism is realism only of a partial kind. In most Oriental and in much early Italian painting, the three-dimensional world is incompletely realized; and in some recent pictures the representation of the third dimension is deliberately avoided. The painter sees what is in front of him in the flat. He notes contours, silhouettes and local colours, but does not represent solid form. The *Madonna and Child Enthroned* (565) by a pupil of Duccio is an example. Artists of this type do not represent space and distance, but identify the plane of the picture with the plane of the ground. Pisanello has done this in the *Vision of S. Eustace* [(1436), see Pl. 8] though the Saint and each of the animals taken separately have some solidity.

The command of three dimensions grew up gradually. Thus Botticelli in *Mars, Venus and Satyrs* [(915), Pl. 24] represents solid figures in an area of little depth against a vague background; whereas Pintoricchio in the *Return of Odysseus* (911) represents a spacious world, inhabited by unsubstantial beings.

The representation of texture and of structure are distinct. The structural ideal demands the explanation of the form of the objects, how one surface articulates with another and what forms underly the surface. Texture is the *quality* of the surface, its hardness, softness, smoothness or roughness. Painters primarily concerned with texture often neglect structure, as Correggio has done in parts of his 'Ecce Homo' (15). Conversely artists, aiming at the explanation of structure, often make textures even and hard, as Mantegna has done in the *Agony in the Garden* [(1417), Pl. 18]. Velazquez has rendered both structure and texture in *Venus and Cupid* [(2057), Pl. 65].

The representation of movement, to be discussed in Chapter IX, may or may not accompany the structural ideal. Ugolino's *Betrayal of Christ* (1188) is an example of what Mr Berenson calls 'disembodied movement', unaccompanied by solidity. In Michelangelo's *Entombment* [(790), Pl. 31] movement and structure are both represented.

A definition of the two main realistic methods, the structural and impressionist ideals may be expressed thus: the structural ideal is concerned with fact; the impressionist ideal with effect. Or, on an analogy with speech: the structural artist explains; the impressionist suggests. The structural aim is to make the form of what is represented *more* clear to the untrained spectator than it would be were the object itself in front of him. The impressionist aim is to paint its appearance only. The structural artist, when representing a human being, studies anatomy, when representing a mountain studies geology. The impressionist deliberately forgets any scientific knowledge he may possess and paints only what he sees. The structural artist paints what he knows is there.

It may be objected: 'How is it possible to represent what is there except by representing what one sees? A painter is not a sculptor. He does not construct actual three-dimensional form. He can only imitate its appearance on a flat surface.' The answer is that the structural artist must certainly use what he sees as a basis for representation; but actual appearances are often indefinite or blurred, especially if separated by atmosphere; even the appearance of a near object, seen with sharp contours, does not always explain the object's form; the structural artist therefore, in addition to painting what he sees, uses various devices for *emphasizing* form and structure.

Of these devices the most important is line, either actual outline or the sharpening up of contours. Outline is not an imitation of anything seen, but a pure convention for determining the boundary between an object and its surroundings, or between two parts of an object. Outlines are, in fact, interpretations, not representations, of seen appearances.

The most original artist in history was probably the prehistoric being who invented outline. He saw, let us say, a white goat, silhouetted against the green grass; and instead of representing a white mass against a green mass, he invented the new idea of making a diagram of the boundaries dividing the goat from its background. His method is so familiar to us now that we are apt to forget that there is anything strange about 'drawing'. We almost imagine that outline literally represents what we see. As a child brought up among pictures, I even once supposed that objects were surrounded by black outlines too thin for me to perceive. So much can art pervert perception.

The artist who aims at precision must make use of line. He must begin with an outline, which may or may not be subsequently covered up. The use of uncovered outlines of appreciable thickness is the readiest way of explaining structure. How much structure is explained depends on the quality and accuracy of the outline and these again depend on the painter's knowledge. Outline does not *ipso facto* result in structural truth (see Pls. 2 and 4). On the other hand the drawings of Leonardo, who pushed scientific inquiry as far as any artist, show how much form precise outline can express, even when unsupported by contrast of light and shade. This also applies to the *Portrait of a Lady* [(758), Pl. 23] by Baldovinetti, though here the sharp contours take the place of outlines: contrasts of light and shade are reduced to a minimum and the structure of the nose (bone above and cartilage below) and of the neck (the sterno-mastoid muscles coming in front of the larynx) are explained by contour alone.

The quality of an outline can even reflect the emotional attitude of the painter. The outlines in Crivelli's *Annunciation* (739) are strong and firm; those defining the features and hair of Botticelli's *Young Man* (626) are tender in addition.

The method in covering the initial outline, while leaving the contours sharp, occurs in Van Eyck's *Man* (222) and Memling's *Young Man at Prayer* (2594). As painters became more interested in atmosphere and texture, outlines were used less. In Titian's *Bacchus and Ariadne* [(35), Pl. 36] they have been alternately exposed and covered. Veronese, on the other hand, in *Unfaithfulness* [(1318), Pl. 49] surrounds the central figure throughout with a brown outline, varying in thickness, but only occasionally interrupted. It is also possible greatly to soften or blur a contour, without losing the firmness of a linear foundation (see p. 35).

A second method of making structure clear is to supplement the contours by contrasts of tone, i.e. of light and shade. In Caravaggio's *Christ at Emmaus* [(172), Pl. 52], where the aim is to give the form an immediate appearance of solidity rather than structural subtlety, the tonal contrasts are strong, but the contours not more than broadly accurate. Conversely in Holbein's *Duchess of Milan* [(2475), Pl. 39] the contours explain the form more precisely, but the form at first looks flat, because the contrasts of tone due to its projections are so delicate (see also pp. 111, 112, 155).

Cézanne discovered that the structure of an object could also be explained by a third method, the rendering of colour. His discovery may be simplified and expressed thus. Supposing a large cube of white material to be placed on sandy ground of an orange hue and supposing the sky to be blue, one of the cube's vertical faces and its upturned horizontal face may be of precisely the same tone (i.e. degree of lightness or darkness), but of totally different colours. They may be receiving the same strength of sunshine and neither surface be darker or lighter than the other; but the image of the vertical surface will be orange by reflection from the sand, and that of the horizontal face blue by reflection from the sky. Thus form may be explained by colour apart from tone, though not apart from contour. More often, however, some tonal contrast accompanies the emphatic contrast of colour.

In Cézanne's *La Montagne Sainte Victoire* [(Courtauld Institute), Pl. 78] the structure of the mountain depends upon all three. Broad brush-strokes explain where the visible shadowed planes meet the unseen planes on the further side; and the shadowed planes are distinguished from those in sunshine by being darker and bluer.

Study of Cézanne shows that the structural ideal itself can be of different kinds. A painter may emphasize large facts of form and ignore detail, as Cézanne did. Or he may particularize minutiae at the risk of losing his grasp of the main structure. Moreover, he may build up structures that resemble those in Nature either closely or hardly at all.

This second distinction may be considered first. Many fifteenth-century Italians must be described as structural, though the structure they represent, without being intentionally distorted, is partially or almost wholly untrue to life. This applies to the draperies in Tura's *S. Jerome* (773), to the mountains and rocks in Mantegna's *Agony in the Garden* [(1417), Pl. 18], even to the legs of Mars in Botticelli's *Mars, Venus and Satyrs* [(915), Pl. 24]. In all these cases the painter has been a potential sculptor. His aim has been never to represent anything in the flat picture, until he has first apprehended it as solid form. He has conveyed it in terms of solid structure, even though that structure bears little resemblance to anything in Nature.

The structural often coincides with the sculpturesque. Objects in structural pictures often share the limitations of sculptured reliefs, their hardness, their immobility and their dependence upon linear, and neglect of aerial, perspective. Aerial perspective implies that the image of the distant object is less distinct in contour, less contrasted in tone (see p. 24) and cooler (i.e. bluer) than that of the near object; linear perspective, merely that the image of the distant object is smaller than that of the near object. In the fifteenth century, Italian painting and low relief sculpture trespassed upon each other's domain. The painters, in their search for solidity, thought, often unconsciously, in terms of statuary and low relief. The Florentine ideal tended to be marble; the Paduan and Ferrarese ideal to be bronze.

As representation improved during the fifteenth century, the limitations of the sculpturesque lessened. The rocks in Leonardo's *Virgin of the Rocks* [(1093), Pl. 29] are not only solid, but are also geologically probable and exist in atmosphere. The figures in Michelangelo's *Entombment* [(790), Pl. 31] are anatomically faultless; and even the textures represented have as much variety as could be rendered in marble, but not more.

Structures, closely resembling and widely differing from the natural, often occur in the same picture; so do detailed and generalized treatments of structure. In Uccello's *Rout of San Romano* [(583), Pls. 16 and 17], though the horses are simplified and conventionalized, certain details of the armour and the profile of the young squire are rendered with delicate minuteness. The danger of the detailed method is that, in the search for minutiae, large forms tend to be forgotten. This fault occurs in three pictures of such different periods as Gregorio Schiavone's *Madonna and Child* (630), Dou's *Poultry Shop* (825) and Dyce's *Pegwell Bay* (1407). Fine examples of the recording of essential structure and omission of minor forms are: Petrus Christus's *Edward Grimston* (lent by the Earl of Verulam); Zurbaran's *S. Francis* [(5655), Pl. 57] and Seurat's *La Baignade* [(T.G. 3908), Pl. 79]. Attention to detail is combined with a grasp of the large facts of form in Dürer's portrait of his *Father* [(1938), Pl. 38] and Rembrandt's *Françoise van Wasserhoven* (?) (775).

The structural ideal appeals more to the twentieth-century mind than the impressionist ideal. If anything be sacrificed, we prefer it to be atmosphere rather than structure. But this ought not to blind us to the development of some of Europe's greatest painters. Titian, Velazquez and Rembrandt all began as structural artists, primarily concerned with explaining form, and ended as impressionists, primarily concerned with suggesting atmosphere. Or rather they ultimately reconciled the two aims. Titian in the *Mother and Child* (3948) has made the solidity of the forms convincing through the separating mist. His late work showed the benefit of his early training. For all its softness it was never vague.

CHAPTER VIII

THE IMPRESSIONIST IDEAL

THE word 'Impressionism' first came into being in the 1870's, when Claude Monet called a picture: 'Sunrise—An Impression.' Since then it has been used in many different senses, one of which is concerned with appearance rather than fact (see p. 29). The Impressionist paints what he sees rather than what he knows. He cares for aerial, more than for linear, perspective (see p. 32).

The followers of Monet, who led the movement in the later nineteenth century, were absorbed almost exclusively with problems of light and atmosphere. Structure interested them little. Degas and Renoir, who cared more for humanity, specialized in momentary pose and expression, seizing upon main appearances and eliminating detail. Manet began as a painter of contemporary life, reacting from the classical and romantic schools. His originality lay in this and in his simplified treatment of silhouettes of light and dark. Later, under Monet's influence, he studied colour in relation to atmosphere.

As soon as these painters were appreciated, it was discovered that their aims were not entirely new and soon Rembrandt, Velazquez and Hals and the later Turner and Constable and others were called 'impressionists'. The word has become so general that art historians have even referred to a style, prevalent in Italy before the Christian era, as 'Pompeian impressionism'. The word is used in a great number of different senses. 'Decorative impressionism' is discussed briefly on p. 16; other meanings are as follows:

Impressionism sometimes means the recording of an instantaneous, as distinct from a continuous, effect. This kind of impressionist is concerned in portraiture with gesture, movement and expression, in landscape with momentary light and shadow. Hals's *Man with a Glove* (2528) is an instance. The portrait is not structural. No sculptor could carve a head from the information given him by the artist. The record of the momentary expression on the faces is due to the accurate placing and proportioning of the areas of dark and light in relation to each other. The boundaries of these areas are not accurate in direction, but largely the accidental result of the economy of brush-work necessary to so rapid a record.

The contours of the *Man with a Glove*, unlike most contours associated with impressionism, are hard and definite. Sharp edges, due to quick execution not to careful drawing, occur in many sketches by Constable such as *Salisbury Cathedral* [(1814), Pl. 73] and *Hadleigh Castle* (4810), in which the aim is at recording momentary light, weather and atmosphere, rather than form.

Many of Turner's later works, such as the *Interior at Petworth* (1988) and *Rain, Steam and Speed* (538), are also impressionistic in that light and atmosphere are given more importance than structure; but the general effect of these, unlike that of Constable's sketches, is soft, partly because of the blurred edges and partly because of the delicate differences of tone (see pp. 24, 99). In most landscapes by French Impressionists, such as Pissarro's *Louvre* (T.G. 4671) the forms are merged in the surrounding atmosphere. This helps the effect aimed at, but involves the danger of the vagueness and formlessness from which most of Monet's later paintings suffer.

Yet a blurred edge need be no excuse for shirking draughtsmanship. Ingres said that even smoke should be described by line. By this he did not mean that an actual outline must be used, as in Blake's clouds, but that even a softened contour should be under control (see p. 31). Its direction and the degree of its softness should be intentional, not accidental. There is a great difference between a blurred edge that bounds an understood form and one that ignores structure. In Nature the visual image of a contour varies from the sharpness of tin to the softness of cotton wool, with an infinite range between these extremes. This is finely realized, without any sacrifice of solid structure, in Crome's *Moonrise on the Marshes of the Yare* [(2645), Pl. 71].

The problem of edge is closely allied to the problem of focus. If we look at an object intently and make it the centre of our field of vision, we see other objects as more or less blurred, according as their image is far from or near to, that centre on our retina. Rembrandt and Velazquez were the first to make full use of this optical phenomenon. In Chapter IV it was noted that in Rembrandt's *Portrait of Himself at 34* [(672), Pl. 60] his right eye is drawn in more detail and placed in a stronger light than anything else. In his *Portrait of Himself when Old* [(221), see Pl. 61] the principle is the same, but the transition from what is in focus to what is out of focus more sudden (see also pp. 157 ff.).

Focus of some kind is necessary to unity of design. Some things must be subordinated to others. Especially in landscape, if everything is sharply defined, the total effect will be disjointed. Canaletto, in *The Stone Mason's Yard* (127), and Crome, in the *Windmill on Mousehold Heath* (926), have given more precision to the middle distance than to the foreground, which is treated as out of focus.

This corresponds with normal vision better than the Pre-Raphaelite method of representing everything near or far with the same degree of detail.

At this point extremes meet. Some impressionists also ignore focus and sacrifice the coherence of their work. They ignore it by treating everything as *out of* focus, just as the Pre-Raphaelites do by treating everything as *in* focus.

The term 'impressionist' has been applied on the one hand to Rembrandt and Velazquez because they gave *more distinctness* to some things than others, and on the other to Monet and Pissarro because they gave *equal indistinctness* to everything.

In history the two ideals, structural and impressionist, have often alternated with each other. One tendency is frequently a reaction from the other and an attempt to stress an aspect of truth, overlooked by the previous generation.

In Christian Europe Giotto made the first important attempt at the structural, in contrast with the flat pattern methods of his predecessors. Most of his fourteenth-century successors reverted to flat pattern; and the structural ideal was not consistently pursued until Masaccio adopted it in Florence and was followed by such painters as Piero della Francesca in Umbria, Mantegna at Padua and Tura at Ferrara. The sculpturesque tendency of the Florentines reached its climax in Michelangelo. The Umbrians, especially Raphael, combined it with command of space.

Meanwhile Masaccio's Flemish and Dutch contemporaries were learning an outlook almost as structural from sculpture in wood. But the soft gradations of atmosphere, which their medium of transparent oil enabled them to represent gradually modified the woodenness of their work (see pp. 142-3). Softness of atmosphere and texture were further developed by the Venetians, after Antonello had taught them the Van Eyck medium. In the sixteenth century many modifications of the structural ideal took place. Correggio's *Venus, Mercury and Cupid* [(10), Pls. 40 and 41] is textural and atmospheric as well as structural; and in Titian's *Vendramin Family* [(4452), Pl. 44] atmosphere is as important as shape. The Flemings too, from Patenier to Bruegel, paid increasing attention to aerial perspective.

The greatest of the painters of the seventeenth century, except Nicolas Poussin, became, especially in their old age, more impressionistic than structural. Velazquez and Rembrandt paid increasing attention to softened edges due to atmosphere. And Rubens, great draughtsman though he was, often put colour and light before form, as in the background of the *Rape of the Sabine Women* [(38), Pl. 53]. Claude, the first scientific painter of outdoor lighting, and many contemporary Dutch landscape painters were as much concerned with atmosphere as with drawing.

In the eighteenth century Canaletto and Wilson at their best maintained a just balance between the structural and impressionistic ideals. Guardi, a pioneer in the open-air sketch, was almost purely an impressionist. In France Watteau in his devotion to Rubens, had overthrown the grand style and by his aerial vistas prepared the way for the works of Gainsborough and Fragonard, which were often free renderings of light, rather than exact statements of form. Several of Hogarth's sketches were also purely impressionistic.

The neo-classical revival of the later eighteenth century, which culminated in Jacques Louis David, brought a reaction in favour of exactness, and severity of line. Blake, who called *chiaroscuro* a 'demon', represented another aspect of the same tendency. The Gothic revival, which reached its zenith in the mid-nineteenth century, was so far the ally of classicism that both favoured clear-cut definition. Ingres' love of linear precision made him a pioneer in the admiration of the earlier Italians. In the 1840's the cult of both the Italian and the Flemish primitives affected the English Pre-Raphaelites, typical exponents of the structural ideal at its most minute and least monumental.

Meanwhile by 1800 Turner and Constable had begun their careers. Much of Turner's later work and most of Constable's sketches were impressionistic in their concern with effect. Constable's spacious breadth affected Delacroix, the leader of the romantics. Corot and Delacroix had impressionistic phases. Thus the impressionists proper, Monet and Pissarro and even Manet and Renoir were not entirely unheralded. Constable and his French followers had prepared the way. Later, Monet rediscovered in England the later works of Turner, from which he learned many of his ideas about light and colour.

No sooner had the French impressionists come into general favour than a reaction from their limitations, later to be called Post-Impressionism, set in. Seurat in Paris and Cézanne at Aix-en-Provence each sought to create something more solid. Seurat adopted the impressionistic technique of dividing light into spots of pure colour, eliminating browns and greys; but gave a simplified solidity to the forms of his finished works that makes any Monet look flimsy by comparison. Cézanne also sought the three-dimensional coherence that command of structure alone can give. After his early romantic phases, he became the pupil of Pissarro, from whom he learned to observe colour in relation to light. But, whereas Pissarro recorded such effects for their own sake, Cézanne did so as a means of explaining form (see p. 31). Cézanne then was a rebel, not so much from impressionism itself as from its limitations. He greatly extended the scope of impressionistic discovery and, like other painters of the first rank, largely reconciled impressionism with the structural ideal.

During the present century, in so far as painters have accepted realism as their ideal, Cézanne's influence has been the strongest. There has also been an impressionistic tendency of a more limited kind, based on the school of Monet. There has been cubism, the aim at simplifying structure even more than Cézanne did; and there has been, in England, something like a return to the Pre-Raphaelite ideal of painstaking attention to small forms. These last two movements, opposed though they are, both aim at describing structure; and at present, apart from deliberately non-realistic art, the structural painters seem to be more powerful than the impressionists.

CHAPTER IX

DISTORTION

THE preceding three chapters are concerned with the ways in which pictures may resemble appearances or explain structure. This chapter and the next deal with the converse aspect of the problem, that is, the ways in which appearances and structures are changed in painting, how far this is inevitable and for what reasons it is, or is not, desirable. Non-realism is no more a desirable end in itself than realism, but only justifiable (like realism) as a means of reaching some particular result, such as the expression of an emotion or the co-ordination of a design.

Some distortion is inevitable in a work of art (see pp. 3 and 5) partly because the artist inevitably emphasizes and exaggerates what he loves or hates; also, if he is to express himself clearly, he must select, simplify, organize and re-combine rather than merely record. Distortions due to emotion tend to be more instinctive, and those due to reason more deliberate; but it is perfectly possible for reason to work subconsciously and for feeling to work consciously. (For distortions due to the dictates of the brush and the pigment, see Chapters IV, XXIV and XXV.)

Recently the work of Matisse exemplifies extreme distortion due to enjoyment of brush-work. That of Utrillo exemplifies less extreme distortion due to enjoyment of pigment. That of Van Gogh provides examples of both. The requirements of pattern lead to various kinds of distortion (see under § (ii), p. 93). Linear design, though based upon truth of perception, often also involves distortion (see under § (vii), p. 76).

I have already stated some reasons for distortion by valuing expression and coherence above representation; by showing that some kinds of realism are difficult to combine or even irreconcilable, that the impressionist sacrifices structure, and that the structural artist exaggerates, adds to, or even alters appearances. For distortion implies *some* adherence to truth. Before the appearance of an object can be seen to have been distorted, the object that has inspired the painter's image must be recognizable. We speak of some pictures as representations of appearances and of others as derivations from appearances; but actually the difference between the most abstract design by Picasso and the most photographic example of Dutch topography is one of degree, not of kind.

The structural ideal involves several types of distortion described in Chapter VII: the use of outline is interpretation rather than representation; structural fact and fiction can be combined; the painter who emphasizes large structural facts eliminates minor structure; and the painter who is absorbed in details of form often fails to explain larger structural relations.

It is impossible to define at what moment simplification becomes distortion. Cézanne simplified forms with a geometrical bias. He discovered that a mountain was in the main conical in form, a building cubic, the human forearm cylindrical, the human head (with modifications) ovoid, etc. His reduction of all forms to some simple geometrical solid led to the cubists, who treated all forms as cubes or series of cubes. The discovery of geometry *in* Nature and what I should call the infliction of geometry *upon* Nature often occur in the same painting.

There are distortions due to newly acquired anatomical knowledge; such are the exaggerated muscles of the archers in Pollaiuolo's *Martyrdom of S. Sebastian* (292) and the prominent bones of Tura's *S. Jerome* (773). Some distortion inevitably results from the tendency of structural artists to ignore softness of texture.

Other distortions are the result of a bias more philosophical, more emotional. These may be considered under the following five headings:

(i) Idealization.	(iv) Combined Imagery.
(ii) The Grotesque.	(v) The Representation of Movement.
(iii) Caricature.	

(i) IDEALIZATION

Idealization sometimes means the representation of what is general rather than particular. A pine tree in a Chinese landscape is a type (or, as Mr Eric Newton says, an 'essence') of all pine trees. It is intended for the *idea* of a pine tree, almost in the Platonic sense. To this idea all the particular pine trees seen by man imperfectly approximate.

The expression of the typical often becomes confused with the expression of the admired. The normal is thought of as the perfect and the perfect as the normal type; but artists of different periods or nationalities differ widely in what they think perfect or normal. This particularly applies to ideals of the human body and countenance.

On the whole, slimness and tallness have been more admired by Europeans, but Rubens and Bruegel are notable exceptions. It has often been remarked that when a type of woman is admired, examples of the type come into existence.

The painter goes further and deliberately invents impossible proportions, e.g. the long back of the Virgin in the *Vision of S. Jerome* (35) by Parmigianino. The improbable smallness of the hands of the *Lady* (1433) by Roger Van der Weyden or his pupil also show an admiration for a non-existent elegance. On the other hand admiration for a voluptuous fullness has led Palma Vecchio in his *Flora* (3939) to omit the hollow below the neck and between the collar-bones.

The endeavour to represent ideal human proportions often leads to absence of character. The lesser portrait painters of Italy, in their search for dignity, often achieve insipidity. So do most later attempts to revive the idealized proportions and physiognomy of Attic Greek statues.

Exaggerations and distortions due to moral preferences are also frequent. The tall bodies and small heads of the Saints in Michelangelo's *Entombment* [(790), Pl. 31] suggest that they belong to a nobler order of beings than that of common humanity. The boniness of Tura's *S. Jerome* (773) is partly due to his asceticism. El Greco increasingly exaggerated the slimness and tallness of his figures, in order to express their spirituality, as in his *Agony in the Garden* [(3476), Pl. 50] and *Purification of the Temple* [(1457), Pl. 51].

Distortion then may be the result of the exaggeration of what is admired. It has often been associated too narrowly with the exaggeration of what is disliked or held up to ridicule. The exaggeration of ugliness may be of two kinds, according as the aim is to create an ideal type or to emphasize the particular characteristics of an individual. The *grotesque* is a convenient name for the first and *caricature* for the second.

(ii) THE GROTESQUE

The *grotesque*, then, is a branch of idealization. The grotesques of medieval art, nominally symbolic of evil, were often the outcome of joyous energy. The distortion often consisted in combining the head of one creature, the trunk and forelegs of another, the hind-legs of a third and the wings of a fourth. The pure grotesque occurs little in the National Gallery; but the Devil, trodden down by S. Michael in Crivelli's '*Demidoff Altarpiece*' (788), is a good example.

The so-called 'caricatures' of Leonardo are more sophisticated expressions of the same spirit; each feature may be the exaggeration of something observed, but so combined as to create an ideal type.

(iii) CARICATURE

Although the word 'caricature' is of Italian derivation, the real pioneers in this art were the Flemish and Dutch. Their portraits tended always to stress individuality at the expense of dignity (see Chapter XIII), to make a face live for all time as the face of an individual requires *some* exaggeration, however slight.

In Bruegel's *Adoration of the Magi* [(3556), Pl. 43], among all the sixteen *faces*, there are only two of which the proportions of the features are impossible; in the remaining fourteen the exaggerations are too slight to defy probability. Bruegel, therefore, is not strictly a caricaturist. The National Gallery has no examples of caricature proper.

(iv) COMBINED IMAGERY

The painter's concern is not with single optical images, but with the after-images arising from them in his mind. The after-image recorded in the picture will often be a combination of many images beheld at different times. The grotesque animals of medieval art (see above) and the ancient Egyptian convention for the human figure, seen partly front view and partly in profile, are examples.

It is only comparatively lately that painters have aimed at representing appearances seen within a limited space, at a single instant of time; and even apparently realistic art has frequently departed from this ideal. Still more lately artists have returned to earlier ideals of combined imagery, which, though superficially less realistic, derive from visual experience.

Combined imagery is the only method by which a painter can record the movement of time. In Turner's *Frosty Morning* [(492), Pl. 72] the frost seems to melt before the increasing warmth of the sun. In his *Evening Star* (1991) the sun seems to sink, while the mists rise and the sky and the sands darken. The result is due partly to a combination of successive effects; but how we know that in one case light is increasing and in the other diminishing remains mysterious. In *Rain, Steam and Speed* (538) he has represented also the rapid motion of the approaching steam engine by making the funnel of the engine darker in tone and sharper in edge than anything else, so that its position in aerial perspective is nearer than in linear perspective.

(v) THE REPRESENTATION OF MOVEMENT

The camera can represent rapid motion in three ways: the snapshot records the instantaneous image on the retina; the 'slow-motion picture', a series of such images; and the ordinary cinema, the same series at the actual rate of their occurrence. Of these methods, though all represent an optical image, only the last records what is seen, i.e. apprehended by the brain. Merely to receive on the retina is not to see. Seeing is a continuous, not an instantaneous act. Our after-image of a movement is a composite impression of instants put together by the memory. For this reason an instantaneous photograph of rapid movement looks even less like what we remember seeing than a slow-motion film. A figure in such a photograph appears to be struck motionless as though by Medusa's head. This applies also to paintings in which one instant, occurring during continuous motion, has been accurately recorded. Thus in Piero della Francesca's *Baptism of Christ* [(665), Pl. 20] the youth who is stripping looks as if he would never extricate himself from his garment. On the other hand in Botticelli's *Nativity* [(1034), Pl. 28] the angels fly convincingly, because the record is not of one instant but of several instants combined. The representation of movement justifies the distortion, the angels' flight being expressed partly by the lengthening out of their figures in the direction of their motion. In fact all successful renderings of rapid movement depend upon what has been called by the ugly phrase 'a synthesis of successive instants'.

Other examples involve even more distortion. In Titian's *Venus and Adonis* [(34), Pl. 37] Venus's right leg is impossibly long compared with her left leg; but only by this means could it be shown that she had her back to Adonis before she turned to throw her arms round him. The record of a single pose could never express all this. On the same principle, Venus in Botticelli's *Birth of Venus* (Uffizi) appears to be floating, just because she does not balance upon her feet.

In the *Birth of Venus* the effect of movement is increased also by Venus's blowing hair and by the flying cloaks of Zephyr and Flora. A nude or tightly clad figure, to appear in rapid motion, must in some degree be distorted. But if a figure has long hair, a loose cloak or scarf, or even a loose skirt, distortion may be less necessary. Drapery can do much to express movement. It indicates not only where the body is now, but where it was before. The robes of the angels in Botticelli's *Nativity* [(1034), Pl. 28] are tightest where their bodies press forward against them and loosest where they flutter behind their backs. In Tintoretto's *Origin of the Milky Way* [(1313), Pl. 48] the cloak of Jupiter explains the direction and speed of his movement.

It is easier to represent weight without movement or movement without weight than both together (see p. 29). In Duccio's *Annunciation* (1139) both figures appear to move, though only partly solid.

Giotto, because he mastered weight, is less strikingly successful with movement. On the other hand several later painters, such as Lorenzo Monaco in *Legends of S. Benedict* (4062), were like Duccio in mastering movement without substance.

Except for Masaccio himself, most of the sculpturesque painters of his generation were less successful with movement. Piero della Francesca's very accuracy prevented him from solving this problem. Pollaiuolo, who was the first consistently to attempt structure and movement together, solved the two problems pleasingly in *Apollo and Daphne* (928). In the later fifteenth century the structural painters were as much concerned with movement as with substance itself. An example is Mantegna's *Triumph of Scipio* (902).

A climax in the representation of masses in motion is reached at a later date in Rubens's *Rape of the Sabine Women* [(38), Pl. 53].

Watteau because of his good memory succeeded with movement in *La Gamme d'Amour* [(2897), Pl. 66], whereas Chardin's typical successes such as *The Lesson* [(4077), Pl. 67] are static. To a temperament less sensitive than Chardin's, dependence on models may be a snare. Frith's *Derby Day* [(615), see Pl. 74] lacks the alertness of Hogarth's brilliantly remembered *Calais Gate* [(1464), Pl. 68].

A painting or drawing then can call up an image of movement, as no single photograph can. The photograph can only record a phase; the painting can also record a succession of phases.

This applies equally to the representation of animals. The instantaneous photograph has proved that at a given instant of time no creature puts both front legs right in front and both hind legs right behind, as the running hound and hare do in Pisanello's *Vision of S. Eustace* [(1436), see Pl. 8], but no more scientific method of suggesting rapid motion has yet superseded this convention, which has lasted from medieval times to the sporting prints of the nineteenth century.

CHAPTER X

ABSTRACTION AND SURREALISM

PHOTOGRAPHY has banished the need for the once useful type of picture that accurately but mechanically recorded facts. The paintings of the lesser topographers of the past are valuable records but not works of art.

Photography has influenced painting in two opposite ways: (i) towards the imitation of its effects; (ii) towards the concentration on what is outside its scope. The first tendency is responsible for much that is dull; but the surprises of the camera may well have suggested methods of design to such painters as Degas (see p. 16). The reaction from photography, however, and the consequent stress on what the camera cannot achieve have had much more important results.

These include two more non-realistic tendencies in painting:

(i) Abstract and 'Constructivist' Art;
(ii) Surrealism.

Abstract Art means the designing of shapes and colours to satisfy the eye, with the minimum of realistic representation. Surrealism means the recording of images arising in the subconscious mind. These aims, in theory incompatible, can in practice be combined. Both tendencies have existed in the earliest works of art; their only novelty is their formulation as conscious aims.

(i) ABSTRACT AND 'CONSTRUCTIVIST' ART

In the past the most extreme type of abstract art never claimed to be more than decoration. The artist covered surfaces of wood or wall with geometrical shapes, often repeated. His work had no pictorial claims. The modern production of similar results—an extreme type of abstract art known as 'constructivism'—does claim to be pictorial, without (in extreme cases) justifying the claim (see p. 14). In such cases the colours may have been inspired partly by visual experience, but their dependence upon past vision is too slight to warrant their being regarded as works of imagination.

All art thrives within *some* limitations, but too many limitations become restrictions to freedom of expression. A geometrical exercise may appeal to the decorative, but hardly to the imaginative sense. If carried out by ruler, compasses, etc., it communicates little of the artist's emotion. If drawn by the hand (a method entailing infinite subconscious variations from mechanical precision), it can express more, but not enough.

Constructive designs in line alone may be described as almost one-dimensional, though they can call forth images in two or three dimensions. Designs of flat areas of colour rigidly emphasize the fact that a picture is a two-dimensional surface. Sometimes, however, the colours are contrasted so as to suggest different distances from the spectator. Red is thought of as nearer than blue, because of the effects of aerial perspective.

These aims are as far from representing appearances as is possible in painting, being derived only to a minimum extent from visual experiences. There are other kinds of abstract art, which, without being obviously representational, depend more closely upon vision.

In its origin the word 'abstract' means 'taking or drawing away', in the special sense of taking away and contemplating in isolation some quality from an object possessing that quality. When we contemplate 'courage', we are separating *one* of the qualities from the rest of those possessed by this or that courageous person. Analogously, a more realistic picture represents a particular man by stressing as many of his characteristics as possible, his tallness, his thinness, the size of his nose, the length of his fingers, the colour of his hair, the awkwardness of his gait, etc. An abstract picture, on the other hand, seeks to express one only of these qualities as shared by all individuals possessing it, to express the general quality of having red hair as distinct from the other qualities of a particular red-haired person.

It may be here objected that such abstraction is impossible in painting, an art essentially concrete in the materials used and in the images conveyed. The objection may be met by two arguments already put forward. First, it is impossible to represent all the characteristics of an individual person in one picture. Some aspects must be sacrificed, if others are to be emphasized, so that to concentrate on one aspect at a time is only carrying selection a stage further.

The second argument in favour of abstraction depends upon memory and the after-image (see pp. 12–14). The character of the after-image is affected by the painter's subconscious emotions; and consequently abstract art and surrealism are more alike in practice than in theory. The abstract artist, in pursuit of the decorative, draws inspiration from what he has seen, the choice of which is inevitably partly determined by his emotions. The surrealist, in seeking to reveal his subconscious emotions, depends on what he has seen optically, however he may distort it; nor can he afford to ignore design. Otherwise surrealism becomes mere illustration in the narrowest sense (see Chapter XI), just as abstract art, if it has no emotional visual experience behind it, becomes (again in the narrowest sense) mere decoration.

The recording of the vision of the mind's eye is the first necessity of self-expression; but only under certain conditions does it automatically result in clarity. A young child may obtain intense satisfaction from painting pictures, which *for him* record lucidly the visions of his mind. To an adult the *raison d'être* of this record may be completely obscure, so that nothing but the intensity of the creator's satisfaction is communicated.

To paint a good abstract picture requires unusual gifts both of sensibility and of clear pictorial eloquence. When Picasso paints a harlequin with a violin and bounds his areas of flat colour entirely with straight, and mainly with oblique, contours, he knows completely what patterns of gay colour and what jerky changes of direction he wants to record and how to make these experiences clear to the patient spectator. Or to take a less classical example, when Ivon Hitchens remembers a grey-green copse seen dimly in half sunlight, and again a high-backed crimson chair beheld at dusk, he records the combined images with such convincing beauty of colour and pigment, that the expression of the mysterious vision becomes lucid.

Such masterpieces of sensibility are inspired by, and appeal to, emotions largely subconscious, though they are not usually described as surrealistic.

The passion for geometry may have a connexion with the even more prevalent passion for machinery. Machinery, the one thriving creative activity of our age, is itself an art; and many pictures have been painted to demonstrate its power. Sometimes the artist is a wholehearted admirer of mechanical achievements, sometimes a hostile critic. In both cases he is right to seize for inspiration upon a force so important in life. But if mechanical objects are his sole subject, his art is liable to become narrow.

The constructivist geometrical pattern and the exclusive representation of mechanical objects have much in common emotionally, though differing as pictorial aims in one important respect: namely, that the painter of the first accepts the flatness of the surface to be covered and the painter of the second seeks to represent the image of recession upon that surface.

In early painting, patterns that include vegetable forms, however conventionalized, by referring more closely to past visual experience than patterns exclusively geometrical, approach nearer to one of the requirements of a picture, but frequently fail to fulfil another requirement, that of unity. Thus the horizontal bands separating the scenes in Margaritone's *Madonna and Child with Saints* (564) do not in themselves constitute pictures, because bounded by no inevitable termination. On the other hand the best modern constructivist designs, though failing as visions, do achieve unified compactness. Nor are unity and even vision absent from the Margaritone altarpiece, taken as a whole. The proportion of the parts and their relation to the total shape have been calculated to a nicety.

The mosaicists and painters of the Byzantine tradition created shapes, the meaning of which even their illiterate contemporaries understood. Many of these shapes, such as the halo, the symbol of sanctity, had no foundation in the world of appearances. Others might resemble natural forms but slightly. A small mouth was understood to mean purity and a large forehead intellect, etc. Each saint was recognized by his symbol. Relative stature was arranged according to spiritual importance. The appeal was primarily neither to the spectators' decorative sense, nor to his memory of appearances, but to an arbitrary system of conveying ideas, accepted and made possible by the common culture of the Christian Church. The method is less suited to our individualistic age. When Picasso wishes to convey, say, nobility by a horse, and, say, brutality by a bull, his symbols require to be explained.

Thus, while photographic art and constructivist art, for apparently opposite reasons, both fail to appeal to our fullest imaginative vision, the more arbitrary type of symbolic art can only appeal if the symbols are understood. Pictures can hardly ever be fully appreciated without *some* reference to extraneous associations. The mistake of constructivist art lies in attempting to do without associations, and the mistake of symbolic art in depending upon nothing else.

(ii) SURREALISM

Surrealism, being derived from associations, may be regarded as a branch of symbolic art. As a conscious aim, surrealism is almost impossible to achieve. First, there is an inherent contradiction in consciously recording the visions of the subconscious. That the subconscious has played an undoubted part in the great art of the past is evident to the critic after the event. But the artist of the past was less introspective. It never occurred to him consciously to exploit his subconscious mind, of which he had never heard. The conscious exploitation in modern art of subconscious emotions, by destroying spontaneity, deprives pictorial vision of half its value. The best modern surrealists do not know that they are surrealists.

The word 'surrealism' implies that the images of the mind are of greater aesthetic value than the normal objective images from which they are derived. In practice it is convenient to describe as surrealistic only such pictures as have been inspired by dreams or conditions of mind akin to dreams.

The dream of the present-day surrealist is often a nightmare of pain, fear and despair. There are even insincere painters, who make up nightmares never really experienced, in the spirit of the hack-writer of a ghost story.

Of the genuine surrealists, who really have nightmares and really express them, many have considerable power, so that their pictures command the spectator's attention. Chirico in particular, in his early work, achieves organic completeness and communicates the conviction that his visions are of importance. Others are narrower in their appeal. The nightmares of the abnormal, though disturbing to behold, may remain partly or wholly obscure.

In addition surrealism raises the question of what emotions are worth expressing (see pp. 3 and 162 ff). Many surrealists appear to be utterly humourless and joyless. If their work is erotic, the eroticism is inhibited and sad, and makes one long for Rubens or Boucher. It seems sad that they should delve into the meanest mental morbidities, when the world outside can supply inexhaustible inspiration.

Hieronymus Bosch, El Greco, Goya and Blake (among other artists of the past) are frequently regarded as forerunners of surrealism; and, except that they were all quite unconscious of their aims, the classification is justified. Each artist was impelled by an emotional urge unlike in kind, but like in the strength, which led to distortions of normal vision. Their works have the reality of dreams. Bosch believed in devils, and his visions of them were derived from memories of tormenting insects and animals, and the most malevolent aspects of humanity. What he derived from humanity can be seen in the *Crowning with Thorns* (4744), where the tormentors' expressions are distorted by exclusively evil passions. In other cases his visions departed farther from reality and combined crowds of semi-human, animal and vegetable forms with the consistent incoherence of a dream.

El Greco saw all religious subjects in the light of an exaggerated and tense striving of the spirit, which he shared with the most fervent Spanish Catholics of his day. This led to his visions of flickering lights and attenuated flame-like men, often far more distorted than in *The Agony in the Garden* [(3476), Pl. 50]. Goya, an enemy of the Church, was impelled by his hatred of cruelty and superstition to give forth such visions as *The Bewitched Man* [(1472), Pl. 69], a nightmare all the more haunting because of the absence of distortion in all but one of the forms.

Bosch, El Greco and Goya may each of them be compared with artists somewhat similar, in whom the tendency is less extreme: Bosch with Bruegel, El Greco with Tintoretto and Goya with Daumier. Bruegel's humour, geniality and balanced sanity of mind puts his average work (however exaggerated) outside surrealism; but his appalling *Triumph of Death* (Prado, Madrid) is more haunting and to-day, unhappily, more credible than any of Bosch's dated diableries. Tintoretto could create visions that seemed to come to him in a flash, such as the endless vistas of his *Massacre of the Innocents* (Scuola di San Rocco, Venice). In his nightmare phases, Daumier was nearer to normal vision than Goya: in his *Don Quixote and Sancho Panza* (Courtauld Institute) he is as direct and vivid as his Spanish forerunner.

Surrealistic painting at its best is the outcome of vision and especially of the kind of vision that reason cannot explain. The work of Blake exemplifies this. With an actual model in front of him, he could produce nothing of value. He depended entirely upon those visions, which he regarded as miraculous. The stylistic mannerisms of the resulting pictures can be explained away as imperfect memories of engravings from Michelangelo, Gothic sculpture, etc.; but nothing can explain the power that his greatest designs have to convince and hold the imagination. The *Satan Smiting Job* (T.G. 3340) of 1808 is already haunting; and the later alterations in the engraving of 1825 are all additions to its force; and his joyful visions, such as the engraving of *The Lord answering Job out of the Whirlwind* (B.M.), are equally inspired and compelling.

In the four scenes in the life of S. John (5451–4) by Giovanni di Paolo the perspective, though inconsistent and unscientific, somehow makes space a reality; in *S. John entering the Wilderness* especially [(5454), Pl. 12] the combined imagery and the fact that, when he is on the mountains his feet do not touch the ground, recall the type of happy dream, which is quite as convincing, if quite as irrational, as a nightmare.

CHAPTER XI

ILLUSTRATION

In most Victorian books on painting the descriptions of the pictures relate exclusively to the subject-matter. In many more recent books they relate exclusively to the technique and the design. Neither method is complete. In the best painting, design and subject are inextricably interwoven.

The problem of subject-matter is closely allied to the problem of realism. Those interested in subject only are the same as those who like a picture to 'look real'. Those who speak scornfully of the 'merely realistic' speak equally scornfully of the 'merely literary'. The two problems as they affect portraits and landscapes have much in common, but as applied to figure-composition are distinct. Here the treatment of the subject involves *illustration*, an aim which may or may not accompany realism. By illustration I mean the pictorial expression of a human story. The early *Madonna and Child* [(4741), Pl. 2] attributed to a Pisan artist, though far from realistic, is an excellent illustration. Vermeer's *Lady Standing at the Virginals* [(1383), Pl. 64], though closely imitating appearance, illustrates nothing.

Illustration for some time has fallen into disrepute. In the last century, and even in this, quantities of pictures achieved nothing but the telling of a story. Sometimes even the story itself needed the verbal title to explain it. In any case, story-telling was the painter's sole aim. So long as he did this, he took no trouble to visualize his work as a whole. The result was a total neglect of design. Hogarth's less convincing moralities, Watts's worst allegories, Millais' pot-boilers, Delaroche's *Princes in the Tower*, all broke down for this reason. The admirers of the 'story picture' in this sense do not enjoy the picture itself, but merely use it as a tap for turning on an emotion, which excuses them from needing to look at it any longer. The reaction from such false standards was inevitable. Whistler went to the opposite extreme when he called his portrait of *His Mother* (Louvre) 'An Arrangement in Black and Grey'.

Yet there is such a thing in art as legitimate emotional content, in which associations of the subject may play an important part. This is a merit provided it makes the spectator continue to look at the picture. If the artist has seen his subject aright, he will not neglect design. On the contrary, the design will grow out of the story. His dramatic instinct and decorative sense will go hand in hand, each strengthening the other. Thus, in Lippi's *Annunciation* [(666), Pl. 9] the curved backs of the two bowing figures are necessary for the expression of their mutual reverence and equally necessary for their enclosure within the frame. It is impossible to know which reason came first into the painter's mind. In Titian's *Noli Me Tangere* [(270), Pl. 33] also, the dramatic and decorative necessities are in accord. The curve running up the figure of S. Mary Magdalene to the tree and the curve uniting her arm with Christ's are graceful in themselves and also emphasize the intensity of her sudden change of mood. The alternating sunshine and cloud shadows over the landscape make telling patterns in *chiaroscuro* and also typify the dawning of hope after the night of despair.

These two examples—and hundreds more could be cited from the National Gallery alone—are illustrations in the best sense of the word. The story has inspired the design: and the design not merely represents, but throws light upon, the story.

Another question now arises. How far do such pictures depend upon the subject? Can they be fully appreciated regardless of it? The answer to this cannot be an unqualified 'Yes' or 'No'. After the masterpiece is completed, it *is* possible to enjoy its aesthetic qualities alone, divorced from what they illustrate, to enjoy the language of expression and ignore the subject expressed. To a certain extent one can appreciate line, tone, colour and the like, while ignoring the subject. But by such artificial restrictions one is bound to miss the full flavour of the artist's inspiration. For the great artist always has an idea to express as well as the means of expressing it. He does not think exclusively in terms of aesthetics. For him to think of nothing but design is to narrow the possibilities of design itself. And even the spectator who ignores 'the inward and spiritual meaning' will in practice pass over the subtlest delights of 'the outward and visible form'.

One can enjoy Giotto's frescoes exclusively for the distribution of solid masses, or a 'Bacchanal' by Nicolas Poussin exclusively for the linear design. But a painter who imitates Giotto's composition without the inspiration of Christianity, or Poussin's forms without understanding the pagan spirit, will fail in those very qualities of design which he professes as his aim. A figure placed in a picture solely for a decorative purpose, does not achieve that very purpose so well as one that is also conceived as a human being, capable of human experience.

Painting is not merely an abstract, geometrical and chemical science. Like literature and music, it reflects the temperament, philosophy and environment of the artist.

ILLUSTRATION 53

Art, therefore, cannot be fully understood without a knowledge of the artist's environment. An Oriental, ignorant of Christian tradition, can only partly appreciate a picture of a Christian subject; and an American or European, ignorant of Buddhist beliefs, can admire the lines, colours and external forms of a representation of Buddha; but the full value of these qualities will be felt by him only when he has studied the artist's religion.

Thus, in the appreciation of painting, while reliance on associations alone leads nowhere, the cult of 'art for art's sake', like other *a priori* methods of approach, does not lead very far. Associations are needed as supplements to technical study; but much depends upon their character. If they arouse only the emotions expected by the indolent spectator, they are valueless. If they reveal some idea or current of feeling that affected the artist, they are of value. In most cases, however, a wide and deep study of the ideas and the outlook of the present and bygone periods is necessary.

In England, the Victorian 'literary' approach to art appreciation was succeeded, early in this century, by its opposite, the advocacy of purely technical and aesthetic study. This in turn has been followed by another reaction chiefly due to continental scholars, who rightly treat the history of art as a branch of the general history of society, philosophy and religion. Such learning, used in such a way that grasp of content quickens grasp of form and vice versa, can immeasurably enrich artistic understanding.

For these reasons it would be misleading rigidly to exclude all reference to religious and cultural environment even from a book dealing mainly with other aspects of art. So the three following chapters include brief semi-historical accounts of developments in the treatment of different types of subject-matter. Like Chapters XXVIII, XIX and XXX, they are more concerned with the *quality* of the emotion expressed than with the main topic of the book, the *means* of expression.

CHAPTER XII

CHRISTIAN AND CLASSICAL SUBJECTS

ALL great art is in the widest sense religious, since it expresses not only the pride of creation, but also the humility of wonder. The artist loses himself in his experience and finds himself in it again. He gives forth that which he has been given. He transforms it, so that it is both recognizable and fresh, both old and new.

(i) CHRISTIAN SUBJECTS

A religious spirit in the above sense is not confined to the illustration of Christian themes, although these have inspired some of the noblest examples of it. Portraiture, landscape, pagan subjects and still-life provide equal opportunities for reverence. Moreover, the nominal theme is not always what awakens the deepest feelings of the illustrator. Crivelli in painting the two pictures of the *Madonna and Child with Saints* (724 and 807) has taken the opportunity of introducing the flowers and fruit, which command his real devotion. It is surprising that such examples of transferred reverence are not commoner.

Casual visitors to the National Gallery complain of finding so many pictures of the Madonna. Sometimes, no doubt, the artist must have felt handicapped by having to illustrate so well-worn a theme. Gozzoli's *Madonna and Child with Saints* (283) is somewhat dull. But more often fifteenth-century artists, encouraged by the certainty of public sympathy, found new inspiration in a subject by no means new. Giovanni Bellini, for instance, in all his illustrations of the Madonna and Child, never repeats himself monotonously.

Painting in Europe, until the fifteenth century, was restricted almost exclusively to Christian subjects. Altar-pieces were at first devotional in inspiration: Christ, the Virgin and the Saints were regarded as beings superior to the ordinary human emotions and experiences. S. Francis's teaching gradually modified this outlook. The *Madonna and Child* by a Pisan artist (?) [(4741), Pl. 2] is beginning to be more human; and in the early fourteenth century Duccio's great *Madonna and Saints* or 'Maestà', painted for Siena Cathedral, was carried through the streets in triumph, because the Virgin looked like a real woman. To us she looks less real, but comparison shows her to have more humanity than previous representations. In the large *Madonna and Child* (565) by a follower of Duccio, there is more of the older tradition than in Duccio's own little *Madonna and Child with Saints* [(566), Pl. 3], in which the Child plays with His Mother's veil.

As time went on, the subject of the Virgin and Child underwent a great variation of moods. In general, humanity was increasingly stressed rather than divinity, and the treatment became more episodic and less devotional. This is already apparent in Correggio's *Madonna of the Basket* (23) and the climax of the tendency is reached in Titian's *Mother and Child* (3948), which expresses no exceptional spirituality, but merely whatever is divine in the normal human relationship.

Not surprisingly, the narrative of the Gospels, containing so much to move and uplift the spirit, inspired some of the greatest examples of painting. Many of the finest passages, however, describing the ministry of Christ, were seldom illustrated in the fifteenth and sixteenth centuries. Except for a few accepted subjects, such as the Baptism, Transfiguration, House of Martha and Raising of Lazarus, the tendency was to concentrate on two groups of subject: (i) the beginning, events surrounding the Nativity; (ii) the end, from the Journey into Jerusalem to the Ascension, especially the Passion and Crucifixion.

Of examples in the National Gallery of the early group, Lippi's *Annunciation* [(666), Pl. 9] expresses poetically the unexplained mystery of the supernatural event. Two pictures of the *Nativity* may be contrasted: Piero della Francesca's [(908), Pl. 21], restrainedly and peacefully happy; and Botticelli's [(1034), Pl. 28], wild with demonstrative ecstasy.

Duccio's 'Maestà' (see above) originally included several small panels (now dispersed) representing subjects rarely illustrated. Of these, the *Temptation*, the *Call of Peter and Andrew* and the *Woman of Samaria* are at Washington. The National Gallery possesses the somewhat damaged, but solemn *Transfiguration* (1330), rendered touching by the naïve gesticulations of Elijah, and the beautifully preserved *Christ Healing the Blind Man* [(1140), Pl. 1].

This picture, glowing with colour and delicate in lighting, is one of the Gallery's most prized possessions. The narrative is continuous. The blind man, stooping and anxious, first receives his sight; then throws down his staff, gives thanks and looks joyously about him. Not being a saint, he wears contemporary dress and is smaller than Christ and the Apostles, who have the bare feet and long robes of tradition. Christ's gesture is full of earnest purpose, and the attitudes of the Apostles express their puzzled awe.

Of the imaginary portraits of Christ in the gallery, much the finest is Antonello da Messina's *Salvator Mundi* (673), inspired by a touching sincerity, although little positive character is suggested. The Redemption, which greatly occupied Giovanni Bellini's mind when he was young, is the subject of his devotional picture *The Blood of the Redeemer* (1233), in which the sentiment depends much on the still landscape, clouded except where the sun shines on the distant towers beside the sea.

The Agony in the Garden is illustrated in the National Gallery in four fine pictures: (i) by Borgognone (1077A), who stresses Christ's patience and the quiet of the scene; (ii) Mantegna [(1417), Pl. 18], who makes the tragedy heroic and gives it an heroic setting; (iii) Giovanni Bellini [(726), Pl. 19], who calls forth the image of impending crisis; and (iv) El Greco [(3476), Pl. 50], who expresses with least restraint the bitterness of the moment. In the Bellini, the inconsistency of the sunlight (which comes from three different directions) in no way disturbs the unity. Bellini has remembered a number of effects seen at the same time, when looking in different directions. These and the dramatic subject have made in his mind one complete vision, to which his picture is faithful: the little group of unprotected friends, separated from Judas and the soldiers merely by the small bridge; Christ in the throes of lonely prayer; the three disciples exhausted and asleep; Jerusalem on the hill; the vivid, irrelevant details of trees, houses, fences and streams; and over everything the architecture of the clouds, reddened by the threatening sunrise.

The Crucifixion was often treated devotionally rather than historically, as in Antonello's picture (1166), small in scale but large in design, where only the Virgin and S. John sit contemplatively at the foot of the Cross, against a background of skulls and a landscape of fortifications, and low hills, dotted with trees. Andrea dal Castagno's treatment in another illustration [(1138), Pl. 13], small in measurement but large in conception, is much more tense: the colours are gloomy; the Virgin and S. John are in despair; Christ is dead, and only the penitent thief contemplates with hope the promise of Paradise.

The joyful events of the Resurrection inspired equally dramatic masterpieces. Titian's *Noli Me Tangere* [(270), Pl. 33] is a splendid example of a favourite theme.

Stories about saints gave opportunity for fantasy, as in the Master of Werden's childlike *Conversion of S. Hubert* (252), or the more realistic, but equally attractive *S. Giles and the Hind* (1419) by the Master of S. Giles. The legends of S. Francis were especially popular. Sassetta in his ' Scenes of S. Francis' Life' (4757–63) has exactly recaptured the spirit of the man who regarded all things in Nature as his brothers or sisters and the life of Holy Poverty as the greatest happiness. The *Wolf of Gubbio* (4762) is the most entertaining of the series; but the *Stigmatization of S. Francis* [(4760), Pl. 14] is the most inspired. As often happens in great religious art, the miraculous effect depends largely on the landscape: the red-gold of the coming sunset transforms the little chapel, the olive trees and the steep rocks, seen against the deep blue of the evening sky.

An Italian, when illustrating a miraculous narrative, though he might introduce homely details, so idealized the scene as to prepare the mind for the supernatural. The painters of the Netherlands and Germany treated supernatural events as breaking in upon everyday surroundings with an unexpected shock. For instance, in Robert Campin's *Virgin and Child* (2609) the firescreen is so placed as to become a halo; and in the *Death of the Virgin* (658) an imitator of the same artist represents a human and wholly realistic drama, that contains nothing to prepare the mind for the supernatural group of Christ and the angels, hovering in readiness to receive the Virgin's soul.

In the seventeenth century, both in Catholic and in Protestant countries, many changes took place in the treatment of religious art. New subjects were illustrated, especially from the ministry of Christ and the Parables. Caravaggio deliberately avoided the traditional features of Christ in *Christ at Emmaus* [(172), Pl. 52]. Homely events and miracles were put side by side. In the *Adoration of the Shepherds* (232) by a Neapolitan artist, a mother rebukes a boy for irreverently playing a pipe. In Rembrandt's *Woman Taken in Adultery* [(45), Pl. 58] every actor in the drama (and this includes about fifty figures) has a completely realized identity, based upon insight into the minds of the painter's contemporaries.

Meanwhile in Spain, always a land of extremes, El Greco, some decades earlier, had been treating religious themes in an idealized non-realistic spirit; and Zurbaran, only slightly Rembrandt's senior, was putting miracles and circumstantial events side by side. His *S. Francis* [(5655), Pl. 57], a strange misinterpretation of the most joyous of saints, expresses spiritual strife as forcefully as anything by El Greco, but in monumental concrete terms.

El Greco himself in the *Agony in the Garden* [(3476), Pl. 50] has produced effects so powerful that even adverse reaction is a tribute. The distorted forms, the sharp edges, the violent contrasts of tone and colour, all emphasize Christ's unbearable loneliness and the bitterness of his inevitable choice. The blank void of black sky behind the rock and jutting cloud arouses tense disquiet. On the other hand, there is a weird peacefulness about the moonlit valley on the right, although Judas is there; and mercy is implied by the living plants in the foreground and still more by the texture of the head, arm, wing, and even the robe of the patient angel.

This masterpiece of the counter-Reformation presents an almost complete antithesis to the next type of subject-matter to be considered—the illustration of pagan themes in the fifteenth and succeeding centuries.

(ii) CLASSICAL SUBJECTS

After 1400, pictures of Christian themes were still produced in quantities; but there was also an increasing demand for portraits and (in Italy) for pictures of classical subjects, taken from Greek or Roman mythology, history, or literature. The growing wealth of such families as the Medici, the teaching and reading of the Greek language in the original and discoveries of ancient pagan sculpture, all contributed to this cult. History was less popular than mythology. Such pictures as Mantegna's *Triumph of Scipio* (902), showing antiquarian knowledge and a power to enter sympathetically, almost humorously, into past events, were rare. Nominally historical pictures were a little commoner. A fine example is Veronese's *Family of Darius before Alexander* [(294), Pls. 45–7]. Masterpiece though it is, it is not dramatic. The characters are distinguished Venetian aristocrats, who have chosen, with some slight attempts at ancient armour on the part of the men, to take part in a dignified *tableau vivant*.

Poetry and mythology were more inspiring. The spirit of the Renaissance led to many new modes of thought: a more independent and inquiring attitude towards science and philosophy; the recognition of the beauty of the human form and of various forces governing man's behaviour and the workings of the natural world. Perspective and anatomy were studied; nude figures appeared in painting and sculpture; Venus, though not worshipped as a goddess, was accepted as a personification of feelings deeply affecting the whole of life.

Botticelli's spirituality appears as much in his pagan as in his Christian pictures. Both are inspired by a hunger and thirst for righteousness and for ideal beauty. *Mars, Venus and Satyrs* [(915), Pl. 24] in spite of inequalities of draughtsmanship, expresses fully the grace of the body and its function as the house of the soul. Mars, the fighter, is helpless compared with Venus, who symbolizes emotional and even intellectual powers.

The generation in Italy younger than Botticelli painted subjects of this kind with equal power and more confidence. The pastoral idylls of Giorgione were followed by works like Dossi's *Bacchanalian Scene* (5279) and by Titian's great Bacchanalian pictures, including *Bacchus and Ariadne* [(35), Pl. 36]. Titian fully understood the mixture of ecstatic beauty and brutal savagery that were comprised in the worship of Bacchus. Here he has contrasted the excitement of the revellers, who at their wildest are performing a ceremonial rite, with what interrupts it—the appearance of the startled Ariadne and the impetuous passion that she awakens in the alluring young god, not only of wine, but of all dramatic and choric inspiration.

Some thirty years later, when Titian was about seventy, he painted a *Venus and Adonis*, of which there are several replicas. The execution of neither the National Gallery version [(34), Pl. 37] nor the Prado version quite equals the imaginative conception; in ours, Adonis's head and neck are weak in drawing; but the drama is sufficiently expressed in a superb design. Titian's manner of exalting the theme of love was peculiar to the High Renaissance. Something like it occurs in Shakespeare's sonnets; but no painter after 1600 recaptured the exact flavour; and of painters before 1600 only the other Venetians came near to it. Later painters, in treating the subject, fell short of Titian's in one way or another: by being equally frank, but less poetic like Rubens; or merely physically erotic like Boucher; or sincere but restrained like Poussin; or tenderly ethereal like Watteau. None did justice, as Titian did, both to the dignity and to the intensity of the passion (see also pp. 173–5).

In Titian's *Venus and Adonis* the ardour of Venus meets with no response from the unsusceptible young Adonis, who has been entirely occupied in hunting and has never thought of love. It is part of the sublimity of the Venetians that their actors are completely absorbed in their own drama. Titian's Venus thinks only of Adonis, unlike Correggio's Venus in *Venus, Mercury and Cupid* [(10), Pl. 40], who expects to be admired by the audience.

Bacchanalian subjects were popular in the seventeenth century, largely owing to the admiration for Titian's various Bacchanal pictures; and here again, neither Rubens nor Poussin could reproduce Titian's spirit. Poussin recaptured the idea of the rite, but made the revellers, in spite of all their apparently wild behaviour, essentially decorous dancers. Rubens recaptured the savagery, which did not repel him, but failed to express the ritual.

The gods and goddesses in most paintings of the Renaissance symbolize impulses governing the actions of man. More rarely they personify the forces of Nature outside him: the tree nymph; the river spirit; the genius of the mountain or the thunder; the powers of sun or stars, wind or sea. The sea inspired Tintoretto in particular. Though not itself represented, its effect is implied in the vaporous atmosphere of the *Origin of the Milky Way* [(1313), Pl. 48], in which Jupiter and

Juno are endowed with superhuman stature and an energy and calm that might well control the elements.

Such personifications, human or superhuman, might be termed *allegories*. On the other hand, pure allegories, unsupported by mythological tradition, though the theme of much great literature, have produced little great painting. Most allegorical pictures are dismal failures; when they succeed, the inspiration comes from something other than the subject. Veronese's four so-called allegories, *Unfaithfulness* [(1318), Pl. 49], *Happy Union* (1326), *Scorn* (1324) and *Respect* (1325), are absurdly unconvincing as particular human dramas, though they express magnificently the painter's invariable theme, the beauty and dignity of mankind. A comparable satisfaction with life, expressed in a less static form, is the real subject of Rubens's *Peace and War* (46).

CHAPTER XIII

PORTRAITS AND LANDSCAPES

(i) PORTRAITS

A good portrait depends both on the painter's perception and on the sitter's response. It is a joint effort. The sitter must allow his face to become more than a mask; the painter must get outside himself enough to understand the sitter's mind. The extent to which a likeness reveals individual character varies. It can never do so completely. Reynolds's account of *Dr Johnson* (887) in paint, and Boswell's account of him in writing agree; but each tells something that the other omits. Some portraits, such as Van Eyck's *Man* (222), even though there is no written account of the sitter, carry conviction as revelations of an individuality, never before, and never afterwards, exactly repeated in the world's history.

Some painters have disclaimed the ability to record more than externals; and it may be true that their conscious efforts have been devoted exclusively to searching out physical facts; but this does not preclude an unconscious selection, based on a knowledge of the sitter's mind. Such knowledge must help. When painters attempt portraits before getting to know their sitters, the results are deficient. The ideal is to reveal the mind by means of representing the outward appearance.

Many portraits, though evidently good likenesses, remain enigmas. For instance, do the crooked mouth and suspicious eyes of *Dr Peral* (1951) by Goya indicate nervous antipathy to the painter, partial paralysis, or merely loss of teeth?

Portraiture, like every other branch of painting, must be the outcome of emotion. The painter must be excited by the sitter's having eyes, cheek-bones, a mouth, jaw and nose of a particular shape. He may also be interested in his mental characteristics; but these need not excite his admiration or hostility. He must observe and record; but he may abstain from comment. He may leave the spectator to decide on his own sentiments concerning the man or woman revealed. This ideal of detachment is notably attained by three painters, who differ in other respects: Van Eyck, Holbein and Velazquez. It gives added value to the unquestionable truth of Velazquez's *Philip IV when Elderly* (745).

Some critics hold that such unbiased revelations are the greatest portraits; but that which betrays the painter's prejudices may be more immediately attractive.

It brings us into more intimate contact with the artist. In portraits of women particularly, a cold objectivity may be almost displeasing. Many will prefer Gainsborough's slight, but charming *Miss Singleton* (2638) to Van Eyck's revealing, but formidable portrait of his *Wife* at Bruges. Sometimes, as in Rubens's *Lady* (M. Gulbenkian) a feminine portrait seems to go beyond the representation of an individual and to symbolize the perennial fascination of womankind.

In painting children, the chief danger is the sentimental tendency to represent them not as they are, but as the adult would like them to be. A respectful treatment is combined with searching observation and tenderness in Gainsborough's lovely groups of his *Daughters Chasing a Butterfly* (1811) and *Teasing a Cat* (3812). Velazquez, in the portrait of the baby prince *Don Baltasar Carlos* (Wallace, 12), has achieved pathos without sacrificing truth. Real affection is a spur to vision. It is sentimentality, not love, that is blind.

Portraits of the old provide some striking contrasts. In them Velazquez maintains his objectivity. Van Eyck, too, is, as always, detached. Tintoretto, on the other hand, makes *Morosini* (4004) repellently pitiable, without denying him dignity of bearing. Rembrandt's pathos is different: his own sufferings give him a special sympathy with the aged; but the sorrows of *Margaretha Trip* (1675) have a moral dignity that commands respect.

In contrast, in Dürer's portrait of *The Painter's Father* [(1938), Pl. 38], old age is seen at its most confident and least passive; the impression is of a fiery and alarming temper, sensitivity combined with humour, keenness of brain akin to genius. Pity for old Dürer would be superfluous: pity for the more timid of his friends would be more appropriate. The search for detail, which goes beyond even Van Eyck in thoroughness, has been prompted by deep filial affection.

Intimacy of presentation is commoner in Flemish and Dutch than in Italian and Spanish portraits. The people of the Netherlands valued individuality above beauty; and for the sake of it they even indulged in caricature (see § (iii), p. 42). The tendency is latent in Van Eyck's portraits and apparent in such non-portrait groups as Bruegel's *Adoration of the Magi* [(3556), Pl. 43].

The Italian ideal in portraiture was polite and reserved. Sitters must be represented at their best: handsome, if possible; if not, at least dignified. Often individuality itself was sacrificed to beauty, as in Andrea del Sarto's *Sculptor* (690); Raphael, as in *Julius II* (of which no. 27 is a copy), and Titian (as in the *Vendramin Family* [(4452), Pl. 44] were capable of great insight into men's minds; but no Italian was so ruthless as Van Eyck was in *Jan Arnolfini and his Wife* [(186), Pl. 10].

Italianized Flemish attempts at grandiose portraiture were usually, as in Mabuse's *Man with a Rosary* (656), hybrid and snobbish failures; but Van Dyck, through his Italian training, succeeded in bringing out only such virtues and faults as would please his sitter.

To regard all men as equally dignified and to regard all men as equally absurd are both democratic sentiments; and Veronese's dignified shepherds in the *Adoration of the Magi* (268) bear out this. But the democrats of Holland and England have usually produced the less dignified type of portrait. Hogarth, indeed, was no true democrat. Like the Irishman, he believed firmly that: 'One man is as good as another and a great deal better, too.' His powers are well seen in his group of his *Servants* (1374), each of whom lives as an individual; and even better in the *Shrimp Girl* (1162), a beautiful example of the 'speaking likeness', i.e. the vivid record (usually from memory) of the momentary expression of a face. Frans Hals was the first to succeed fully in this aim (see p. 34); but even his brilliant works are excelled—in feeling, at least—by this unique English masterpiece.

(ii) LANDSCAPES

Towards 1600 a more regular demand began in Europe for three new types of subject: landscape, genre, and still life. Before then, with few exceptions, these subjects had been treated as accessories, subordinate to a portrait or to a religious or mythological illustration.

In medieval times, while Chinese artists had long represented mountains and torrents with enthusiasm, Europeans still shrank from wild natural scenery in fear. The only purpose of a mountain was to retire there and do penance. Cultivated gardens had their attraction; but, in pictures, even these were subordinate to humanity. In the sixteenth century the attitude was only gradually modified. The *River Scene* (1298) formerly ascribed to Patenier, but probably by some other Antwerp painter, was an exception in illustrating no human narrative; then came Bruegel's great pictures of the Alps, such as the *Snow Hunt* and the *Return of the Herd* at Vienna. Meantime in Italy, though landscapes were never the sole subject of a picture, the Umbrians had rendered space and the Venetians sunshine. Giorgione treated the mood of man as dependent on his surroundings. Titian introduced mountains, and Tintoretto the sea, into their backgrounds.

Outside Holland and Flanders, even in the seventeenth century, landscapes would not sell, unless treated as settings for human dramas. Working in Italy,

Claude had to introduce figures into them and call them 'Cephalus and Procris', 'Isaac and Rebecca', and so on. In Holland, such titles were not demanded; but even there, landscapes without figures were extremely rare and Ruisdael is said to have employed a professional figure painter to add them to his foregrounds.

Several tendencies in landscape had their first germ in seventeenth-century painting. The Dutch painters of the period were the first to paint simple scenes, marine, pastoral or agricultural, scenes devoid of any striking features. In addition, the following painters were each typical of a new aim and a new influence: Salvator Rosa, Claude Lorraine, Nicolas Poussin, Rubens.

Salvator Rosa popularized a sentiment known in the eighteenth century as 'the sublime'. It consists of a proud exultation in overcoming the fear inspired by Nature's destructive forces. It governs certain pictures by artists senior to Salvator, such as the *Shipwreck of S. Paul* (3535) by Elsheimer, and *Mountain Landscape* (4383) by Segers. Much later, at a period when it was greatly in vogue, it was vigorously expressed in the dark early works of Turner, such as *Calais Pier* [(472), Pl. 70].

Meanwhile, Claude became the acknowledged painter of 'the beautiful', i.e. of everything sunny, peaceful and soothing. His scientific treatment of sunlight by relative tones (see Chapter XIX) taught an invaluable lesson to Wilson, Corot and Turner.

Nicolas Poussin's landscapes are perfect examples of a conception of balance, met with a little earlier in those of Annibale Carracci and Domenichino (see Chapters XVII and XVIII). Poussin expressed the coherent durability of the ground with a completeness, later equalled only by his great admirer Cézanne and by such of Turner's works as the *Garden of the Hesperides* (T.G. 477).

The ground in Rubens's landscapes is as solid as in Poussin's, but much less permanent. Poussin's soil, like his rocks, his ruins, even his trees, has remained unmoved for centuries (see Pl. 55). Rubens's soil is being constantly worn away by streams or worked away by roots. Poussin was the philosopher of immutability; Rubens of growth and change. In Rubens's *Château de Steen* [(66), Pl. 54] shadows of clouds and patches of sunshine are blown across the fields; horses draw the rumbling cart along the uneven ground; the smaller birds are astir; the sportsman creeps round the bush with his gun; the trees, aware of the fresh September wind, are as much alive as all the other creatures in the scene; sap courses through them, like blood through the veins of man.

Rubens's landscapes were admired and imitated by his successors, but no later work combined all their qualities. Watteau and Fragonard had a comparable command of atmosphere, but less vitality. Gainsborough, as in the *Market Cart* (80) was as sunny and as graceful in his brush-work, but lacked Rubens's structural power. Constable, as in *The Hay-Wain* (1207), was inspired by a kindred spirit and borrowed several of Rubens's technical devices, but without Rubens's grace or control of material.

But in the recording of local colour, especially cool colour, Constable excelled Rubens. In fact, with a few exceptions such as Cuyp, the seventeenth-century landscape painters were somewhat conventional colourists. They made mauves (in skies) greyer and greens either greyer or browner than they saw them. In the next century, Canaletto, and still more Guardi and Wilson, produced lovely records of the colours of the sky; but Constable and Corot were the first to apply the same standards of subtlety to all the colours of Nature.

Landscapes tend to be inspired either by the sense of familiarity or by the sense of strangeness. Most Dutch and many Flemish examples are of the first type. The quiet Dutch mood continued in the less ambitious English water-colours of the eighteenth and early nineteenth centuries, in Gainsborough's earliest land-scapes, in the works of the Barbizon School, in those of Crome and Constable and in many Turners, such as *Walton Bridges* (2680) and the much later *Evening Star* (1991).

Turner's *Frosty Morning* [(492), Pl. 72] expresses an intimate experience in the quietest language. Complete structural and atmospheric knowledge is shown without ostentation. The skilful avoidance of repeated coincidences, so essential to the design, gives it at first the air of a random record. The stage-coach in the distance emphasizes the rural character of the scene; the people are real awkward rustics; the horses, the cart, the spade and wheelbarrow, the very ruts in the road, belong as much to the heart of the country as the subordinated, but indispensable hemlock in the foreground, or the delicately and firmly articulated trees.

To convey intimacy, the painter must have a knowledge of his subject. Mountain scenes, such as *Cader Idris* (5596) by Wilson, who was bred in Wales, are more satisfying than those, such as *The Bridge* (2284) by Gainsborough, who only visited the Lake District once towards the end of his life; and even Turner, with his unequalled capacity for new impressions, was greatest when representing what he had seen often. Such works and all that Constable painted in East Anglia are ample proof also that familiarity is perfectly compatible with awe.

Constable's sketches and Turner's later works anticipated and influenced the French impressionists (see Chapter VIII); but the professed aim of the group led by Monet was primarily optical. Outside this group, though both in their different ways affected by it, Renoir and Van Gogh returned to the earlier ideal of expressing in landscape a mood of Nature, which they combined forcefully with the revelation of their own mood.

Cézanne's mature aims were more intellectual (see p. 31); but for this very reason he reached even more profound, though less immediately understandable, depths of feeling in his paintings of his favourite mountain *La Montagne Sainte Victoire* (see Pl. 78); his intimate knowledge of its form, derived from repeated study, gives his works, whatever passing effects of light he records, whatever unexpected relations to a foreground he discovers, the grandeur of something complete and permanent.

CHAPTER XIV

HISTORY, GENRE AND STILL LIFE

(i) HISTORY

In the eighteenth century the word 'historical' applied to all pictures illustrating lofty, as distinct from trivial, events: from the Bible or ancient literature as well as from public life. Then and in the nineteenth century historical scenes in the narrower sense were more often laid in the distant, than in the more recent, past; but neither the distant, nor the recent subject tended as a rule to be a source of inspiration.

On the other hand, in fifteenth-century Italy the demand for history proper resulted occasionally in a masterpiece. It grew up side by side with the more insistent demand for portraits. Both were encouraged by the revival of Greek and Roman culture, which was partly the cause and partly the effect of attention being transferred from the next life to this world.

Even in comparatively early times palaces had been decorated with frescoes of secular subjects. In the middle ages heraldic art was second in importance only to ecclesiastical art. As early as in 1328 Simone Martini (in a large fresco in the Palazzo Pubblico, Siena) had represented *Guidoriccio da Fogliano* on horseback— a victorious general in a wide landscape.

Between 1454 and 1457 Cosimo de Medici commissioned Uccello to commemorate the Florentine victory under Niccolo Tolentino over the Sienese, in three panels, now in the Louvre, Uffizi and National Gallery [(583), Pls. 16 and 17]. Like the others, our panel expresses nothing of the horrors of war. The battle is treated as a tournament, gay with the chivalric blazonry of heraldic device, tidily arranged upon neat plots of turf, against a tapestry of fruit-trees and rose-bushes, beyond which on the hills toy skirmishes take place on foot. From the realistic standpoint Uccello's conscious aim at correct perspective fails ridiculously; but his unconscious instinct for pattern, fed by his love both of geometry and of naturalistic detail, triumphs over this and over his inconsistent treatment of forms (flat, rounded or sectional) and becomes a source of inexhaustible joy. One of the many aspects of his inspiration was independently expressed later by Andrew Marvell in the lines:

> He hangs in shade the orange bright
> Like golden lamps in a green night.

Such unsophisticated renderings of war were not to reappear in the art of later centuries. There can, therefore, be no comparison between Uccello's battlepieces and Velazquez's grandly human and dramatic *Surrender of Breda* (Prado) or the deliberately horrific renderings of war by Goya and Picasso. In fact, the *Rout of San Romano* stands almost as much alone in the history of European painting, as it stands among the pictures of the National Gallery.

(ii) GENRE

Genre painting has become the accepted term for the representation of everyday contemporary life. The persons must not be recognizable individuals: for then the work becomes a portrait, or, if they are engaged in a pretence of action, as in Hogarth's *Strode Family* (1153) a 'conversation-piece'. Nor must they take part in an event of political importance; for then the group is 'historical'. Nor, again, must the scene suggest a pastoral idyll, an ideal existence outside the ordinary; but the word 'genre' is sometimes applied to Watteau's works, in which the groups, though ideally graceful, were suggested by the observation of the men and women of his day.

Genre painting in Europe developed on lines similar to landscape. Before 1600, groups of figures observed from life, like the gossips in Crivelli's *Annunciation* (739), were subordinate to the main subject. *The Concert* (2486) attributed to Roberti is a rare example of pure genre. Like landscape, genre developed soonest in the Netherlands. Quentin Massys's *Banker and his Wife* (Louvre) was followed by Marinus Van Reymerswaele's unpleasant *Bankers* (944), and then by Bruegel's masterpieces, such as *Peasants Feasting* and *Peasants Dancing* (Vienna).

A steady demand for genre began first in the middle-class republic of seventeenth-century Holland. Dutch genre pictures served a purpose akin to that of the novel. They represented a society, sufficiently like and sufficiently unlike the prospective buyer's own to entertain him. The painter became a shrewd observer and especially trained his visual memory. This training accounts for the vivid spontaneity of such pictures as Brouwer's *Three Boors Drinking* (2569), Steen's *Oyster Feast* (2559) and *Skittle Alley* (2660). It is essential in dramatic genre, that is in representations of character and action.

The mood of dramatic genre pieces can vary considerably. A single painter, such as Steen, is now almost detached, now sentimental, now benevolently humorous, now scathingly satirical. Terborch stressed the elegance of his characters; Bruegel their genial absurdity. Hogarth combined pathos and bitter satire in *Calais Gate* [(1464), Pl. 68]; the result is brilliant, because though he intended to point a moral, he remembered what he had really seen.

There also exists another type of genre painting, which might be termed 'static'. For such work the painter may have his models before him for a considerable time, since an alert visual memory is not needed. In most pictures by De Hooch and in some by Vermeer, the persons represented are scarcely individual. On the other hand, individual character plays a part, however static, in Louis Le Nain's *Resting Cavalier* (V. and A.) in Vermeer's *Cook* (Amsterdam), in Chardin's scenes of middle-class life (see Pl. 67), and in the various groups of card-players by Cézanne.

Les Parapluies [(3268), Pl. 80] by Renoir, though deliberately worked out, is inspired by a momentary impression; *La Baignade* [(T.G. 3908), Pl. 79] by Seurat, by an experience gradually absorbed. Seurat never succeeded in representing movement, and his failure to do so is analogous to the same limitation in Piero della Francesca. *La Baignade* is static, large in scale, classically designed in three dimensions (see p. 95); but the conception depends entirely on contemporary life and is in no sense historical. A conventionally 'classical' group of bathers would have included only heroic nudes. Seurat strikes a deeper note. The ugly bathing costumes, bowler and brown trousers, so useful in providing tones that establish one figure behind another, also contribute greatly to the touchingly plebeian reality of the scene. On the banks of the Seine the sun burns hot; the atmosphere is windless and hazy. The boys have escaped from their work in the factory; but not far; its chimneys are still visible. They are enjoying their outdoor leisure, dawdling and basking; the nearest is too lazy even to undress. Time is forgotten; life is at a blissful pause.

(iii) STILL LIFE

The development of still-life painting in Europe was similar to that of landscape and genre. Pictures devoted exclusively to 'common objects' (food, kitchen utensils, etc.) were first produced in the seventeenth century, in large quantities in Holland, in smaller quantities in Spain and Italy. Caravaggio's influence contributed to the vogue [see his *Christ at Emmaus* (172), Pl. 52]. His one exclusively *Still Life* group (Ambrosiana, Milan) is inspired by an almost Rubensian exuberance, which has been effectively contrasted with the austerity of Zurbaran's *Still Life* (Contini Palace, Rome). The eggs, fish and garlic in Velazquez's *House of Martha* (1375) express a spirit half-way between these extremes.

Before 1600, Flemish and Dutch artists often painted careful studies of the furniture of a room. Among the Italians the painting of flowers was common; Crivelli often put fruit into his foregrounds; and Crivelli, Catena, Ghirlandaio, Antonello and others took a special interest in objects upon shelves—books, jam-pots, carafes, ink-bottles, candlesticks, etc. Such studies were even more keenly pursued by Jan Van Eyck and his successors and by such inheritors of this tradition as Holbein [see his 'Ambassadors' (1314)]; but until the seventeenth century still life was never the sole subject of an entire picture.

It is tempting to maintain that before 1900 Europe produced only two great still-life painters, both of them Frenchmen—Chardin and Cézanne. Still life requires a special kind of imaginative invention. In other branches of painting, the accidents of Nature supply the painter, skilled in selection, with more than half the ideas for a design: mountains will stand, figures will group themselves, sitters will assume poses which will suggest the first impulse, at least, for pictorial unity. The accidental placing of pots and pans, vases and fruit upon tables, is hardly ever so inspiring. The still-life painter has to do all the work of constructing the picture: first in his mind, then on the table, then on the canvas. He must choose his units and then arrange them creatively according to his original inner conception; till this is accomplished the task of representation cannot begin.

Consequently, still life tends to extremes of merit or demerit. At worst it sinks with facility into mere skilled copying. At best, of all forms of representational painting, still life, by exacting an arbitrary choice, approximates most closely, concrete though the units are, to abstract art. It is the subject of some of the dullest pieces of mere representation. It is also the subject of some of the most daring and satisfying inventions of Picasso, Braque and Matisse.

Emotions associated with the objects represented need not be excluded, but must be kept direct and simple. Plutocratic ostentation mars almost all Dutch flower-pieces of the eighteenth century. Even Huysum, the finest decorator of the period, did not avoid it: his *Vase of Flowers* (796) though rhythmically balanced, is restlessly profuse. Fantin Latour's flower-pieces [see (1686)] apart from their greyness and the unenjoyable quality of the paint, are apt to be pretentious. Perhaps oil is unsuited to the rendering of objects so delicate and fragile unless they are treated, as in Henri Rousseau's works, as purely flat patterns, or else the flowers themselves are of the coarse texture of Van Gogh's *Irises* and *Sunflowers* (T.G. 3863).

Contrasts of shape and texture are essential in still-life paintings; and these are most effective when there is economy in the number of objects introduced. This is one reason why the picture of *Pewter, China and Glass* (4562) by Jan Jansz Treck is more satisfying than most paintings of such subjects. Again, the *Study of Still Life* (1258) by Chardin or an imitator attracts because the bread and wine look good; but quality, not quantity, is the source of the attraction; it appeals to the *gourmet* rather than the *gourmand*. It also satisfies by fully expressing the weight and structure of the objects and by reconciling qualities of paint, pleasurable in themselves, with a truthful rendering of the texture of the objects (see Chapter IV).

Here, as in all branches of painting, too great attention to minutiae is distracting. Cézanne, whose still-life painting carries with it an inexplicable authority, always simplifies to some extent and renders no more than the main large facts of form. His brush-work, deliberate and the reverse of graceful, his considered balance and selection, his eye for colour and especially the broken tints of his backgrounds, all contribute to a type of work as impressively monumental as his portraits, landscapes, and the greatest of his figure compositions.

CHAPTER XV

DESIGN BY LINE

THE Italian word 'disegno' means both 'drawing' (definition of form by line) and linear design (relation of shapes by line). The two ideas are closely related; often, too, the greatest draughtsmen are the greatest linear designers; but the gifts are distinct; form may be defined by outlines, as in Bouts's *Virgin and Child with SS. Peter and Paul* (774), without the use of linear organization.

Conversely, it is possible to design by line without leaving outlines round the contours. In Correggio's *Venus, Mercury and Cupid* [(10), Pl. 40], though outlines are avoided and the edges softened, the eye can follow such contours as that from Venus's right shoulder, down her arm to Cupid's right shoulder, elbow, knee and heel.

Drawing, whether by outlines or not, is discussed in Chapter VII (p. 30). Concerning design by line, the problem now to be considered, a word of warning is necessary. Pictorial geometry should not become a fetish. Linear design is analogous to metre in poetry, and should be given as much, but not more, importance. To construct a perfectly regular sonnet is not to be a poet. To invent a perfect linear design is not to create a masterpiece. What the poet has to say should inspire the way in which he says it. What the painter has to express should inspire his design. The painter whose linear design is obtrusive is like the versifier whose metre obscures his meaning. By the great painter or poet the means of expression are often achieved subconsciously. Neither of them twists sense to fit metre or pattern. Bronzino's *Venus, Cupid, Folly and Time* (651) has great stylistic merits; but the poses have been forced into somewhat too rigid a linear scheme. Michelangelo's *Madonna and Child with S. John and Angels* [(809), Pl. 30] is an even more regular linear design; but the natural actions of the figures are what are first apparent.

Rules are made to be broken (see p. 5). Thus, in the *'Wilton Diptych'* [(4451) see Pl. 6] the banner is just not vertical, the ring of angels round the Virgin just not complete, and the implied curve joining the tips of the wings of the farther angels just fails to repeat that joining their faces.

Linear design is the free outcome of a trained vision. Not abstract geometry, but perception of living form suggested to Poussin the continuity of the backs of the men holding the bowl in the *Nursing of Bacchus* (39). Even the folds of S. Mary Magdalene's cloak, dipping regularly deeper as they descend, in Ugolino's *Deposition* (3375), are based on the way that a full garment hangs from two points of support.

It must also be noted that linear design may depend upon the direction, not only of actual contours, but also of whole limbs or even whole figures. Thus, in Michelangelo's *Madonna and Child* [(809), Pl. 30] the left forearm of the angel on the extreme right and the series of forms from Christ's left elbow to the end of the book count as straight obliques, sloping the opposite way from the left upper arm of the same angel and of S. John. Sometimes a limb may do double duty both as a curve and as a straight. In Raphael's 'Garvagh Madonna' (744) the whole of S. John's left arm leads by twisting S-curves to the Virgin's head; but also part of the same arm from the elbow to the wrist counts as a straight, parallel to the left arm of the Virgin.

It would be impossible to give an account of all the ways in which linear relations contribute to a picture's unity; but eleven recurrent methods (mainly relating to the flat pattern of pictures) may now be described:

    (i) Curves and Straights contrasted;

    (ii) Lines echoing, and contrasted with, the Frame;

    (iii) Inward leading lines and avoidance of outward leading lines;

    (iv) 'Trellis-work';

    (v) Repetitions and Echoes;

    (vi) Avoidance of Repetition;

    (vii) Continuous Curves and Curves of Contraflexure;

    (viii) Division by Curves;

    (ix) More Complex Rhythms, based on Nature;

    (x) Symmetry, Balance and Spacing upon the Picture-area;

    (xi) Movement, Stability and Repose.

(i) CURVES AND STRAIGHTS CONTRASTED

All linear design depends upon the interplay of straight lines or curves, or both. Vertical and horizontal straights, actual or implied, are necessary to a picture's stability. Curves and oblique straights are not necessary, but oblique straights add emphasis, and curves grace. When curves preponderate, as in Lorenzo Monaco's *Coronation of the Virgin* (1897), the effect is soothing but lacking in vigour, like *legato* music. When oblique straight lines preponderate, as in Campin's

Virgin and Child (2609), the effect is often jerky and *staccato*. Sometimes, as in Bouts's *Entombment* [(664), Pl. 15], a strongly knit unity is achieved by subordinating short straight lines to long curves.

For a more thorough analysis of the subject (including an account of the different kinds of curve, the circle, ellipse, parabola, hyperbola, etc.) see Ruskin's 'Modern Painters', pt. v, ch. xvii, in which finite and infinite curves are contrasted and curves are related to the laws of natural form. Though there is no space here for such fascinating investigations, one peculiarity may be noted that all curves share in common. A straight line, being the shortest distance between two points, can lead the eye in two directions only; but a curve can spring forth in mid-course in innumerable directions and innumerable minor curves can run into it, like tributaries into a river.

(ii) LINES ECHOING, AND CONTRASTED WITH, THE FRAME

Often the shape of the frame, or part of it, is repeated within the picture. In Lippi's *Annunciation* [(666), Pl. 9] the curve of the frame is nearly echoed in the angel's wing and related to the implied curve uniting the bowed backs of the Virgin and Angel. In Crivelli's *Dead Christ* (602) the curve uniting the arms of the two angels completes the circle begun by the arch at the top. In Vermeer's *Lady Standing at the Virginals* [(1383), Pl. 64] the verticals and horizontals of the instrument and pictures on the wall are emphasized, so that these smaller rectangles echo, or are contrasted with, the relative proportions of the rectangular picture as a whole.

Contrasts with the frame are frequent. In the *Madonna and Child* (275), partly by Botticelli, while the bowing figures echo the circular frame, the design is steadied by the horizontals of the clouds and the Virgin's dress at the neck.

(iii) INWARD LEADING LINES AND AVOIDANCE OF OUTWARD LEADING LINES

Most pictures have some natural centre of interest. It need not occupy the geometrical centre of the picture-area. This centre of interest is often the point of convergence of the main lines of the pattern. In Ugolino's *Deposition* (3375) the curves of the backs of the other saints converge towards, or (from another point of view) diverge from, the heads of Christ and the Virgin.

Just as lines *should* lead the eye *in*, so they *should not* lead the eye out into sides and corners. From the standpoint of flat pattern, the cloud in Crome's *Mousehold*

Heath (689) runs too much into the right-hand top corner, though, when the plants on the left were lighter and repeated more emphatically the slope of the dark bank behind them (upwards towards the left), the pattern must have been happier. From the standpoint of composition, however, the realization that the cloud is moving upwards and forwards above our heads, almost redeems the awkward pattern.

Even more distracting are verticals and horizontals that run into the frame with nothing to stop them. Crivelli in the *Annunciation* (739) just avoids this; the obliques of the divine rays and the peacock's tail and the horizontals of the near façade prevent the vertical corner of the house from cutting the picture into halves.

Horizontals also, if they are of any length, ought not to occur at the sides of a picture. Often in architectural subjects, such as Claude's *Embarkation of S. Ursula* [(30), see Pl. 56], horizontals are repeatedly interrupted by verticals and vice versa. The ideal of such designs is to be self-contained. Rubens's *Château de Steen* [(66), Pl. 54] aims at none of this compactness (see p. 20); here the horizontals break all rules and run out of the picture with nothing to stop them, since the wide fields are seen as fragments of a vaster earth.

(iv) 'TRELLIS-WORK'

Just as horizontals and verticals can be usefully contrasted, so one set of obliques can be checked by another, sloping in the opposite direction. This may conveniently be called 'trellis-work'. In figure subjects the trellis is often made up of arms or legs—sometimes of whole figures. Many examples of this method might be mentioned, from its crude use in Zoffany's *Family Group* (3678) to its consummate application in Veronese's *Family of Darius before Alexander* [(294), Pl. 45]. In Rubens's *Rape of the Sabine Women* [(38), Pl. 53] it brings order out of chaos.

(v) REPETITIONS AND ECHOES

'Trellis-work' is a form of repetition (see pp. 8 and 21). 'Patterns' in the narrower sense are the repetitions of the same shapes at regular intervals (see Ch. I, p. 4). Flat patterns contrasted with each other and with unpatterned areas, occur in Jacopo di Cione's *Coronation of the Virgin* (569). Patterns, conceived in the solid, occur in the armour of Piero della Francesca's *S. Michael* (769).

Repetition with variety is an extension of the idea of repeated patterns. In Uccello's *Rout of San Romano* [(583), Pl. 16] the same undulating curve (in one case in reverse) is almost exactly repeated, but at varied intervals, in the horses' backs; but no two horses' heads or pairs of hoofs reach the same height.

In Botticelli's *Mars, Venus and Satyrs* [(915), Pl. 24] the intervals between the curved backs of the satyrs and between the various oblique limbs are more regular; but the varieties of natural form prevent monotony. Freedom is also introduced by the slope of the tilting staff, repeated in the rising sequence of the satyrs, but *just not* repeated in the sequence of the hands. In Poussin's *Bacchanalian Revel* (62), many arms and legs are parallel, though the intervals between them vary.

Difference of scale sometimes accompanies sameness of direction. In Giovanni Bellini's *Pietà* (3912) the small right arm of one of the angels repeats the angle of the large right arm of Christ. In Botticelli's *Birth of Venus* (Uffizi), the shape of the shell is repeated again, much magnified, in some of the main enclosing contours.

In some designs, while exact repetition is avoided, there occur what may be described as *echoes*. In Botticelli's *Primavera* (Uffizi) several of the arms are nearly parallel to each other, but not quite. In Titian's *Vendramin Family* [(4452), Pl. 44] the curves of the backs of the three men are slightly varied, the hang of the sleeves of the two oldest is similar, but not the same, whereas the angles of the heads are contrasted.

(vi) AVOIDANCE OF REPETITION

When a painter's chief aim is verisimilitude, he often avoids repetition, just as a writer of prose avoids blank verse. Throughout Hogarth's *Marriage à la Mode* pictures (T.G. 113–18) the distance between any two heads is never the same. In Turner's *Sun Rising Through Vapour* (479) no two boats are of the same shape or of the same visual magnitude. In his *Calais Pier* [(472), Pl. 70] he has made a correction; the implied line joining the tops of the two nearest masts was once parallel to that joining the two tallest masts; to prevent this the nearest mast was shortened.

(vii) CONTINUOUS CURVES AND CURVES OF CONTRAFLEXURE

A long continuous curve recurs in the finest natural forms. It also calls up an image of the bold gesture of the artist. When Michelangelo painted the Sistine ceiling, he must have swung his brush, not from the wrist or even from the elbow, but with a sweep of the whole arm from the shoulder. Continuity in pictures can be of three degrees, consisting:

(a) of a single curve absolutely unbroken;
(b) of a curve with slight gaps in it caused by the structure represented;
(c) of an implied curve with large gaps in it, linking together two parts of a design.

The first degree of continuity occurs in Tintoretto's *Origin of the Milky Way* [(1313), Pl. 48; in Jupiter's cloak]. The second degree is frequent in contours of nude figures, e.g. in Veronese's *Unfaithfulness* [(1318), Pl. 49; in the arms and shoulders of the woman]. The third degree of continuity cannot be rigidly distinguished from the second. In Titian's *Noli Me Tangere* [(270), Pl. 33] there are but slight breaks in the curves connecting Christ's back with the rising hill.

In tracing continuities with larger gaps in them than this, one may become over-ingenious; but there can be no doubt that in Van Dyck's *Villiers Brothers* (3605) the S-curve which connects the lower edge of George's cloak with Francis's left shoulder is intentional.

Several of the curves described above are S-curves or curves of *contraflexure* with a double bend in them. S-curves are valuable as links between the different parts of a design. In Tintoretto's *S. George and the Dragon* [(16), Pl. 42] the design is enclosed by two large S's (one reversed) which cross each other, forming roughly a figure 8.

(viii) DIVISION BY CURVES

If part of a picture has to be separated from the rest, curves mark off the division more effectively than straight lines, which tend to break the unity of the design. Curves, while they separate, also connect. Thus, in Botticelli's *Nativity* [(1034), Pl. 28] curves enclose each of the four groups; the flying angels above, dancing in a ring; the angels on the roof; the Holy Family, the introducing angels and the magi and shepherds; the angels below and the three men whom they embrace. The implied curve connecting the feet of the dancing group is repeated in that connecting the tops of the fir-trees. Had the fir-trees been all of the same height, the dancers would have formed a second picture, bounded by a horizontal line. Similarly, in El Greco's *Agony in the Garden* [(3476), Pl. 50] the curve of Christ's sleeve runs into the ellipse enclosing the sleeping disciples.

(ix) MORE COMPLEX RHYTHMS, BASED ON NATURE

It is tempting to use the vague word 'rhythm' for a sequence of lines, more easily perceived than described in words. Nature is full of such sequences. In Claude's *Cephalus and Procris* (2) the leaves of the tree are blown by the wind into a cyclic rhythm. In Spinello Aretino's *Two Apostles* [(276), Pl. 5] the regular diminution in the curls of the hair and beards is an idealization of fact. Similar observation, combined with stylization, occurs in all successful treatment of drapery. Even the robes in Tura's *Madonna and Child Enthroned* [(772), see Pl. 22] are based on the behaviour, not of cloth perhaps, but of metal. In the best examples not only are actual folds of drapery recorded, but from all the possible folds in Nature a selection is made of those that will help the design. In Titian's *Noli Me Tangere* [(270), Pl. 33] the smaller folds are tributaries to the main curves; in Correggio's *Madonna of the Basket* (23) every seemingly accidental flutter contributes to the consistency of the whole.

(x) SYMMETRY, BALANCE AND SPACING UPON THE PICTURE-AREA

The notion of symmetry in relation to a vertical axis (see p. 22) applies both to design in the flat (upon the picture-area) and to composition in the solid (within the picture-volume). In Raphael's '*Ansidei Madonna*' [(1171), Pl. 32] the rigid symmetry of the architecture and grouping is contrasted with the asymmetry of the poses of SS. John and Nicholas. Two-dimensional symmetry occasionally occurs in relation to a horizontal axis as in Velazquez's *Venus and Cupid* [(2057), Pl. 65]; see pp. 158, 159. The effect can be caused by the reflection. In Botticelli's *Primavera* (Uffizi) the Graces' arms and hands are symmetrically related to an oblique axis.

Balance (see p. 22) involves a perpetual risk. In Tura's *Allegorical Figure* (3070) the throne is slightly to the left of the geometrical centre and the figure is slightly to the right. For Holbein's *Duchess of Milan* [(2475), Pl. 39] see pp. 155, 156.

(xi) MOVEMENT, STABILITY AND REPOSE

In relation to the problem of movement, there are two kinds of good design: design expressive of repose only, and design expressive of both movement and repose.

Stability is also to be contrasted with movement, though it indicates a state less restful than repose.

The representation of a figure in movement depends primarily on the accurate recording of its appearance, including the combined recording of after-images (see pp. 42–4). This accurate record naturally also decides the part (dynamic, static or reposeful) that a figure plays in the design of a picture as a whole; but this part may be further emphasized by stressing the curve, verticality, horizontality or obliquity of a limb, or of an entire figure. Thus linear emphasis upon movement, stability or repose is an important branch of linear design.

Horizontal lines or directions usually emphasize repose. The horizon of a flat landscape, recumbent figures and animals stretched across the picture from side to side, are each restful in their effect. But under particular circumstances horizontals may perform the exactly opposite function of expressing extreme speed. In Titian's *Bacchus and Ariadne* [(35), Pl. 36] the horizon is reposeful and the top of the chariot stable, but the horizontal clouds behind Bacchus emphasize the swish of his cloak through the air.

Vertical lines and directions usually emphasize stability. Cossa's *S. Vincent Ferrer* (597) is monumentally immobile in pose. In Titian's *Venus and Adonis* [(34), Pl. 37] Adonis's right leg and in Tintoretto's *Origin of the Milky Way* [(1313), Pl. 48] Juno's right leg act as pillars steadying an otherwise restless design. But again, under particular circumstances, a vertical direction may emphasize a condition other than static. In pictures of the Last Judgement a figure may be falling downwards, and this direction is, of course, vertical. In *Bacchus and Ariadne* [(35), Pl. 36] the left leg of the girl with the cymbals (vertical in direction) expresses an abrupt break in the dance immediately following the clash of her cymbals, and caused by her sudden stop on seeing Bacchus leap. This implied vertical continues up her figure and, by cutting across the implied oblique that leads from the heel of the man with the snakes to Bacchus's shoulder, produced an effect, analogous to a pause in music.

When movement is represented, the natural direction of dancing, running or flying figures is oblique. But in static compositions, depending on cones or pyramids, two sets of limbs, sloping in opposite directions, may act as buttresses supporting the main cone. The word 'cone' is here used rather than triangle, because solid, rather than flat, geometry is now the topic. The cone form of the castle on the sands is the surest way of distributing weight. So in painting the conically disposed figure or group produces the most stable effect. In Andrea del Sarto's *Madonna and Child with SS. John and Elizabeth* (17) there are two cones supported by a 'trellis' of obliquely sloping limbs (see p. 75).

What is represented as being a cone becomes in the picture a triangle. And a triangle standing on its base is soothing, just as the sight of a triangle poised on its point is disturbing. For, no matter how ably three-dimensional facts are represented, the shapes made by the lines and areas upon the flat picture-area are of primary importance. In Veronese's *Family of Darius before Alexander* [(294), Pl. 45] a triangle (light in tone), poised on its point, is left over between the secure triangle of Darius's family and the secure triangle (partly hidden) of the figures in the left foreground; but this insecure triangle is made less conspicuous by the irregular shape of the monkey, by the rectangular balustrade supporting him and by the distant pillars.

In many designs, curves emphasize neither stability nor movement, but merely introduce an element of grace. But occasionally a curve emphasizes movement more complex than can be suggested by a straight oblique. Thus, in Tintoretto's *Origin of the Milky Way* [(1313), Pl. 48] the curve of Jupiter's cloak and the under-curve of his body indicate that he is flying towards the spectator and on reaching Juno has changed from a downward to an upward direction. In Ingres' *Madame Moitessier* [(4821), Pl. 75] the contour of the dress at the neck, by leading to the contours in the mirror, achieves both a two-dimensional relation of lines and areas and a three-dimensional relation of volumes

CHAPTER XVI

PERSPECTIVE

IN Europe the power of representing the three-dimensional world upon a picture's flat surface has depended to a great extent upon perspective. Some knowledge, therefore, of the principles and limitations of this 'science' is useful both in painting and in the appreciation of painting—always provided that perspective is regarded, like other methods of representation, not as an end in itself, but as a means towards the clarified expression of visual experience.

The practical application of perspective, explained in various treatises on the subject (such as R. G. Hatton's 'Perspective for Art Students'), is outside the scope of this book; but a few relevant general considerations are here necessary, in preparation for the two chapters on Design in Three Dimensions.

Consistency in working out vanishing points, etc., is by no means always accompanied by the power to present impressions of spatial depth to the imagination; and conversely some pictures, such as the 'Scenes in the Life of S. John the Baptist' [(5451–4), see Pl. 12] by Giovanni di Paolo, who disregards linear perspective, nevertheless succeed in transporting us imaginatively into a world of space.

The effect of recession in these pictures owes something to aerial perspective (see p. 32), especially in *S. John entering the Wilderness* [(5454), Pl. 12], but more to an inexplicable instinct for so distributing the flat shapes upon the picture-area, as to suggest a receding picture-volume, alternately filled and empty. This instinct is frequently met with in Oriental art; so is the use of combined imagery which occurs in Pl. 12 (see pp. 42 and 50).

The ancient Chinese method of landscape painting (see p. 19), by recording a continuous series of images upon a long scroll, can represent distances much vaster than is possible by European methods of perspective; for the Chinese artist is a traveller, whose gaze is constantly shifting, whereas the European renders only what can be seen from a fixed position, without moving his head.

On the other hand, perspective, just because it involves a limited field of vision, is reducible to rules. Linear perspective, as ordinarily applied to a picture vertically placed, implies a vertical picture-plane. The picture-plane is the imaginary transparent plane through which the artist sees what he represents. The picture is an opaque substitute for the imaginary picture-plane. To illustrate perspective, teachers have painted on actual glass. The picture-plane is normally a few feet from the painter's eye. Besides depending on the fixed position of the artist's head, perspective assumes that he represents what he sees with one eye only; that the distance from the eye to the picture-plane is fixed and that the direction of vision is perpendicular to the picture-plane. Thus, if the picture-plane is vertical, the direction of vision is horizontal. Because we see with two eyes and can only relate the near foreground to the background by shutting one of them, it is impossible to represent the appearance of very near objects according to the laws of perspective.

The single vertical picture-plane also excludes the representation by perspective of objects at our feet or above our heads. Van Gogh's *Chair* (T.G. 3862) cannot be judged by accepted laws, because it has been seen through two picture-planes, of which one is vertical, so that vision is directed horizontally, and the other oblique with the lower edge nearest the artist, so that his vision is directed obliquely downwards.

The *picture-volume* (i.e. the three-dimensional space represented in the picture) often resembles a theatrical stage, bounded by rectangles and seen from a central, or nearly central, position. The vertical picture-plane is parallel to, or coincides with, the curtain and the direction of vision perpendicular to it and horizontal. The level of the spectator's eye may vary considerably, but, if the picture-plane remains vertical, must never be high enough or low enough to make the direction of his vision oblique.

If the painter's ideal is to be compact, the stage may be of unlimited depth from curtain to backcloth, but must be severely limited above, below and at the sides. Claude, though a master of three-dimensional volume, emphasizes distances from the spectator to the horizon more than distances that carry the eye upwards or sideways beyond the confines of the visible stage (see also pp. 19–20, and compare Pls. 54 and 55).

On the other hand, Hobbema in the *Avenue at Middelharnis* (830) emphasizes all three dimensions equally: inward depth by the ruts in the road and the diminishing visual magnitude of the trees; lateral width, by the flat horizon, and the boundaries of the fields parallel to it; height, by the position of the tall trees in relation to the clouds above them.

In discussing perspective, it should be made clear whether the line, surface or volume referred to belongs to the three-dimensional organization of forms represented, or to the two-dimensional area on which it is represented. For instance, a line that is *represented as being horizontal* should be distinguished from one which is represented by a *horizontal line*. I usually refer to the second type of line as *visually horizontal* or as having a *horizontal image*.

'Image' is a clearer word in this connexion than 'appearance'. For instance, it is true to say that the *image* of a distant object is smaller than that of the same object near at hand, but misleading to say that the distant object *appears* smaller than the near object; for the spectator never judges the distant object to be in fact smaller. Similarly, instead of describing receding parallel lines as *appearing* to meet in a point, it should be stated that the *images* of certain lines, parallel in fact, meet visually.

In relation to the box stage, the familiar terms 'horizontal and vertical', applicable both to straight lines and to planes, need to be supplemented by other less familiar terms. This is because all horizontal planes are parallel to each other, but not all horizontal lines. On the other hand, all vertical lines are parallel to one another, but not all vertical planes.

New terms are therefore needed to distinguish vertical planes parallel to the picture-plane, from vertical planes perpendicular to it. New terms are also needed to distinguish horizontal lines parallel to the picture-plane from horizontal lines perpendicular to it. New terms are not needed for vertical planes obliquely placed with regard to the picture-plane, nor for horizontal lines that, if produced, make with the picture-plane an angle other than a right angle.

For convenience I describe horizontal lines parallel to the picture-plane as *lines of width*. Such horizontal lines retain their horizontality in their image and are always represented by horizontal lines on the picture.

Horizontal lines perpendicular to the picture-plane I describe as *lines of depth*. These are usually represented by oblique lines. Their image only becomes horizontal when they are on a level with the eye. It becomes vertical when they are directly above, or directly below, the eye.

Vertical planes parallel to the picture-plane I describe as *frontal*. These play an important part in composition, since lines and areas occurring upon their surface are unaltered by perspective. Lines of width (which are always horizontal) are also important, in that they mark the intersection of horizontal with frontal planes.

Vertical planes perpendicular to the picture-plane I describe as *vertical planes of depth*. Lines of depth mark the intersection of vertical planes of depth with horizontal planes. Although lines of depth are representations of horizontal lines, the fact that they are seldom represented *by* horizontal lines prevents their having so restful an effect upon the eye as lines of width. This is an instance of the fact that, however representationally skilful the designer in three dimensions may be, he can never afford to neglect attending to two-dimensional pattern.

CHAPTER XVII

DESIGN IN THREE DIMENSIONS

COMPOSITION in three dimensions never succeeds unless accompanied by pattern in two. On the other hand, good pattern can exist without composition, and can succeed even when composition is confused. Uccello's attempt in the *Rout of San Romano* [(583), Pl. 16] to represent solid forms in relation to the receding ground and to define a lucid three-dimensional design from them has failed; but the two-dimensional lucidity of the picture owes much to the attempt.

The two aspects of design can enrich each other, though their reconciliation often involves problems. It is usual to avoid improbable coincidences, but occasionally painters seem to seek them out. In Foppa's *Adoration of the Magi* [(729), Pl. 27] the lower contour of the Child's right hand coincides upon the picture-area with the contour of the Virgin's right hand, and the top of the bare-headed squire's head with the top of the neck of the horse behind him, though three-dimensionally the latter are separated by an appreciable volume of air. Similarly, in Cézanne's *La Montagne Sainte Victoire* [(Courtauld Institute), Pl. 78] the near contours of the fir-trees repeat the far contours of the mountain in a way that in other hands would have been affectation, but here has the inevitability of genius.

De Hooch was an adept at extracting pattern from three-dimensional relations of shape. In his *Courtyard of a Dutch House* [(794), Pl. 62] he echoes the gable of the pump in the gable of the distant house, though the buildings face different ways.

Just as the painter has to reconcile three-dimensional clarity with two-dimensional grace, so the sculptor has to consider the two-dimensional image of his statue or group (e.g. of the contours seen from every aspect) as well as its three-dimensional coherence. Michelangelo has followed the low-relief ideal in the *Madonna and Child with S. John and Angels* [(809), Pl. 30]; whereas, if the group in his *Entombment* [(790), Pl. 31] were carved in the round, the contours of the forms, seen from every position, would be as rhythmic as from the view-point chosen for the painting.

Some generalizations concerning pattern apply in an extended sense to composition. Just as in two-dimensional design the *general direction* of a limb may count as a straight or curve regardless of its *particular contour* (see p. 73), so in three-dimensional design the *general form* of a figure or group may count as a single geometrical solid (cube, pyramid, cone, etc.), regardless of its *particular form* in detail. Again, just as a line may continue after interruption, so a solid form may, although interrupted, be regarded as continuous: e.g. the cone of which the apex is the head of Christ in Mantegna's *Agony in the Garden* [(1417), Pl. 18]. Thirdly, a limb, two-dimensionally considered, may slope upon the picture-area in one direction; but three-dimensionally considered may slope within the picture-volume in a different direction.

Composition is also like pattern in its alternations of emptiness with fullness. Just as two-dimensional balance depends upon the proportions on the picture-area of full to empty areas, so three-dimensional balance depends upon the represented proportions of weighty volumes (figures, building, etc.) to the empty volumes of air surrounding them.

There follows a description of some of the methods of three-dimensional design, many of which can be combined. The account is not exhaustive: the ways of relating solid forms within the picture-volume is almost endless. Here, as with other aspects of design, the best compositions are often the least regular; here, as always, Nature is the greatest inspiration.

The following are some of the methods and problems affecting three-dimensional design:

(i)	The Ground-plane;	(vi)	Low Eye-levels;
(ii)	The Mass or Group;	(vii)	High Eye-levels;
(iii)	The Cone;	(viii)	Measuring Points in Composition;
(iv)	The Cube;	(ix)	Near Foregrounds.
(v)	Two Ideals of Unity;		

(i) THE GROUND-PLANE

In composition the ground-plane is by far the most important of the horizontal planes represented. The patternist considers the picture-area only. The three-dimensional designer gives equal attention also to the ground.

(ii) THE MASS OR GROUP

When many figures are represented as touching or nearly touching each other, the shape made by the whole group that they form is more important to the design than that made by each figure singly. Though it cannot be described by a single geometrical term (such as a modified hemisphere), the figures in Bouts's *Entombment* [(664), Pl. 15] belong as much in the physical sense to a single group, as they do emotionally in community of feeling.

(iii) THE CONE

For the advantage of the cone in distributing weight, see p. 79. It is a favourite form for the Madonna and Child, seated and enthroned. The two principal figures represented in Masaccio's *Madonna and Child* [(3046), Pl. 7] could have been carved out of a cone of marble with a minimum of cutting away. An implied cone encloses the figures in Leonardo's *Virgin of the Rocks* [(1093), Pl. 29], though there are greater gaps in it. Mantegna's *Agony in the Garden* [(1417), Pl. 18] is based upon seven cones represented as solidly interrelated (see also above). The figure of Zurbaran's *S. Francis* [(5655), Pl. 57] also occupies a modified cone. That of Christ in El Greco's *Agony in the Garden* [(3476), Pl. 50] forms a pyramid on a square base.

In Raphael's '*Ansidei Madonna*' [(1171), Pl. 32] the cone of the Madonna and Child is placed on an almost cubic throne; and the steps leading to it become increasingly wider upwards, to emphasize the central concentration of the weight; the solid volumes and the volumes of air are distributed with perfect architectural coherence. Its excellence may be compared with the insecurity of Costa's *Madonna and Child with Saints* (629), where a heavy cone mass surmounts the stone framework of a vista.

(iv) THE CUBE

In groups of figures the cube is less frequent than the cone, though solid rectangular formation is not uncommon. Architecture in composition is often most effective when of the simplest geometrical form. In the *Landscape with Figures* [(40), Pl. 55] by Nicolas Poussin, one of the massive buildings consists of two cubes and the other is scarcely more complex.

(v) TWO IDEALS OF UNITY

Cones, pyramids, solid rectangles, cylinders, spheres and irregular solids are the units of three-dimensional composition. In more complicated designs many units make up the whole. In Veronese's *Family of Darius before Alexander* [(294), Pl. 45] the group round Alexander stands on a rectangular base, whereas the family of Darius and the chamberlain form a modified cone, and the group on the left part of another cone. The groups are united by their firm relation to the ground as well as by the trellis-work pattern (see p. 75) of the arms and the halberds.

In static designs, of which Raphael's achievements are typical, each unit has a complete balance in itself. On the other hand, in many 'baroque' pictures of the seventeenth century, the units, taken singly, are often insecure and unbalanced. The balance of Pietro da Cortona's *Rape of the Sabine Women* (Capitoline Gallery, Rome) depends on three separate top-heavy groups of equal importance. Each group on its own account is unstable and kept in control only by opposition with the other equally unstable groups. This also applies to a modified extent to Rubens's *Rape of the Sabine Woman* [(38), Pl. 53]; cf. also p. 20.

(vi) LOW EYE-LEVELS

The height from which the painter sees and represents the floor of his stage affects his design. Looking at the actors from too low down in the pit prevents the floor on which they stand from being visible and obscures their relation to one another in space. Mantegna in his wall painting of *S. James led to Execution* (Eremitani Chapel, Padua; now destroyed) did not entirely overcome this difficulty, in spite of the rapid diminution in the visual height of the actors as they recede. The confusion does not arise in his later *Triumph of Scipio* (902) because, though the floor is unseen, the stage is one of little depth.

There are two reasons for choosing a low eye-level, one psychological and the other realistic. To 'look up to a person' implies respect. So artists, who aim at emphasizing the dignity of their actors, often place them on a platform above the audience. The second reason for the low eye-level applies to the picture high on the wall, to be seen by a spectator of normal stature, standing on the floor. The picture reproduces for him the image of actual persons standing on a higher level than himself. If the floor of an actual stage were above the level of his eye, he would not see it. So it is hidden in the picture.

In paintings intended to decorate very high positions in a room, the eye-level is sometimes taken so low, that the picture-plane becomes oblique instead of vertical. For instance, the persons and the architecture in Veronese's four allegories (1318, 1324–6), including *Unfaithfulness* (Pl. 49) would cease to give the present impression of toppling over away from the spectator, if they were hung many feet higher. The present hanging, however, is fully justified by making it possible to see how the paint was applied.

In Veronese's *Family of Darius before Alexander* [(294), Pl. 45] the eye-level is high enough to make the floor on which the main actors stand just visible. Even here there would have been confusion if all the figures had been placed on the same height of ground. By grouping most of the distant figures upon a higher platform, so that those nearer never obscure our view of them, the dignity of the low eye-level has been combined with a clarity of spacing, usually obtained only by looking down on the ground from a height.

(vii) HIGH EYE-LEVELS

Composition with a high eye-level will be more conveniently analysed in connexion with the use of frontal planes and of vistas and balanced masses (see pp. 93, 94). It only needs to be pointed out here that the larger the area of the ground represented, the better is the opportunity for what Mr Berenson calls 'space-composition', that is three-dimensional design in relation to the ground-plane. And in order to represent a great stretch of ground, the eye-level must be fairly high, as in Perugino's *Christ giving Keys to Peter* [(Sistine Chapel, Vatican), Pl. 34].

(viii) MEASURING POINTS IN COMPOSITION

Measuring points, as they are called, determine the distance at which the spectator should stand in order to obtain the maximum illusion—or rather *reminder*—of reality. In De Hooch's *Interior of a Dutch House* [(834), Pl. 63] this distance is about 4 ft. 6 in. This result, which depends on the assumption that the tiles are represented as square (i.e. as deep as they are wide) can be worked out by diagrammatical and geometrical proof, too lengthy for inclusion here. It can also be tested by observing the picture from different distances.

In this case the measuring points, which determine the gradual diminution in visual magnitude of the depths of the squares as they recede, are the points of convergence of the lines running through their diagonals. These meet on the horizon outside the picture. If the visual depth of the squares had been more nearly equal to their width, the ideal distance of the spectator from the picture would have been less.

In the seventeenth century the Dutch owner of the painting of an interior liked to tell his friends singly where to stand in order to 'see how real the picture looked'. Hoogstraten's *Peep-Show* (3832) is painted on the ceiling, floor and walls of the inside of a box and has to be seen with one eye through one of two peep-holes. Perspective is applied to horizontal as well as vertical surfaces; and the eye, the position of which is necessarily fixed, is directed obliquely as well as horizontally. The ideal distance for seeing Dutch pictures varies greatly. Carel Fabritius's *View of Delft* (3714) is intended to be seen from only a few inches away. The spectator's precisely determined position suited the comparatively small house, for which such works were intended.

Many Italians, on the other hand, applied perspective to their larger paintings in a more general way, more suited to large buildings, where they would be seen by many spectators at once from near or far. They therefore often avoided those devices for precisely determining measurements in inward depth (such as the chessboard of tiles) and relied solely on vanishing points and aerial perspective, which give a less precise and more general impression of space. An example is Perugino's *Christ giving Keys to Peter* [(Sistine Chapel, Vatican), Pl. 34], in which, although measuring points must have been used in representing the divisions of pavement, these are represented as oblong, not square, and there is nothing to indicate the proportion of their depth to their width. So the effect of recession, though lacking the force (almost amounting to illusion) that Dutch perspective has when seen from the right position, remains generally convincing as seen from whatever distance.

(ix) NEAR FOREGROUNDS

Vermeer achieved masterpieces of three-dimensional composition, by combining the nicest taste in two-dimensional pattern, with a complete grasp of the relations of the objects to the ground-plane. In his pictures of interiors the area of the ground represented is often only a few square feet, but the position of every person and thing upon it is deliberately planned. The vague spatial relations in Ter Borch's *Guitar Lesson* (864) and even Ter Bruyghen's *Jacob and Laban* (4164) bring out by comparison Vermeer's superiority.

Unlike De Hooch, Vermeer often placed objects—such as the 'cello in the *Lady Seated at the Virginals* (2568) in the near foreground, with hardly any space between them and the picture-plane. The tendency first became marked in the work of Caravaggio, whose influence spread to Ter Bruyghen and other Utrecht painters. Vermeer's early *Christ in the House of Martha* (Edinburgh) indicates clearly his connexion with the Utrecht School. Caravaggio's *Christ at Emmaus* [(172), Pl. 52] and Guido Reni's *Lot and his Daughters* (193) are characteristic examples of the use of near foregrounds. The method makes for forceful realism and gives opportunity for striking juxtapositions of foreground with background, but is suited only to compositions without much inward depth. It also limits the near figures to half-lengths or at most three-quarter lengths, since a near person standing at full length cannot be seen as a whole through a single picture-plane.

CHAPTER XVIII

DESIGN IN THREE DIMENSIONS (*continued*)

THE following are some further problems and methods affecting three-dimensional design:

  (i)   The Use of Frontal Planes;
  (ii) Frontal Planes in Relation to the Ground-Plane;
  (iii) Vistas and Balanced Masses upon the Ground-Plane;
  (iv) Contrapposto;
  (v)   Foreshortening, Projection and Recession;
  (vi) Obliquely Placed Masses and Vistas;
  (vii) Precarious Balance;
  (viii) Methods of Decorating Ceilings.

(i) THE USE OF FRONTAL PLANES

In orderly composition the frontal plane, parallel to the picture-plane, has a peculiar value. Painters of the most diverse types have chosen to represent vertical surfaces, directly facing them at equal distances from the picture-plane. A great advantage of the frontal plane in design is the fact, already noted (see p. 83) that the image of shapes upon it are not distorted—and in particular that lines upon it, horizontal in fact, remain horizontal in the picture (see also p. 79). A deliberate preference for frontal planes is seen in such different examples as Holbein's '*Ambassadors*' (1314), Chardin's *House of Cards* (4078) and Van der Heyden's '*House in the Wood*' (1914).

A vertical plane with horizontal boundaries that is factually nearly, but not quite, frontal to the spectator, necessitates if precisely represented, lines in the picture that are nearly, but not quite, horizontal. Such lines are so awkward and disturbing to design, that painters, to avoid them, will represent a plane, actually seen slightly obliquely, as though it were perfectly frontal. Titian, for instance, in the *Vendramin Family* [(4452), Pl. 44] has made the sunlit face of the altar perfectly frontal. If it were frontal, the shadowed face, perpendicular to it, would be invisible. But Titian has wisely sacrificed literal realism to repose of design. The platform in Catena's *Warrior adoring the Infant Christ* (234) and the virginals in Vermeer's *Lady Seated at the Virginals* (2568) have been drawn on the same principle. Numerous other examples of this designer's licence might be mentioned. One that occurs in Manet's *Bar of the Folies Bergères* [(Courtauld Institute), Pl. 77] provokes especially frequent discussion. In real life, presuming the counter to be parallel to the mirror, if we could see the reflection of the girl and of the man addressing her, our image of the horizontal edge of the counter would be slightly oblique. But it makes a much better pattern as it is, perfectly horizontal.

(ii) FRONTAL PLANES IN RELATION TO THE GROUND-PLANE

In the earliest and simplest three-dimensional designs, a single group of figures is arranged frontally across the stage. Giotto has done this in the *Death of S. Francis* (Bardi Chapel, S. Croce, Florence). Botticelli in the *Primavera* (Uffizi) has continued the same method of type of design. During the fifteenth century the Italians, especially the Umbrians, gradually extended it by introducing a series of frontal planes at regular intervals of distance from the spectator and generally seen from a high eye-level.

Piero della Francesca in the *Flagellation* (Urbino) arranged the main group frontally, at a distance from the group in the foreground, which is also frontal. His eye-level is below the heads of his actors, though appreciably above the ground. So the near group is to the right of the far group to prevent its being hidden. A decade or two later, Perugino, in his *Christ giving Keys to Peter* [(Sistine Chapel, Vatican), Pl. 34] by taking an eye-level considerably above his actor's heads, so arranged the groups that the feet of the distant figures are only twice hidden by the heads of those nearer, and large empty spaces of ground occur between each frontally placed group or building and that beyond it, thus gradually leading the eye away to the far distant mountains.

Composition had by this time become a rival to architecture. Raphael adopted the general scheme of Perugino's fresco in his own *Marriage of the Virgin* (Brera, Milan). In Raphael's *School of Philosophers* [(Stanza della Segnatura, Vatican), Pl. 35] composition in three dimensions reached a perfection never since excelled. In the frontal placing of the groups there is some likeness to Perugino's fresco; but the eye-level is only just above the heads of the near actors, and the further figures are on a higher platform, so that their heads are above the horizon. Space is extended in all directions beyond the confines of the fresco. The vertical planes of depth in the architecture and the lines of depth give emphasis to the space from foreground to background; the frontal planes and lines of width to the space from side to side; and the vertical lines and the dome-like vistas of open sky to the dimension of height.

(iii) VISTAS AND BALANCED MASSES UPON THE GROUND-PLANE

Compositions take on a different character, according as the central space in the picture is full or empty. In simpler examples, where a cone-shaped mass is centrally placed, as in Giovanni Bellini's *Madonna of the Meadow* (599), the only opportunity for vistas occurs on each side of the main cone. Sometimes, where a single figure dominates, as in Borgognone's *Christ Carrying the Cross* (1077B), the vista occurs on one side only. Sometimes the vista, though central in the picture, is partly interrupted and hidden by some prominent figure or object in the foreground, such as the tree in Raphael's *Vision of Scipio Africanus* (213).

The system of propping up the main masses of weight against the frame, instead of placing them centrally, began to occur in Italian art towards 1500. In Correggio's '*Ecce Homo*' (15) though the main figure is near the centre, all the others are grouped round the four sides, so that the frame is felt to give them support.

From these uses of the vista and of lateral masses there gradually grew up a system of balanced composition, later favoured by certain landscape painters. Though subject to innumerable variations, it depended always on relating masses to the ground-plane. In Piero della Francesca's *Baptism of Christ* [(665), Pl. 20] the flat pattern upon the picture-area does not completely balance; too much occurs on the left; but, when the forms are perceived as solidly related to the ground, the impression of balance is restored; the two trees on the left and the angels under them are balanced on the right by the youth who is stripping, the four Orientals by the stream and the more distant tree.

An example of a single distant vista between two masses is the *Golden Age* (1173) attributed to the studio of Giorgione. Both Raphael and Titian developed the device, the latter especially in his *Worship of Venus* (Prado, Madrid). It takes on a formal aspect in Sebastiano del Piombo's *Raising of Lazarus* (1).

In seventeenth-century Italy the single vista between balanced masses had become an accepted landscape recipe. Domenichino's *Landscape with S. George and the Dragon* (75) and Claude's *Marriage of Isaac and Rebecca* (12) are composed on a principle, imitated by landscape painters for two centuries. In such designs the centre of the stage, though there may be figures upon it, is kept comparatively clear, except in the extreme distance, which usually culminates in a building or mountain. The vista leading to the distance is not always exactly centrally placed.

The balanced masses may be arranged in pairs, equidistant from the spectator or on the principle of a zigzag ground-plan—say a near mass on the left, balancing a farther mass on the right, and then a still more distant mass on the left, and so on, so that the total weight on one side is represented as approximately equal to that on the other. Turner introduced great varieties into this method of composition, as in *Crossing the Brook* (497) and the *Fighting Téméraire* (524).

The above method is not the only way of achieving balance upon the ground-plane. In Turner's *Frosty Morning* [(492), Pl. 72] there are three vistas, two of them oblique in direction. In Wilson's *On the Wye* (1064) the vista is partly interrupted. Piero della Francesca's *Nativity* [(908), Pl. 21] has two vistas. In Seurat's *La Baignade* [(T.G. 3908), Pl. 79] the main group of receding masses occurs on one side of the river only. Each of Cézanne's great achievements in landscape depends upon a slightly different principle.

(iv) CONTRAPPOSTO

Until about 1500, the general tendency of Italian design was to avoid foreshortening and to arrange groups in a frontal plane. The ground-plane might recede and the figures might stand firmly upon it; but the three-dimensional composition was always rigidly controlled by a sense of the flat pattern made by the picture on the wall. After about 1500, other methods of design, often described as 'baroque' and reaching a climax in the seventeenth century, came into being. A tendency of baroque design is to break up frontal planes by foreshortening, projections and recessions, obliquely placed masses and what is called 'contrapposto'.

Contrapposto is defined by Mr Berenson as the turning of the body on its own axis. In a single figure the hips are turned one way, the shoulders another, and the head in a third direction. Such a pose may give to a single figure the force of well-designed sculpture. In Raphael's *S. Catherine* (168) the cone shape, out of which the saint could have been carved, gains vitality from the contrasts in direction of her head, shoulders and hips. In Parmigianino's *Vision of S. Jerome* (33) the contrapposto of the Madonna contributes real, if mannered grace.

(v) FORESHORTENING, PROJECTION AND RECESSION

Foreshortening is often combined with contrapposto. In 'baroque' compositions, an arm or leg, or sometimes a whole figure, instead of sloping *across* the stage (on a plane parallel to the picture-plane) and appearing in its full length, often slopes towards, or away from, the spectator. A balance is established, made up of alternate projections and recessions. If one figure leans back away from us, another must lean forwards towards us, as in *Peace and War* (46) by Rubens. In the flat pattern of Rubens's *Rape of the Sabine Women* [(38), Pl. 53] 'trellis-work' (see p. 75) is conspicuous; but also, if a map were made of what is happening upon the ground, a number of alternating zigzag directions would be traced of zigzag figures swaying from background to foreground.

In Veronese's early *S. Mary Magdalen Laying Aside her Jewels* (931) the combination of contrapposto, foreshortening, projection and recession produces a more static effect. All these methods of design also occur in the *Purification of the Temple* [(1457), Pl. 51] by El Greco. Their effect is sometimes of stability, sometimes of movement. Just as some parts of a good composition must always be stable, so preferably some figures or parts of figures should be unforeshortened. Thus in Tintoretto's *Origin of the Milky Way* [(1313), Pl. 48], where much foreshortening and movement towards us and away from us occur, Juno's torso is seen unforeshortened in a frontal plane.

(vi) OBLIQUELY PLACED MASSES AND VISTAS

As designers became more confident about perspective, they depended less on the frontal plane and were more ready to place rectangular or cubic buildings or groups of figures at an oblique angle with the picture-plane. The Flemings were pioneers in the three-quarter view portrait, as seen in Van Eyck's *Man* (222.) The Italians at first tended to represent the countenance either in profile or in front view; but by the later fifteenth century Giovanni Bellini had already begun to place his figures at an oblique angle with the picture-plane, as in his *Madonna and Child* (3913). The idea was carried much farther by Titian in the *Madonna of the Pesaro Family* (Frari Church, Venice) where the throne itself is obliquely placed. In Bruegel's *Adoration of the Magi* [(3556), Pl. 43] and in El Greco's *Agony in the Garden* [(3476) Pl. 50] almost all the masses are also obliquely related to the picture-plane.

The composition of Rembrandt's so-called *Night Watch* [(Amsterdam); see copy by Lundens, N.G. 289] is a good example of foreshortening, projection and recession, and obliquely directed movement. In his *Woman Taken in Adultery* [(45), Pl. 58] the architecture, to which the groups are solidly related, is seen at an oblique angle. The distance is seen through an oblique vista in Rubens's *Watering Place* (4815) and Watteau's *La Gamme d'Amour* [(2897), Pl. 66].

(vii) PRECARIOUS BALANCE

Another peculiarity of 'baroque' and 'rococo' design might be described as the principle of precarious balance (see p. 22). Thus, in G. D. Tiepolo's *Building of the Trojan Horse* (3318) the wooden horse may be regarded as a mass in stable relation to the ground. From this mass a number of forms project, to the left, to the right, towards and away from the spectator in all directions. A much finer example of this principle occurs in Rubens's *Rape of the Daughters of Leucippus* (Munich).

Many of the above 'baroque' methods of design were anticipated by the 'Mannerists' of the sixteenth century, who also had a tendency to place important events in the sides and corners of their pictures, as in Pontormo's *Joseph in Egypt* (1131).

A note on names of styles is needed here. 'Mannerist', 'baroque' and 'rococo' are all names for extravagant styles. Mannerism, which prevailed in the sixteenth century and culminated in El Greco, implies emotional eccentricity in reaction from the calm, orderly style of Raphael's *School of Philosophers* [(Vatican), Pl. 35.] The 'baroque' style, of which Rubens was the greatest exponent, tends to stress movement as much as, and weight more than, mannerism. 'Rococo' art which flourished in the eighteenth century is conveniently described by the word 'light' in three different senses: light as opposed to heavy; light as opposed to dark; and light as opposed to serious.

(viii) METHODS OF DECORATING CEILINGS

When the Italians of the fifteenth century and later were commissioned to decorate a ceiling, their command of perspective offered new possibilities. A ceiling might be decorated in two ways: either the painter might represent his scene as beheld through a vertical picture-plane, and then transfer it, so to speak, to the horizontal plane of the ceiling; or he might represent it as though the actors were actually perched on clouds or lofty supports above the spectator's eye. Work carried out in the first method must be seen from one side of the building; otherwise the picture appears endways on or upside down. Michelangelo's frescoes on the ceiling of the Sistine Chapel, Rome, and Guido Reni's *Aurora* (Casino Rospigliosi, Rome) of about 1612 were painted on this principle.

Ceiling paintings designed by the second method in theory demand that the spectator should stand on one spot, though on that spot he may turn round and look at them from every direction. The earliest of them is Mantegna's ceiling in the Ducal Marriage Chamber at Mantua, painted between 1468 and 1474. In Correggio's various ceilings at Parma the method was elaborated and imitated in a number of seventeenth-century paintings, of which the most scientific was Pozzo's ceiling of S. Ignazio, Rome, of 1690.

In some examples of the second method the spectator is expected to face a particular way. This applies to Guercino's *Aurora* (Casino Ludovisi, Rome) of 1621-3, and to Rubens's *Apotheosis of the Duke of Buckingham* (or *Arundel?*) (187), a sketch for a ceiling, which looks best as usually hung, so that the Duke's head is above his feet.

The *laws* of perspective, applied to ceilings by the second method, remain unchanged; but their *application* works out so differently as to give the design a new character. The picture-plane is now horizontal and the direction of vision vertical. Vertical lines have taken the place of lines of depth and are represented by lines meeting in a vanishing point immediately overhead. There is no horizon and nothing that gives the security of a visible ground-plane. The under-faces of horizontal planes parallel to the ground are visible frontally, but their upper faces (e.g. of ledges supporting figures) are invisible. Design, in fact, is subservient to a pseudo-realism, which deprives it of the quality of repose.

CHAPTER XIX

THE RENDERING OF LIGHT

LITERAL realism in painting is impossible, among other reasons because of the impossibility (with rare exceptions) of reproducing in paint the full range and contrast of tone, apparent in Nature.

By 'tone' I mean the *degree* of *lightness* or *darkness*, perceptible in an appearance, natural or pictorial (see p. 24). By 'the *highest* tone' I mean what is *lightest*, by 'the *lowest* tone' what is *darkest*, in the area discussed. Between these extremes, the number of tones is infinite, as is the number of 'tones' (in the musical sense) reproducible by the violin and the subtlest differences as difficult to perceive. The '*half-tones*' are approximately half-way between the lightest and the darkest passages.

'Tone' relates here exclusively to lightness and darkness, apart from colour, i.e. from redness, blueness, yellowness, etc. I avoid using 'tone' in another sense often given to it, when describing the general colouring of a whole picture as of 'a golden tone', 'a silvery tone', 'a warm brown tone', etc. For this concept a better word would be 'tonality' or 'complexion'.

The tones of Nature require, as a rule, to be treated *relatively* by the painter, i.e. translated into the tones at his disposal. Even if the source of light (sun, lamp, etc.) be excluded from the picture, the contrast in Nature between what is in full light and what is in dense shadow is usually much greater than the contrast between the lightest and the darkest pigments that the painter can use. A few contrasts, such as those seen in the distance on a grey day, can be literally reproduced in oil; but with most effects this is impossible. The difference of tone between a Rembrandt lit by direct sunshine and the same picture seen in a dark corner is much greater than the difference of tone produced by dark and light paint.

In Nature, tone is due to two factors, acting in combination: (i) *incidence of light;* (ii) *local tone.* Let us consider in Nature any image, perceived as of one tone throughout, say that of the roof of a house. It is darker, say, than the sky above it, and lighter than the interior of the house seen through the windows. Its tone is due, first, to *incidence of light,* i.e. to its spatial relation: (*a*) to the source of light (the sun, e.g. to the angle at which the sun's rays hit it, directly or indirectly); and (*b*) to the spectator, to whom it will appear lighter or darker according to his distance from it and to the angle at which his vision hits it. Its tone is due, secondly, to *local tone*, i.e. to the intrinsic lightness or darkness of its *material* (tile or slate, etc.), i.e. the degree of its intrinsic capacity of reflecting or absorbing light. Material also, of course, affects colour; and this aspect of colour is called *local colour*. Local colour, however (redness, blueness, etc.), must be distinguished from *local tone* (darkness or lightness due to material).

Incidence of light can cause much greater contrasts than *local tone*. The contrast between two objects of the same local tone, one placed in direct sunshine and one in dense shadow, is much greater than the contrast between two objects of different local tones placed in the same light.

Nature possesses a vast *scale* of tones, some strongly, and others barely perceptibly, contrasted with each other. The scale of tones at the painter's disposal is much smaller, though it also includes both striking and delicate contrasts.

The actual *means* that the painter employs to represent incidence of light is *local tone*. Since contrasts due to local tone are comparatively small, it is impossible for him literally to reproduce Nature's full range of tonal contrast. To represent them at all his treatment must be *relative*; and on that one word *relative* the whole argument of this chapter hangs. Nature's great contrasts have to be translated into something smaller and her small contrasts into something smaller still.

In Nature extremes of tone are invisible. We cannot look at the sun nor see into the darkness of a moonless and starless night; but what we can see is immense. If we are in a dark room long enough, we can make out objects by perceiving faint differences of tone. If we pass from such a room into the open, though we are dazzled at first, we can soon adjust our eyes to the higher key. A picture, which is concerned with *one* impression, cannot possibly record such adjustments. In an outdoor painting of a near house the windows must be represented, as they appear, in slight variations of dark tone. Conversely, in a picture of an interior, the main contrasts of tone must be those perceived inside the room, and everything outside the window can be represented only by the slightest variations of light.

The treatment, if it is to bear any resemblance to truth, must be relative. Painters have dealt with the problem in a variety of ways. Most of these have been described by Ruskin in the chapter on Turnerian Light ('Modern Painters', pt. v, ch. III), in which he gives a numerical table of three methods of treating Nature's tones. From this chapter is derived much of what follows. It contains many illuminating analyses not included here; but there are also some additional observations in the following account:

The painters whose methods Ruskin describes are Rembrandt, Veronese and Turner. I propose to describe nine methods in all, four unscientific and five scientific. Painters typical of the four unscientific methods are: (i) Jacopo di Cione; (ii) Titian; (iii) El Greco; (iv) Constable. The five scientific methods (which are no more meritorious than the unscientific methods) occur in the works of (v) early Turner; (vi) Rembrandt; (vii) Veronese; (viii) Claude and middle-period Turner; (ix) later Turner.

(i) JACOPO DI CIONE

In the *Coronation of the Virgin* (569) by Jacopo di Cione, as in most primitive pictures of all schools, more attention has been paid to local tone than to incidence of light. The striking contrasts are between garments of a light and of a dark material, not between what is in light and what is in shadow. Those who treat tone in this way are usually identical with the flat-pattern realists. Another example is the 'Wilton Diptych' [(4451), see Pl. 6; see also p. 28].

(ii) TITIAN

Titian in *Bacchus and Ariadne* [(35), Pl. 36] has recorded *separately* many true relations of tone; but, taken as a whole, the tone of the picture is arbitrary. Different passages represent different times of day. For dramatic purposes most of the sky is darker, in relation to the flesh of the principal sunlit figures, than it would ever be in real life. And no attempt is made consistently to base the relations of tone as a whole on Nature's proportion and sequence.

(iii) EL GRECO

The method of El Greco is even more arbitrary. In his *Agony in the Garden* [(3476), Pl. 50] the pattern depends on incidence of light, not on local tone; but the light has no consistency of direction, and though intermediate tones occur, the highest and the lowest tones alternate in a manner that disregards natural effect. Something like this treatment occurs also in Tintoretto's paintings in the Scuola di San Rocco, Venice, such as the *Baptism of Christ*.

(iv) CONSTABLE

Constable's treatment of light, though not based, as a rule, on scientific grading of tone, is more objective. In his *View of Hampstead* (1275) the sky is treated in one range of tone and the earth in another. He felt the contrast between the dark clouds and the lighter part of the sky to be so important that he made it almost as strong as in Nature, but failed to indicate that, though these clouds were dark compared with the rest of the sky, the whole sky, dark clouds included, was light compared with the whole earth. (With a few rare exceptions this is always the case, provided no part of the earth receives the direct rays of the sun.) Claude or Turner would have been more cautious with the lesser tonal contrasts.

Yet Constable's method produces a truer effect than Ruskin, the consistent advocate of 'truth', would allow. It appeals to the emotions and to the memory. Our eyes are not, as a rule, trained to remember tone; and when we see a cloud darker than the rest of the sky, the difference in what is usually a dome of light impresses itself upon our memory, so that a Constable vividly reminds us of what we saw and how we felt. A more scientific treatment could hardly have conveyed the tenseness of the thunderstorm in his *Salisbury Cathedral* [(1814), Pl. 73].

(v) EARLY TURNER

In his earlier oils, Turner's treatment of tone is less expressive than Constable's, but more scientific in that the relations of tone as a whole are based more closely on those of Nature. In *Calais Pier* [(472), Pl. 70] the contrast between the lightest light and darkest dark is as great as the medium will allow, though less than in Nature; but such a contrast could only be obtained at the cost of loss of colour. In *Calais Pier*, colour is confined to the half-tones, because only black paint will give such strong darks, and only white paint such strong lights; whereas in the real scene the blackness of the dark sky and sea would have been modified by purples, blues and greens, and even the white foam might have shone with rose or gold. These colours could have been recorded in paint, only by keeping the darkest tones lighter and the lightest tones darker.

(vi) REMBRANDT

The blackness of *Calais Pier* compares unfavourably with even the darkest Rembrandt. Rembrandt's range of tone is considerable, but smaller. This makes it possible for him to treat the darkest shadows not as black, but as golden brown. Instead of pushing the contrast of tone as far as his medium will allow, he makes the contrasts greatest among the lights and smallest amongst the darks. His extravagance of contrast at one end of the scale of tone drives him to economy of contrast at the other. It is also the direct cause of the darkness (golden gloom though it be) which takes up the largest area in his pictures.

For instance, in the *Rabbi* (190) the contrast between the highest light (on the side of the nose) and the next highest light (on the cheek) is as great as in Nature; and that between the light on the cheek and the shadow under the cheek almost as great. But among the darks a large difference in Nature becomes a small difference, only just perceptible in the picture (as in the gradations of shadow behind the Rabbi's head and the contrast between this background and the hat). Rembrandt's superiority to his imitators is often shown most of all in his management of these delicately contrasted darks. The tones of his *Portrait of Himself when Old* [(221), see Pl. 61] follow a similar system.

This method had great dramatic advantages, but was more suited to indoor than to outdoor scenes. It also somewhat restricted his colour. In order to be luminous, the large areas of shadow in his pictures are always warm, i.e. tending towards orange, in colour (see p. 117); and even his lights and half-tones are more often warm than cool; reds and yellows are in excess of blues and mauves, which are usually greyish.

Leonardo, who was Rembrandt's precursor in this treatment of tone, was even more restricted in his use of colour. On the other hand, Correggio, who adopted the same method, managed to combine it with colour schemes of much subtlety and variety.

(vii) VERONESE

Veronese's method, which is the converse of Rembrandt's, gives great opportunities for colour. In the *Family of Darius before Alexander* [(294), Pls. 45–7], the contrasts at the dark end of the scale are given a force almost equal to Nature's, and consequently, because of the restricted possibilities of paint, those at the light end, though based on Nature, are translated into something more delicate; and, exactly on the converse principle to Rembrandt's, a large proportion of the picture is light in tone. Just as Rembrandt's skill is tested by gradations of darks, Veronese's is shown in gradations of light.

The difference between the shadows in the dark blue robe of Darius's mother and those in the less dark red breastplate of Alexander is nearly as great as in Nature. But the contrast between the sky and the two tones of the balustrade in front of it is considerably less. The sunlit portions of the balustrade are just perceptibly lighter than the sky and the shadowed portions just perceptibly darker; in Nature these contrasts would be greater. And none of this background, pale and light though it is, is as light as the faces and white portions of the dresses of Darius's wife and daughter, where the sun shines on them in the foregound.

The method is ideal for Veronese's purpose. He can work in a full range of colour, including blues and mauves. He can do full justice to differences of local tone. The large proportion of light tone gives gaiety to the scene.

This also applies to the later figure compositions of Rubens, such as the *Rape of the Sabine Women* [(38), Pl. 53] in which the treatment of tone is the same as Veronese's.

The disadvantages of Veronese's method would only become apparent were it applied to landscape proper, since the delicate difference of light tone would have insufficient force for representing a long series of receding trees, buildings or mountains.

(viii) CLAUDE AND MIDDLE-PERIOD TURNER

Turner in his middle period treated tone by a method based on Claude's and more suited to landscape than either Rembrandt's or Veronese's. Whereas Rembrandt used large areas of delicately gradated darks and Veronese large areas of delicately gradated lights, Claude reserved his most delicate treatment for the half-tones. These half-tones, like Rembrandt's darks and Veronese's lights, occupied the largest area in his works. In his *Embarkation of S. Ursula* [(30), see Pl. 56] the differences of tone at each end of the scale are subtle, but are subtlest of all in the half-tones. The same applies to Turner's *Crossing the Brook* (497).

One advantage of this method is the possibility it gives of reinforcing scarcely perceptible differences of half-tone by easily perceived differences of colour. In painting, colour is best differentiated among the middle tones. Turner takes full advantage of this in the *Bay of Baiae* (T.G. 505) in which there is more contrast of colour than in *Crossing the Brook*, though the treatment of tone is the same. Where tonal differences between distant shadows defy perception, the farther shadow is cooler, i.e. bluer.

(ix) LATER TURNER

Ideal though this method was, it did not satisfy Turner after 1830. It failed to give him the scope he wanted for rendering colour. A full contrast of colour was not possible among the strongest lights or strongest darks. It was now his ambition, as in *Norham Castle: Sunrise* (T.G. 1981), to give a shadowed mountain or castle all its blueness, a near cow (also shadowed against the light) all its redness and, above all, the source of light, the rising sun, all its yellowness. In order to do so, and at the same time to base his relations of tone on Nature's, he restricted the total range of tone, so that the highest lights are less light and the lowest darks less dark than in *Crossing the Brook*. In so far as the colour of *Norham Castle* looks strange, it is because the *colour* contrasts are *absolute* and the *tone* contrasts *relative*.

Turner's first method, then, was to force the contrasts of tone and thereby limit severely the possibilities of vivid colour; his second method to diminish the contrasts of tone and make colour contrasts possible except among the extreme lights and darks; and his third method to diminish tonal contrast still further, so that full justice could be done to colour throughout. The final method was also used by Monet in such pictures as *Vétheuil: Sunshine and Shadow* (T.G. 3262). It does not consist in ignoring or falsifying tone after the manner of cheap paintings of flower-gardens and sunsets. On the contrary, all the more attention has to be paid to the tones of Nature, before all her contrasts, great or small, can be translated into contrasts so much smaller.

A minutely gradated treatment of tone is not the only way of expressing truths of light. Constable's work shows the advantage of other methods. Cézanne's work, which is eminently luminous, is broadly true in the differentiation of tones without being specially subtle: the subtlety comes from the nuances of colour (see p. 31).

The landscape painter has to make his choice between making tone contrasts or colour contrasts more important. Crome in the *Moonrise on the Marshes of the Yare* [(2645), Pl. 71] has treated both relatively. The tonal contrast, though more delicate than in Turner's *Calais Pier* [(472), Pl. 70], is strong enough to make an almost monochromatic colour scheme necessary. The colours are relative, not absolute; but their coolness or warmth is based on true appearance also. To do justice to the blues and silvers of moonlight, a much more restricted range of tone would be required, such as Whistler used in his *Nocturne in Blue and Silver* (3420).

In good oil painting the contrasts of tone are less even than those of which the medium is capable. In water-colour, the total range is even more restricted; at the same time, the whole key of tone is considerably raised. The darks have less strength than in oils, but the lights may be much lighter, even reaching the whiteness of paper itself.

It is not always advisable literally to base *all* the tonal relations on Nature's, even when aiming at a close reminder of appearances. In De Hooch's *Interior of a Dutch House* [(834), Pl. 63] the window panes are no lighter than the sunlit cap and apron of the principal woman. To make them lighter, as they would be in real life, would involve introducing an awkward emphasis in a corner and destroying the balance of tones and the focus upon the figures.

Again De Hooch's *Courtyard of a Dutch House* [(794), Pl. 62] represents a grey day when the light comes, not from one spot, but suffused through the cloudy sky as a whole, which would all be lighter than anything on earth. De Hooch has made it lighter than the whitewashed bricks of the shed and pump, but not lighter than the lady's white cap and the trimmings of her dress. Doing so would have destroyed the total tonal balance and made impossible those delicate gradations of tone on which the painting of his sky depends for atmosphere.

CHAPTER XX

DESIGN BY LIGHT

SOME of the methods of rendering light described above imply corresponding methods of design. This is particularly true of the designing of flat pattern by contrasting local tones.

Incidence of light was first recorded for realistic, not used for decorative, purposes. Contrasts due to it occur in Giotto's paintings of the early fourteenth century, such as the *Death of S. Francis* (Santa Croce, Florence) in which they reinforce outlines in giving the forms solidity, but the *design* depends upon line and solid mass rather than upon tone. Occasionally, however, as in the *Mockery of Christ* (Arena Chapel, Padua) Giotto's pattern of tone (both local and otherwise) in addition to its realistic value, plays an important part in his design.

This is also true of many paintings by Masaccio, who revived and extended Giotto's monumental and sculpturesque aims nearly a hundred years after his death. In his *Madonna and Child* [(3046), Pl. 7] Masaccio has investigated effects of sunshine, such as the light reflected in the shadow of the lute held by the angel on the left, and treated the shadows in the Madonna's blue cloak and crimson underdress as one continuous tonal area, resulting from the direction of the light.

Few of Masaccio's Florentine successors took full advantage of his discoveries; Uccello, as in the *Rout of San Romano* [(583), Pl. 16] and later Botticelli, as in *Mars, Venus and Satyrs* [(915), Pl. 24], depended for tonal pattern almost solely on local tone. The fifteenth-century Sienese were in the main even more backward in this branch of realism; but Sassetta's 'Scenes in the Life of S. Francis' (4757–63) show him a pioneer in landscape and atmosphere; the division into sunshine and shadow of his *Stigmatization of S. Francis* [(4760), Pl. 14] is especially bold and broad.

Piero della Francesca, who must have seen these paintings by Sassetta in Borgo San Sepolcro, carried the study of atmosphere further. In one fresco of the *Vision of Constantine* (S. Francesco, Arezzo) he recorded stronger contrasts of light and shade than in any previous Italian painting, and gradated the tones subtly between these extremes, so as to produce a dramatic balance in light and shade. This fresco, however, had no imitators; and *chiaroscuro*, the use of light (especially incidence of light) for decorative or dramatic purposes (see p. 26) did not become a regular method of design in Italy until the days of Leonardo.

In Jan Van Eyck's *Jan Arnolfini and his Wife* [(186), Pls. 10 and 11] the total effect of light and shade depends about equally upon local tone and incidence of light. Incidence of light has become more important in Antonello's *S. Jerome* (1418) and Bruegel's *Adoration of the Magi* [(3556), Pl. 43].

Some of the methods of design by light and shade (many of them combinable) may now be considered under eight headings:

(i) Proportion and Balance of Light and Shade;
(ii) Linear Design enforced by Light;
(iii) Unsymmetrical Lighting;
(iv) Silhouettes and Counterchange;
(v) Focus by Light and by Shadow;
(vi) Concentrated Lighting and Diffused Lighting;
(vii) Breadth of Tone and Broken Lighting;
(viii) The Pre-Raphaelite Attitude towards Light.

(i) PROPORTION AND BALANCE OF LIGHT AND SHADE

In general, one side of a picture should not be given up to too much light in contrast with the other. The proportion of the picture allotted to areas of light, dark and half-tones varies according to the artist's aims. Reynolds noted that most painters, in distributing the light in their pictures, 'allowed not above a quarter for the light, another quarter to be kept as dark as possible and the remaining half to be kept in mezzotint', adding that Rubens admitted more light and Rembrandt less. These proportions, it may be noted, are the result of the two painters' respective methods of rendering light (see pp. 102–4).

The relative size, distribution and placing of areas of light and dark are usually worked out instinctively; but Reynolds reduced them to rules. By making rough sketches of the distribution of tone in work by other artists (such as Rubens and Rembrandt) he trained his eye for tonal balance and variety. His landscape backgrounds lack the atmospheric truth of Gainsborough's, but succeed better as tonal patterns than those of his imitators. For instance, Reynolds's *Captain Orme* (681) compares favourably with Raeburn's *Lt.-Col. Bryce McMurdo* (1435).

(ii) LINEAR DESIGN ENFORCED BY LIGHT

The various methods of linear design (see Chapter xv) would have a confusing effect on the eye unless supported by contrasts of tone. For purposes both of realism and design, drawings may depend on line only; but in painting, outlines or contours attain their full decorative appeal, only when the forms they enclose are lighter or darker than their background. In Tintoretto's *Origin of the Milky Way* [(1313), Pl. 48] the upright direction of Juno's leg is emphasized as a light shape against darker tones.

(iii) UNSYMMETRICAL LIGHTING

In Leonardo's fresco of the *Last Supper* (Santa Maria delle Grazie, Milan), the inward running lines of the architecture and the undulating pattern of the hands of the arguing disciples all converge symmetrically at the centre, the head of Christ; but the tonal design is unsymmetrical, because the light is represented as shining, as in the Refectory containing the fresco, from windows on the spectator's left upon the wall on his right, leaving the wall on his left (which in the fresco has no windows) in shadow. A similar design, symmetrical in line and unsymmetrical in tone, occurs in Bramantino's *Adoration of the Magi* (3073). In Reynolds's *Nelly O'Brien* (Wallace Collection, 38) the symmetrical figure in the light is contrasted with subordinate, unsymmetrical gleams in the dark background.

(iv) SILHOUETTES AND COUNTERCHANGE

A figure or object represented in a picture is often treated as an area of nearly the same tone throughout, either a dark area against a light background or vice versa. This effect, known as a *silhouette*, may depend on local tone or incidence of light or both; the tones within the area may vary much or little; the contrast with the background may be great or small; and the contours may be sharp or blurred, or of varying definition. In portraits, the background is often in half-tone (sometimes with slight gradations), while most of the figure is dark and certain parts—say the face and hands—are light. This applies to Moroni's *Lawyer* (742) and to *S. Paul* (3590) by an unknown seventeenth-century Spanish artist. Manet in his *Olympia* (Louvre) has made a striking use of a light silhouette against a dark background.

The use of *counterchange* is an extension of the use of the silhouette. A darker area against a lighter backgound is contrasted with a lighter area against a darker background. Counterchanges due to local tone occur throughout Uccello's *Rout of San Romano* [(583), Pl. 16]. In Van Eyck's *Arnolfini* [(186), Pl. 10] they depend also on incidence of light. Titian in the *Holy Family* (4) has treated the Virgin and Child as a light area against the dark rocks, and S. Joseph's head and left sleeve as a dark shape against the light sky, each area, within its lightness or darkness, being also subject to delicate modifications of tone.

Reynolds maintained that 'some part of a picture should be sharp and cutting against its ground', but added: 'if it be relieved on every side it will appear as if inlaid'. In Titian's above-mentioned *Holy Family* and in his *Vendramin Family* [(4452), Pl. 44] the figures owe some of their solidity as well as their texture to slight varieties in softness and sharpness of contour. Soft edges and the gradations of tone of the background in Chardin's *The Lesson* [(4077), Pl. 67], besides contributing to the atmosphere, give variety to the two silhouettes.

In Carel Fabritius's *Man in Fur Cap and Cuirass* (4042) the darker upper sky is the background, both for the still darker cap and hair and for the lighter face. Against the light lower sky are silhouetted the still lighter collar and the comparatively dark coat. A slight difference of tone between an object and its background is often effective, as in Avercamp's *Winter Scene* (1346) where the almost centralized house is emphatic, though it is little darker than the sky behind it. Compare also the principal tree in Turner's *Frosty Morning* [(492), Pl. 72].

(v) FOCUS BY LIGHT AND BY SHADOW

The above account of silhouettes implies something of the system of focus. (For focus in its optical aspect see pp. 35, 36.) It was Leonardo who first concentrated the strongest light on the most important incidents and subordinated the accessories by keeping them in shadow; see his *Virgin of the Rocks* [(1093), Pl. 29]. Correggio used it subtly in the *Madonna of the Basket* (23), and with even greater skill in *Venus, Mercury and Cupid* [(10), Pls. 40 and 41], in which the strongest light is on the tip of Cupid's wing.

Focus by light was further elaborated and perfected by Rembrandt, as in both of his portraits of *Himself at 34* [(672), Pl. 60] and of *Himself when Old* [(221), see Pl. 61 and p. 35]. In his early portrait of *Françoise Van Wasserhoven*(?) (775) he made the collar lighter than the face, as he saw it; but in the later *Margaretha Trip* (1675) he concentrated interest on the face by making the lights on the forehead, cheek and nose stronger than any part of the white collar. The result compares favourably with the literalness of the prominent white collars in Thomas de Keyser's *Constantin Huygens with his Clerk* (212).

Subjects or groups of secondary importance can be subordinated in a picture by being lit less strongly than the main group. In Geertgen tot Sint Jans's *Nativity* [(4081), Pl. 26], two of the three sources of light are supernatural. The primary source is the Christ Child; the second source the angel in the distance; and the third source the little fire on the hill. To conceive of such an effect in the everyday world is impossible, since a source of light cannot be perceived as a form, so that the shape of a luminous Child would be invisible. Correggio in his famous *Nativity* (Dresden) made everything else receive light from the Child and the Child receive light from some near unseen source. Rembrandt in the *Adoration of the Shepherds* (47), hid the lantern, the source of light, behind the nearest shepherd, but so near to the Child as to suggest the supernatural tradition without violating the laws of normal appearance.

In the *Woman Taken in Adultery* [(45), Pl. 58] Rembrandt gave importance to his various groups by the relative strength of their illumination: the main group receives the strongest light; the worshippers by the altar are lit by a secondary light; and the beggars low down on the right and the figures climbing the steps are in luminous shadow. Terborch has achieved an almost equal success in the *Peace of Münster* (896) and Hogarth's lighting in *Calais Gate* [(1464), Pl. 68] has not fallen far below Rembrandt's standard in skill; but the opaque brown fog in Maes's *Idle Servant* (207) shows the danger of adopting this convention without trained perception.

The Venetians also developed an analogous, but less emphatic system of focus by light. In outdoor compositions they often concentrated the light upon the figures by making the sky dark in proportion to the figures (see p. 101). Van Dyck's *Charles I* (1172) and most eighteenth-century English portraits follow this convention. In Gainsborough's *Daughters Chasing a Butterfly* (1811), time has exaggerated the darkness of the background. On the other hand, Gainsborough's own later portrait of *Captain Wade* (Baroness Burton) is remarkable for the light sky, based on actual appearance.

The above are examples of emphasis by light. On the other hand, in landscapes where there is much light sky, trees, etc. are accentuated as shapes of dark against it. So, too, in figure composition, emphasis by shadow, e.g. the head of Christ in Titian's *Entombment* (Louvre) can be most effective. In Goya's picture the *Bewitched Man* [(1472), Pl. 69] the background is in darkish half-tone, against which the priest's dark clothes and light face and hands are both contrasted.

(vi) CONCENTRATED LIGHTING AND DIFFUSED LIGHTING

Leonardo began a tendency, which reached its climax in the art of Caravaggio and his followers, to merge most of the forms represented in gloom, except where they are caught by a single concentrated ray of light. Such lighting, by emphasizing solid projection (see p. 31), can produce results both dramatic and melodramatic, as in Caravaggio's *Christ at Emmaus* [(172), Pl. 52] and Guercino's *Incredulity of S. Thomas* (3216). In Reynolds's portrait of *Dr Johnson* (887) the features are emphasized further by keeping the darkest shadows flat and simple and giving them sharp edges. On the other hand, when delicacy of form was to be expressed, as in Gainsborough's *Daughters* (1811) the palest shadows are often used.

Diffused lighting, as opposed to concentrated lighting, occurs out of doors on grey days, and indoors when a room is well lit by large windows but is not in direct sunshine. Its representation in painting entails some sacrifice of the more obvious effects of solidity. Strong contrasts of tone, if they occur in such pictures, depend upon local tone rather than upon incidence of light, as in Holbein's *Duchess of Milan* [(2475), Pl. 39] and Velazquez's *Philip IV when Young* (1129).

Between the above extremes of concentrated lighting and diffused lighting there occurs, in painting as in Nature, an infinite range of intermediate possibilities.

(vii) BREADTH OF TONE AND BROKEN LIGHTING

Painters who aim at stately grandeur tend to keep their lights together and their shadows together in broad continuous areas of light or dark. In the *Landscape with Figures* [(40), Pl. 55] by Nicolas Poussin, large areas of dark and half-tone are relieved by small accents of light.

In earlier Italian paintings the landscape backgrounds tend to be broken up into a number of tonal contrasts, as also in Mantegna's *Agony in the Garden* [(1417), Pl. 18]. On the other hand, the landscapes in Giovanni Bellini's *Agony* [(726), Pl. 19] and also in Andrea dal Castagno's *Crucifixion* [(1138), Pl. 13] are treated broadly—the earth as one dark area and the sky as one light area, within which are subordinate variations of tone.

The principle of broad distribution of tone can be carried out in different ways. The main tonal design of Turner's *Calais Pier* [(472), Pl. 70] consists of two nearly contiguous lozenge-shaped areas of light, surrounded by darkness occasionally modified; in his *Evening Star* (1991) the light sky and the dark sea and sands are divided by a horizon which is interrupted only by the mast on the left and the rolling vapours on the right.

To ignore breadth of tone is usually to destroy unity as in Dyce's *Pegwell Bay* (1407). Corot's *Bent Tree* (2625) suffers from a similar fault; the softer edges prevent so niggling an appearance; but the tones of the foliage are too varied and merge into each other too vaguely to allow of true breadth of tonal design.

Corot's own earlier *Claudian Aqueduct* (3285) and Constable's *Malvern Hall* (2653) are refreshing examples of tones broadly and simply contrasted and distributed.

Painters frequently combine a general breadth of tone with broken lighting in detail. Within the dark areas are small accents of light, and within the light areas small accents of dark, as in Tintoretto's *S. George and the Dragon* [(16), Pl. 42], Lawrence's *Queen Charlotte* (4257) and Constable's *Cornfield* (130).

(viii) THE PRE-RAPHAELITE ATTITUDE TOWARDS LIGHT

Holman Hunt and Millais rebelled against the *chiaroscuro* of their elder contemporaries, such as Leslie, who merged the subordinate parts of their compositions in would-be Rembrandtesque, but in fact opaque, gloom. In aiming at truer lighting, Hunt and Millais usually failed in tonal consistency, just as in aiming at gay colour they often achieved mere gaudiness; but their records of reflected light and reflected colour, piecemeal though they were, represented a reaction from stagey conventions which have never since returned—a reaction in favour of the study of sunlight, which was carried out with much greater scientific consistency half a generation later by the Impressionists and Post-Impressionists of France. The latters' aims, already discussed in Chapters VII and VIII, are further considered in the ensuing chapters on Colour.

CHAPTER XXI

COLOUR

THE theory of colour harmony is at present largely a matter of speculation. Musical harmony (in the limited sense) is an exact science, depending solely on the *pitch* of the notes played together or in succession. Colour harmony depends on three considerations (shortly to be defined), tone, hue and saturation, and also upon the proportion of space allotted to each colour and upon their juxtaposition or non-juxtaposition.

In the past, painters have succeeded as colour harmonists by a combination of instinct and training, unsupported by theory. Most lovers of pictures also base their colour preferences on instinct, backed by experience; but some discussion of colour is here necessary, though much is little more than guess-work.

It is convenient to consider colour under the following headings:

(i) Tone and Colour;	(vi) Primary Colours;
(ii) Neutral Colours;	(vii) Tone, Hue and Saturation;
(iii) Colours of the Spectrum;	(viii) Hot and Cold Colours;
(iv) Pure Colours;	(ix) Mixture and Divisionism.
(v) Complementary Colours;	

(i) TONE AND COLOUR

Tone (see p. 99) is the degree of lightness or darkness of an appearance, apart from its redness, blueness, etc. The tonal appearance of a luminous object, such as the sun or a candle, results from the intensity of the light proceeding from it towards the eye, and that of a non-luminous object from the intensity of the light reflected by it. *Tone* depends on *quantity* of light. The *colour* in the appearance of an object depends on the *quality* of the light proceeding from, or reflected by, the object. Rays of visible light vibrate in wave-lengths (so many millionths of an inch) which vary according to the colour. Of the colours of the spectrum, violet has the shortest, and red the longest, wave-length

(ii) NEUTRAL COLOURS

Whites, blacks and greys (in which there is no trace of red, blue, orange, etc.), are known as neutral colours. Light is made up of a range of colours of different wave-lengths. Grey, black and white surfaces reflect or absorb all these wave-lengths at equal intensities; white mainly reflects them, and black mainly absorbs them. Coloured surfaces absorb some wave-lengths and reflect others. Surfaces the colour of which is *pure* (i.e. unmixed with neutrality) absorb all the wave-lengths of colour, except the single wave-length which they reflect.

(iii) COLOURS OF THE SPECTRUM

When the sun's rays by passing through particles of water cause a rainbow, the white light is split up into a series of its component wave-lengths of colour. These colours (which can also be produced by a glass prism) are known as the colours of the spectrum. They are of maximum *purity*, i.e. unmixed with grey, and include red at one extremity and violet (somewhat bluer than the flower of the name) at the other. Between the extremities is an infinite range of colours, each merging into the next, arranged in an order which is indicated by the following, by no means exact, names: red; orange; yellow; citron; green; turquoise; blue; violet.

(iv) PURE COLOURS

All the colours of the spectrum are pure (free from grey) but not all pure colours are on the spectrum. There are pure colours, not on the spectrum, mixtures of red and violet, described as 'maroon', 'purple', etc. and due to a *combination* of wave-lengths.

The accompanying circular diagram (see p. 119) helps to explain the meaning of complementary colour and of saturation, but, except in the *order* of the colours, has no relation to the spectrum (which would be indicated better by a straight line); nor are the proportionate distances between the colours proportioned the same as on the spectrum.

The circumference of the outer circle on the diagram symbolizes a series of pure colours of the same tone. The ten colours, red, orange, yellow, citron, green, turquoise, blue, violet, purple, maroon, are indicated by their initials: R, O, Y, C, G, T, B, V, P, M. Between these (the names for which are approximate) an infinite series of intermediate colours must be imagined. The colours between red and violet (including maroon and purple), which do not belong to the spectrum, are included in the diagram because of their purity.

(v) COMPLEMENTARY COLOURS

Every colour has a colour complementary to it, and every pure colour has a pure colour complementary to it. This means that if the two colours are of the same tone and each occupies half the area of a circular colour top, the appearance of the top, when spun, is neutral grey. On the outer circle of the diagram complementary pure colours are arranged diametrically opposite each other: red and turquoise; orange and blue; yellow and violet; citron and purple; green and maroon. Similar pairs of complementaries occur among all the intermediate unnamed colours. N, in the centre of the circle, stands for the single neutral grey that an optical mixture (as by the top) of these complementary colours will produce.

Physiologists recognize the principle of complementary colours. A neutral grey placed next to a vivid (nearly pure) colour, will seem to contain that colour's complementary. If one stares long enough at an area of vivid red and then looks at an area of white, one sees the complementary colour, turquoise, upon the white area.

(vi) PRIMARY COLOURS

Red, blue and yellow used to be regarded as the three primary colours. Green was sometimes included as a fourth. The theory, based on chemistry rather than on optics, is rejected by most scientists, on the ground that colour depends on wave-length and that any selection of particular colours from a continuous series is arbitrary.

Yet I cannot help thinking that the difference between red, yellow, green and blue, must have some cause besides mere words or mere associations, though it has yet to be discovered. It may be due to the chemical effect of the colours upon the eye. It is felt to be a difference in kind, not merely a difference (like that between light and dark) in degree.

There seem to be certain landmarks in the series of pure colours, at which a change in kind takes place; and the four words, red, yellow, green and blue, whether or not precise, at least correspond with broad categories of colour that are felt to differ fundamentally. For instance it is impossible not to think of violet as a blue with a little red in it, although in terms of wave-length it is as unlike red as possible.

(vii) TONE, HUE AND SATURATION

These are three distinct attributes of any given colour, by which it can be described in contrast with another colour. *Tone*, as indicated, means lightness or darkness, apart from redness or blueness. *Hue* denotes degree of blueness, redness, etc.; i.e. it denotes colour itself in a restricted sense, apart from tone and apart from purity. The colours on the outer circle of the diagram differ in hue alone. They are also, all of them, *pure*, i.e. of *maximum saturation* (though not all of them belong to the spectrum). Neutral colours have no saturation. If colours are 'vivid' (i.e. nearly pure) their saturation is high; if they are 'dull' (inclined towards neutrality), their saturation is low. In the diagram (which concerns colours of one tone) saturation is measured by distance from the centre; hue by position upon the circumference. The inner circle indicates colours half-way between neutrality and purity, i.e. colours of medium saturation.

In practice pure colour and dead neutrality are rarely seen in Nature and still more rarely in painting. A vivid red in a picture usually has some brown in it; and a grey has some brown, green, purple or blue. We are commonly surrounded with colours of varying saturation, described by such words as 'brown', 'chocolate', 'slate-grey', 'olive green', 'dove colour', etc.

(viii) HOT AND COLD COLOURS

The non-scientific expressions 'hot and cold', 'warm and cool', etc., are frequently applied by artists to colour, and in particular to hue. Since they are indispensable in discussing colour harmony, their meaning must be defined. The phrases are due to association. Red and orange are associated with fire and called 'hot'; blue and violet with shadows in snow and called 'cold'. This does not always correspond with the weather. Most of the colours in Turner's *Frosty Morning* [(492), Pl. 72] are orange browns, etc.—colours described as warm, though a cold day is represented; and in many pictures of the sea, blue predominates, though the weather represented is warm. Yet it remains convenient to speak of colour schemes as of weather, to blame some for being hot or cold, and praise others for being warm or cool.

There may be a physical cause for these psychological epithets. Of the colours of the spectrum, red, the 'hottest', has the longest wave-length and is caused by the smallest number of vibrations; violet the 'coldest', has the shortest wave-length and is caused by the greatest number of vibrations. The colours of the spectrum from red to violet become gradually cooler; of the pure colours outside the spectrum (see diagram), maroon is cooler than red and purple cooler than maroon, but warmer than violet.

(ix) MIXTURE AND DIVISIONISM

It seems probable that the diagram accounts for every conceivable colour of a given tone, but with one important proviso, that the discussion concerns an area homogeneous in colour throughout. Under these conditions of mixtures completely amalgamated, the equal mixture of two complementary pure colours of the same tone results in neutrality; that of two slightly differing pure colours in an intermediate pure colour; that of two greatly differing pure colours in a colour of lowered saturation. The effect of mixing a pure colour with an equal quantity of neutral grey is the same as that of mixing it with a small quantity of its complementary. Thus the colour X in the diagram opposite, a somewhat dulled (or 'brownish') reddish orange, could be obtained (among other means) by mixing a large quantity of reddish orange *either* with a smaller quantity of neutral grey *or* with a still smaller quantity of bluish turquoise.

If a water-colourist decides that some grass in his picture is too vivid, he can make it duller by superimposing either a wash of grey or a more diluted wash of the complementary of green, i.e. maroon. In practice he will probably use the complementary, especially if he intends the colours not completely to mix.

Many of the richest effects in Nature and in painting result from small particles of contrasted colour, closely interwoven, but not completely mixed. I have seen a field in late August, which, by reason of the red seeds and green blades of grass, could be described only as reddish green, not as grey, nor as greyish red, nor as greyish green. In water-colour such an effect can be produced by mixing with the green pigment a red that has a tendency to granulate in small spots. In the 'olive green' of many Italian pictures, red, as well as green, yellow and grey, is separably discernible. Such incomplete mixtures are unformulated attempts at the 'Divisionism', subsequently carried out by Seurat, who in *La Baignade* [(T.G. 3908), Pl. 79] has represented the grass by juxtaposing frequent touches of green with less frequent touches of red, yellow and even blue.

It is implicit in the preference of all the greatest colourists, for variegated, rather than monotonous, surfaces of colour. Both the tempera painters (see Chapter xxiv) and the oil painters (see Chapter xxv) superimposed contrasted colours upon one another, so that the under-painting was alternately revealed and concealed, e.g. the red under the grey in the architecture of Lippi's *Annunciation* [(666), Pl. 9].

CHAPTER XXII

DESIGN BY COLOUR

COLOUR has an unique power of arousing emotion. When a picture of little merit attracts or a recognized masterpiece repels, the cause, when analysed, will often be found to be its colour. About no other aspect of painting do individuals feel more strongly or differ more widely. Because of this, the practice of inventing

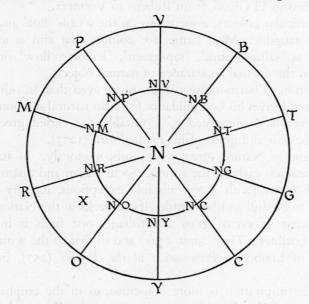

DIAGRAM OF COLOURS. (See p. 115)

rules and the making the examples fit them (never the way to judge of *any* branch of design) is peculiarly inapplicable to colour.

Conclusions about colour owe more to feeling than to reason. One may feel convinced, but one cannot prove that El Greco in painting the *Purification of the Temple* [(1457), Pl. 51] understood and controlled the emotional implications of the colours he used, and that the Master of Moulins in the *Meeting of Joachim and Anna* (4092) failed to do so.

Many people early in childhood choose a 'favourite colour' and only learn later that colour harmony (in painting or room decoration, etc.) depends on the *relation* of two or more colours to each other. To prefer blue to red is almost as meaningless as to prefer B-flat to E-natural, except that in practice the colour is often subconsciously preferred in relation to other colours, e.g. (in the case of clothes) those of the chooser's complexion.

Similarly the preference for the colour schemes of certain pictures may be affected by the colours already decorating a particular room. Or again it may be due to subconscious associations, causing the taste to fluctuate according to mood from Fra Angelico to El Greco, from Rubens to Vermeer.

Regarding particular colours, associations (as the words 'hot' and 'cold' show) are often more tangible. Most names for colours that aim at an unattainable precision (such as 'salmon-pink', 'sap-green', 'lemon-yellow' or 'heliotrope') are derived from the normal appearance of natural objects.

For the invention of harmonious colour, more even than in other branches of his art, the painter derives his best guidance from his natural surroundings. Theory alone could never have suggested to Constable the varied greens, the subtle mauve-greys, the reds and golds of his *Flatford Mill* (1273).

The inspiration of Nature often works subconsciously. In Italy and Spain grass loses its freshness early in the spring. So in Italian and Spanish pictures the green robes of Saints (with a few notable exceptions, e.g. by Veronese and El Greco) tend to be dull and brownish. If one seeks in the National Gallery for a robe reminiscent of vernal grass and foliage, one finds it in the cloak of S. Matthew in Lochner's *Three Saints* (705) and in that of the woman on the left in the Master of Liesborn's *Presentation in the Temple* (257), both works by Northern artists.

Sometimes the inspiration is more conscious, as in the emphasized, but not exaggerated, reds of De Hooch's two pictures of the *Courtyard of Dutch House* [(835 and 794), Pl. 62].

Some of the greatest colourists, such as the Venetians, Rubens, Velazquez and Rembrandt, have been peculiarly sensitive to the variations of colour due to light. This applies notably to the treatment of flesh, which is normally rather warm in the lights (though cool in the highest lights of all), cool in the half-tones and warmest in the shadows. Painters like Bronzino, who ignore this, fail to attain the rich variety of those who record it.

In the painting of drapery also, changes in colour due to light need to be studied and recorded. This practice is one of the main reasons for the richness of the colour of the Venetians, for example for the superiority of the colour of Gentile Bellini's *Adoration of the Magi* (3098) to that of Mantegna's *Madonna and Child with Saints* (274).

In figure composition the chief opportunity for saturated colour occurs in the draperies. Leonardo, as in the *Virgin of the Rocks* [(1093), Pl. 29], and Raphael, as in the '*Ansidei Madonna*', [(1171), Pl. 32], tended to give the most vivid colours to the light sides of garments, which meant, since they used strong contrasts of tone, that the shadows of their draperies were less colourful and inclined towards blackness.

On the other hand Michelangelo, most of the Venetians, Rubens, Rembrandt, and Watteau wisely reserved their most vivid colour for the shadows of clothes and kept the light side of them whitish (i.e. less saturated), thus avoiding blackness without losing contrast of tone. Examples are: the cloak of the first king in the *Adoration of the Magi* (1160) attributed to Giorgione; the man's dress in Watteau's *La Gamme d'Amour* [(2897), Pl. 66]; also the cloak of the nearest turbaned man in Rembrandt's *Woman taken in Adultery* [(45), Pl. 58]. All these painters visualized their work from the beginning in terms of colour (see also p. 26).

The colour of any observed object, like its tone, results from two combined causes: local colour, i.e. that of the material of which it is made; and reflected colour, due to light and surroundings. In their zeal to record colour due to the second cause, the French impressionists frequently understated local colour. In practice this one-sided attitude often had happy results. In *Les Parapluies* [(3268), Pl. 80] Renoir has treated the darker surfaces mostly as blue, but a blue subject to constant change, reflecting now green or turquoise, now violet or purple, always vibrating, never monotonous. (For Cézanne's use of colour see p. 31.)

Exclusive emphasis on local colour, at least in later more realistic periods, often leads to the dull and platitudinous (as in much of the green vegetation of Courbet). Local colour is also usually all that interests those who regard drawing as all-important and colour as something to add at the end to a completed design, as Ingres has done in *M. de Norvins* (3291).

Methods of relating colours may now be considered in more detail under the following headings:

(i)   Juxtaposition and Propinquity;
(ii) Simplicity and Repetition;
(iii) Balance, Distribution and Proportion.

(i) JUXTAPOSITION AND PROPINQUITY

Two colours may have one effect—perhaps harsh—when immediately contiguous, and another—perhaps harmonious—when an area of a third colour is placed between them. In other cases the mere introduction into the picture of the third colour saves them from harshness, and, as it were, resolves the discord.

The juxtaposition or propinquity of two colours usually increases their apparent difference of hue. If orange is next to purple, the orange looks yellower and the purple bluer. Greys next to more saturated colours seem to contain their complementary (see p. 116). Thus in Rembrandt's *Adoration of the Shepherds* (47) the Virgin's skirt, being painted in a grey, looks blue, because of the surrounding warm colours. In Dürer's portrait of his *Father* [(1938), Pl. 38] the reddish cloak and background gives added yellowness to the face. On the other hand two patches of colour that closely resemble each other but are separated by areas of a contrasted colour, appear almost identical (see below, p. 122).

(ii) SIMPLICITY AND REPETITION

Nothing is less pleasing than a conglomeration of too many colours, as in Frith's *Derby Day* (615), though it contains fine separate passages of colour relation [see Pl. 74].

Many of the best colour-schemes consist of three main vivid colours. One or all of the three may be subject to variations of tone and saturation and even (to a lesser extent) of hue. Sometimes, as in Whistler's *Nocturne in Blue and Silver* (3420), two colours and a hint of a neutral grey are enough for a colour scheme.

Repetition is the inevitable consequence of simplicity. If a particular colour is introduced in one part of a picture, the same, or a similar colour must occur in another part. In Constable's *Cornfield* (130) the repetition of reds (in the boy's waistcoat, the poppies, the dog's tongue, the sheep's backs, the old man's face and scarf and the distant roofs) might seem forced but for the fact that, in looking at a real scene, the eye, finding a vivid colour in the foreground, automatically seeks for and usually finds its repetition in the background.

Isolated patches of colour should be avoided. An *apparently* isolated accent of red is familiar in the work of Rubens, Claude, Constable and Corot and many others; but the isolation in good colour schemes is never complete. For instance, in Titian's *Noli Me Tangere* [(270), Pl. 33] the crimson of Mary Magdalene's robe is prepared for by the subdued reds, occurring throughout the main area of golden brown. A distribution of colour similar to this was used by many of Titian's successors, when painting outdoor scenes: viz. for the main areas of warm colour, golden brown; for the main cool colour, blue; for 'temperate' colour (if any) a dull green compounded of the above, and red for smaller accents of special emphasis.

In Veronese's *Family of Darius before Alexander* [(294), Pls. 45–7] pale (i.e. light and subdued) versions of the leading vivid colours are introduced into the background and these colours are repeated with increasingly emphatic saturation from middle distance to foreground. This method is combined with splitting up the main colours into variants. The subdued gold of the background reappears in the dress of Darius's wife and subdivides into the vivid orange cloak and lemon yellow stockings of Hephaestion. The pale rose of the background becomes the deeper crimson worn by Alexander and by the Princesses and changes into the single patch of scarlet worn by Darius's son. The distant blue (with grey and violet in it) occurs at its most violet in the chamberlain's cloak, at its darkest in that of Darius's mother, at its most saturated in the plume of one soldier, the sleeve of another and the patterns on the Princesses' garments. Olive green and greenish grey are also repeated in foreground and background. Rubens's *Rape of the Sabine Women* [(38), Pl. 53] follows a similar system, except that the blue of the background becomes black in the dress of the central woman in the foreground.

(iii) BALANCE, DISTRIBUTION AND PROPORTION

Areas of colour should be skilfully distributed, like the reds and blues in Whistler's *Symphony in White No.* 2 (3418), not lop-sidedly, like the crimson reading-desk in Rossetti's *Annunciation* (1210).

Proportion must also be preserved. No two of the leading colours ought to occupy exactly equal areas. On the other hand there ought to be no overwhelming preponderance of warm over cool colour or vice versa. Vivid colour is often effectively distributed more sparingly and interruptedly than colour of a low degree of saturation, as in Uccello's *Rout of San Romano* [(583), Pl. 16].

The proportion of vivid and dull colour suitable to a picture varies with its size. In quite small paintings vivid colours can take up a relatively considerable space; but in general the larger the picture, the smaller should be the proportionate area occupied by highly saturated colour.

CHAPTER XXIII

DESIGN BY COLOUR (*continued*)

I⟨T⟩ is only occasionally possible to analyse why certain relations of colour should contribute to the precise, but indefinable, blend of emotions that the picture conveys.

Regarding hue, the effect of warm and cool colours is only *partly* explained by sensuous associations with temperature (pleasurable or painful). Again in the case of *tone*, the dramatic and associational value of *chiaroscuro* depends on more than the fact that light has mainly joyful, and darkness mainly sad, associations. Conversely, the widespread darkness in Rembrandt's mature pictures (see pp. 102–3) is not his only way of expressing his sense that life (except for a few gleams of joy) is tragic; just as the prevalent sunniness of Rubens's work (see p. 104) is only one of his means of expressing that *joie de vivre*, which he rarely modified, as in the *Landscape: Sunset* (157), by contemplative sadness.

Joy and sorrow, which alternate and are contrasted or blended in all great art, are expressed by all aspects of painting, including colour relations of every kind. Another antithesis, recurrent in all branches of design, that between the stimulating and the soothing (see p. 21) is often conveyed in pictures by the saturation of the colour. Vivid colour, apart from the fact that it is rarer in Nature than subdued colour and therefore less expected, evokes a purely physical reaction, either pleasing or displeasing. Thus the more saturated colours in pictures tend to stimulate and the more subdued colours tend to soothe.

In many paintings the two tendencies balance. In some, one of them preponderates. The colour of Crivelli's *Annunciation* (739) is mainly soothing, partly because of the subdued tints and partly because many of them are near to each other in hue. That of Veronese's *S. Mary Magdalene laying aside her Jewels* (931) is mainly stimulating because of the many (possibly too many) vivid and dissimilar colours; in Claude's *Embarkation of S. Ursula* [(30), see Pl. 56] the vivid colours are fewer and occupy less space, but are dissimilar enough to introduce excitement into the atmosphere of calm.

Satisfactory colour depends greatly on contrast. Three types of contrast all necessary to colour harmony may now be considered: (i) Contrast of Tone; (ii) Contrast of Saturation; (iii) Contrast of Hue.

(i) CONTRAST OF TONE

Both in 'flat pattern' pictures (see p. 28) in which the differences of tone and colour are mainly *local* (see pp. 99–100 and 121) and in more realistic paintings, change of colour is nearly always accompanied by change of tone. Pattern due to colour alone without tonal contrast is avoided, because apt to confuse the eye. The re-enforcement of colour contrast by tonal contrast is needed for clarity of emphasis. So in many pictures, the blue robes of the saints are darker than the red and the red darker than the yellow, the colours being related to each other in what may be called 'The Natural Order of Tone'.

This may be explained thus. If one attempts to illustrate the Colour Diagram (see Chapter XXI) by painting it in the purest colours obtainable, it is almost impossible to combine maximum saturation with equality of tone. In making the colours of the outer circles as vivid as possible, violet is inevitably darker than yellow. The colours become lighter in the following order: violet; blue and purple; turquoise and maroon; green and red; citron and orange; yellow.

Since these tonal differences naturally arise from the search for vivid colours and since all colours need to be tonally contrasted, painters instinctively tend to let *vivid* colours follow the natural order of tone. (To more subdued colours the principle hardly applies.) In Ugolino's *Deposition* (3375) and, though the total tonal contrast is small, in the *Coronation of the Virgin* (568) attributed to Angelo di Taddeo Gaddi, the more vivid colours and tones (all *local*) obey this system. In Borgognone's *Madonna and Child with the two SS. Catherine* (298) (where tone depends more on incidence of light) the vivid colours are also thus contrasted: blue, darkest; then red; yellow, lightest.

Striking reversals of the natural order sometimes occur, when a light blue is contrasted with a darker red, as in the *Virgin and Child with Saints* (4786) by the Spanish Master Paulus. Again in Crivelli's *Madonna and Child with Saints* (807) and Uccello's *Rout of San Romano* [(583), Pls. 16 and 17] light blues disobey the 'natural order'. The reversal of the order has the advantage of unexpectedness and also of emphasizing tonal pattern. On the other hand to give the *same* tonal value to several vivid colours is apt to be confusing, unless, as in Tura's *Madonna and Child Enthroned* [(772), see Pl. 22] or in Foppa's *Adoration of the Magi* [(729), Pl. 27], strong contrasts of tone occur among the less saturated colours.

(ii) CONTRAST OF SATURATION

Pleasing effects seldom depend on vivid colours alone. In the pages of illuminated manuscripts, the black letters and dull parchment often occupy more space than all the ultramarine, vermilion and gold put together. In medieval stain-glass also, black lead and white, transparent glass cover larger areas than the more conspicuous vivid colours. In these instances colours of medium saturation are rare or absent and the contrast is between neutrals and colours of maximum purity. Similarly, in Fra Angelico's *Christ Surrounded by Angels, Saints, etc.* (663), apart from a few garments of brown, much of the effect depends on the blacks and whites (e.g. of the Dominicans in the end panels), which provide a needed foil for the abundant gold, ultramarine and scarlet and the less frequent green, yellow and orange. None of these vividly coloured garments becomes greyer in shadow, though some, like shot-silk, change their hue altogether.

With the growth of realism, vivid and neutral colours were used more sparingly and colours of medium saturation more lavishly, but the contrast between relatively vivid and relatively dull colour was maintained. In Titian's *Mother and Child* (3948) the red cheek of the Child and the Madonna's gold hood, colours subdued in themselves, seem vivid by contrast with the other still more subdued tints. Similar importance is given by Correggio to the Virgin's russet robe in the *Madonna of the Basket* (23).

(iii) CONTRAST OF HUE

Monotony of hue is as displeasing as monotony of tone. A balance of warm and cool colour is desirable, but the contrast between them need not be great. In Constable's *Malvern Hall* (2653) the pink and the yellow-greens are but slightly warmer than the grey-greens and grey-mauves.

In Sassetta's *S. Francis Renouncing his Heritage* (4758) and the *Recognition of the Franciscan Order* (4759) the reds, browns and golds threaten to make the *ensemble* too hot; but while the *Recognition* suffers from awkward distribution, the *Renunciation*, though it contains even more reds, is saved by the placing of the accents of 'temperate' olive-green and cool blue.

In harmonious colour-schemes the number of hues included is severely limited (see pp. 121–2). Except in the case of complementary colours, violent contrasts of hue should occur seldom. Too many should be avoided altogether. One way of avoiding them is to give the entire picture a pervading 'complexion' (see p. 99) like the blue of Cézanne's *La Montagne Sainte Victoire* [(Courtauld Institute),

Pl. 78], within which contrasts of relatively cooler and relatively warmer colours occur.

In many pictures one of the colours, or rather hues, may be called the *dominant*. Apart from tone and saturation, the relation of other hues to the dominant can be of three kinds: (*a*) *similar*; (*b*) *complementary* (see p. 116); (*c*) *discordant*. 'Similar' colours in this special sense do not differ greatly in hue from the dominant; the limit of difference, though not precisely definable, is indicated, if blue is the dominant (see Diagram, p. 119) by including violet and turquoise (and the hues intermediate between each of them and blue) among 'similar' hues, but excluding colours between violet and purple and those between turquoise and green. *Discordant* hues are hues *neither* 'similar' *nor* complementary to the dominant. Thus in relation to a blue dominant, red, citron and green are all in this sense discordant.

In many, but not in all, harmonious colour schemes, a dominant hue occurs. Even when it is absent, the terms 'similar', 'complementary' and 'discordant' describe the relationship of any one colour to another. When a dominant *is* present, the areas devoted to the four types of colour vary greatly in their pro- positions; but usually the *dominant* and the colours 'similar' to it together occupy more space than the *complementary* to the dominant, and the *discordant* colour or colours occupy least space of all. The saturation of all four types of colour also varies greatly; in general the more subdued the colour, the larger the area that it may fill (cf. p. 123). Thus the normally small area allotted to discordant colour may be much increased if its saturation is low.

In typical examples there are *two* colours (or groups of colours) 'similar' to the dominant, which is intermediate between them in hue. Thus in Titian's *Holy Family with a Shepherd* (4) scarlet is the dominant and the colours 'similar' to it (which also differ from it appreciably) are crimson and orange. These colours have complementaries: blue, opposed to orange; olive-green, opposed to crimson. The complementary of the dominant scarlet is the inconspicuous terra-vert (turquoise-grey) implicit in the shadows of the flesh. The olive-green, terra-vert and blue, together occupy a larger area than the crimson, scarlet, and orange combined. In fact scarlet is the dominant, only because it and the crimson and orange are vivid. The discordant colour is the greyish purple.

The inclusion of crimson, scarlet and orange (or two of them) in one harmonious picture occurs surprisingly often in Italian painting of all periods. In three of Giovanni di Paolo's *Four Scenes in the Life of S. John* (5451–4) there appear garments of crimson and garments which are orange in the light and scarlet in the shadow. As in the Titian each of these colours is contrasted with a complementary: olive-green, terra-vert or blue, of which the blue alone is vivid.

Crimson and scarlet are startlingly juxtaposed in the *Madonna of the Iris* (5592) attributed to Dürer, the colour scheme of which arouses controversy. In its favour are the numerous and widespread greyish-greens (complementaries to the red) and the purplish-red (maroon) of the anemone.

When two colours occur in discord with the dominant, they are often complementary to each other like the yellow and violet in Bruegel's *Adoration of the Magi* [(3556), Pl. 43]. In this remarkable painting the dominant is the orange-red of the negro's boot; its complementary the blue-turquoise of the standing soldier's neckcloth. 'Similar' to the dominant are: (i) the crimsons and pinks, to which the warm green is the complementary; (ii) the subdued orange-browns and buffs, to which the complementary is the blue.

In Renoir's *Les Parapluies* [(3268), Pl. 80] blue is the dominant. The hues 'similar' to it are violet and turquoise, the first verging sometimes on purple, the second on green. Complementary to the violet are the small areas of subdued yellow; and to the turquoise the vivid, and often repeated, varieties of orange and chestnut. In discord with the dominant is the citron-green.

As indicated, the colours 'similar' to the dominant usually differ from it considerably and are limited in number. In Renoir's *Les Parapluies* on the other hand (partly because of his attention to reflected colour) almost every hue between blue and violet, violet and purple, blue and turquoise, turquoise and green, is included.

The degree to which two colours are in discord is mainly a matter of speculation. Some day, when the science of colour harmony is more advanced, it may be possible to assert, as of musical notes, that certain intervals between hues produce concord and other intervals discord. At present it is not even known where 'similarity' ends and discordance begins.

The importance, however, of the complementary relationship is confidently established. In Duccio's *Christ healing the Blind Man* [(1140), Pl. 1] there is no 'dominant' colour, but the complementary to the seven varieties of red are the green of the grass and the cooler turquoise green of Peter's cloak. The inclusion of two vivid blues, the dark ultramarine of Christ's cloak and the lighter blue (devoid of violet) of the underrobes of Peter and John is unusual. Their complementaries are the gold-leaf and the many varieties of orange-brown.

In Ingres' *Madame Moitessier* [(4821), Pl. 75] four pairs of complementaries occur. This and the presence of neutral grey and white give some consistency to the daring scheme, though the stimulating aspect of colour is much in excess of the soothing.

In comparison, Piero della Francesca's *Baptism of Christ* [(665), Pl. 20] preserves the just balance between the soothing and the stimulating, among other reasons, because the total number of colours is less, the proportion of vivid colour is less, and the colours are divided into four groups, each member of which is closely allied to the next in hue. In the first group are: a dark subdued crimson, a lighter red pink with less purple in it, a still lighter red with still less purple and quite a pale pink. In the second are *greens*, the approximate complementaries of the first: dark subdued and warm; dark subdued and cool; and grey-green (for the shadows of the flesh). In the third group are blues: dark with grey and mauve in it; lighter with more mauve; lighter still with a little turquoise; lightest of all (for sky), devoid of both mauve and turquoise. In the fourth group are complementaries to the blues: a dark orange-yellow of low saturation; a lighter, less orange, version of the same, and gold. The colour as a whole, altered though it partly is, amply supports the other aspects of the gravely grand design, in instilling peaceful content, mingled with awe.

CHAPTER XXIV

TECHNIQUE: WATER-COLOUR
FRESCO AND TEMPERA

'Nor does it matter to us, who are not artists but art lovers, not cooks but epicures, what the actual process was'; so wrote Lord Conway (then Sir Martin Conway) in 'The Van Eycks and their followers'. The analogy is questionable. Food may be more enjoyable for not knowing what it is made of; but knowledge of painters' methods reveals subtleties that the mere aesthetic epicure may miss.

Anything that brings insight into the working of the painter's mind is a help towards understanding his fresco message; and his mind is necessarily partly concerned with technique. So it is an advantage to know what limitations his medium imposes and what positive qualities it encourages (see Chapter IV).

The practising painter's reactions to pictures (past and present) are often most illuminating; but too trusting a dependence upon them may be mistaken. His aims limit the number of the great masters from whom he can profitably learn; and this restriction may unconsciously limit his appreciation also. Yet he may easily be too uncritical in another respect, in disproportionately admiring mere skill.

The critic of to-day sometimes falls into the opposite trap. Nauseated by the many paintings displaying dexterity and nothing more, he may regard incompetence as evidence of sincerity. This is as though he hated glibness so much as to believe that to be an orator one must stammer. No doubt Constable was greater than Etty, because Constable had a great deal to say which he often expressed imperfectly, whereas Etty, for all his fluent language, said very little. But Rubens was greater than Constable, not only because he had even more to say, but also because of his complete mastery of the language of painting.

Some account of technical methods then is needed here. But there are many important questions on which I shall not touch: e.g. the chemical aspect of painting, the preservation and cleaning of pictures, the permanence of particular pigments or methods of procedure. For all such matters the following books are useful: Max Doerner's 'The Materials of the Artist' (G. G. Harrap, 1935); D. V. Thompson's 'The Practice of Tempera Painting' (Yale University Press, 1936); 'La Conservation des Peintures' (Office International des Musées, 1939).

The painter's methods must work up to a prepared result. He must know when to work at fever heat and when to wait for days or even months for the paint to dry. The inner vision must constantly be remembered as the reason for the act of painting; but until this vision has been fully expressed, the fervour that inspired it must be controlled, while mere matter is being moulded to give it expression.

No general rules about technique can be laid down. It would be absurd to assert that a painter ought always to display his brush-strokes or always to conceal them, that he ought always to work minutely or always broadly, always directly or always in a complex series of layers. Vermeer's smooth manner of presenting a sunlit wall is essential to the effect of light produced; smooth surfaces by Mieris are mere surfaces of paint. The visible brush-strokes of Tintoretto and Rubens express the flutter of a cloak or the growing tendrils of the vine; Sargent's brush-strokes are often meaningless. Dürer's minuteness in drawing hair is inventive decoration, derived from perception; Baldung's is mere calligraphy. The breadth of a Veronese or a late Velazquez produces a precise result; the so-called breadth of a Raeburn is often mere slovenliness.

Particular media must now be briefly described. In each method of painting, the medium which *binds* the pigment together is mixed with a *diluent* by means of which it is liquidly applied to the *ground*.

For convenience the methods of painting now to be dealt with are classified:

(i)	Encaustic;	(v)	Gold-leaf and Silver-leaf;
(ii)	Fresco;	(vi)	Raised Gesso;
(iii)	Water-colour and Gouache;	(vii)	Tempera and Oil combined.
(iv)	Tempera;		

(i) ENCAUSTIC

In this medium the colours are mixed with melted wax. Greco-Roman artists working in Egypt in the third century painted portraits on mummy cases in this way. The main tool was apparently something like a palette knife; but there is evidence also of the use of the brush. Work had to be done quickly before the wax cooled; so that the rapid, summary sketch of essentials was often more alive than many portraits more laboriously finished. The portrait of a *Woman* (1260) (now at the B.M.) gives a vivid impression of a witty personality.

(ii) FRESCO

In true fresco the colours are mixed with water only and applied to the lime plaster of the wall while the lime is still damp (i.e. 'fresh'). The lime of the wall absorbs the painting and acts as the binding medium. Normally the plaster remains damp for little more than a day. Some re-touching (in which the pigment is sometimes mixed with lime and sometimes carried out in tempera) is possible after the plaster has dried; but the best frescoes contain the least retouching. Thus fresco painting requires even more decision than work in other media. Alterations are possible only by removing and reapplying an area of plaster.

The leading quality of fresco is transparency. It is somewhat pale in appearance, contrasts of light and dark being restricted. When the plaster dries, the colours are several times lighter than when first applied. Strong darks are normally unobtainable. Classical examples of frescoes are those by Giotto in the Arena Chapel, Padua, and Raphael's *School of Philosophers* (Pl. 35) in the Vatican.

Wall-paintings in large buildings are usually on a bold scale, and bounded, not by frames, but by the architecture itself; divisions, if needed, consist of painted borders. In dry climates, as in Florence and Rome, frescoes last hundreds of years; in damp climates, as in Venice and England, they often fade quickly. There are not many frescoes in the National Gallery. Ambrogio Lorenzetti's *Heads of Four Nuns* [(1147), Pl. 4] is a fragment in excellent condition. The *Madonna and Child* (1215) by Domenico Veneziano has suffered in being transferred from plaster to canvas. Perugino's *Adoration of the Shepherds* (1441), which was transferred later when the process was better understood, is in a better state.

In *fresco secco* (as distinct from true fresco) the paint is applied to plaster that has dried for a considerable period. The pigment is mixed with something besides water: lime, egg, size, or some other medium. The effect is apt to be less transparent than in a true fresco, but lasts better in damp climates like England's. Most medieval wall paintings in English churches are in some kind of *fresco secco*.

(iii) WATER-COLOUR AND GOUACHE

In water-colour painting (another transparent medium) the diluent is water and the binding gum arabic. The ground is normally paper. In the Saxon illuminated manuscripts of the school of Winchester, colour was applied in a similar transparent way to enrich pen-drawings on parchment or vellum; in other illuminations, white was mixed with the lighter colours giving them the quality of *gouache*.

In water-colour the darkest tones can be darker than in fresco, but attempt to rival the darks of oil always looks forced. On the other hand, for the strongest lights the paper itself may be used without appearing raw, as so light a surface would in any other medium. The lighter half-tones may be painted in several superimposed washes after each underwash has dried; but the darker the final tone is to be, the fewer should be the washes used to produce it.

The medium demands directness and does not suit finished portraiture; but it is a mistake to regard it as adapted merely to rapid sketches and rough impressions. In the best examples the washes are added to a firm structure of precise, selective drawing, as in the sound tradition of Girtin, Turner and Cotman. The paint in a water-colour should be applied thinly enough to show the surface of the paper underneath. The power of water-colour to represent forms, now clearly seen, now lost in mist and cloud, reached perfection in ancient Chinese landscapes.

A method of combining pure water-colour with gouache is to put in the accents of high light in white paint, or paint mixed with white; on coloured paper this is unavoidable; but on white paper, it needs to be done with strict economy. Other devices for dealing with small accents of light are to *take* them out with a brush or to scratch them out with a knife; but the freshest in effect is to *leave* the accents out as small areas of uncovered paper surrounded by washes of colour.

Opacity is the leading characteristic of painting in *gouache* or body colour, that is, water-colour mixed with white. In *gouache*, as in fresco, the tones dry lighter than when first applied. *Gouache* is suited to the flat decorative conventions of a poster; also, in combination with gold leaf and black ink, to the richly coloured patterns of an illumination. A fine example of a medieval illumination, in which Chinese white is mixed with the colour, is the *Illuminated Letter B* (3089) by Lorenzo Monaco. Until the fifteenth century, whatever solidity in single figures was attempted was within the limitations of this medium. Ultramarine (lapis lazuli), more precious than gold itself, looks especially rich when mixed in varying proportions with white.

From the fifteenth to the early seventeenth century, the English portrait painters in miniature continued the illuminators' method of working with water and gum on parchment fixed to a card. Some of the colours were mixed with white, notably the favourite ultramarine background; but the painting of the face was usually transparent and the shadows extremely pale and delicate. Since the portrait was to be held in the hand, no attempt was made at an illusion of projecting form by contrasts of shadow; but structure was revealed with great precision of line.

The miniature's delicacies of detail, tone and colour were imitated in life-sized Elizabethan portraits, such as *Queen Elizabeth* (N.P.G. 2082), often lacking in vigour, but sensitive. The later converse fashion of treating a miniature as a reduced oil painting, as in the work of Samuel Cooper, has less to be said for it.

(iv) TEMPERA

The word 'tempera', though used of various media, strictly refers to egg. In most Italian panel pictures of the fourteenth and fifteenth centuries, the paint was mixed with yolk of egg as the binding medium and water as the diluent. The use of white of egg appears to have been mainly confined to work in gold-leaf.

Tempera is suited to work on a moderate scale, not more than 6 ft. in maximum measurement. It encourages a rather cool range of subtly varying colours and a range of tone greater than in fresco, but less than in oil. Under normal clean, dry conditions, paintings in tempera last better than those in any other medium.

Tempera is a semi-transparent medium. The panel is usually primed with a smooth coat of white *gesso* (plaster of paris and size) which is left completely to dry before the application of paint. This whiteness is partly, but never wholly, hidden by the covering series of thin layers of paint, a number of which are needed to give the picture a solid and even appearance.

Transparency and opacity are relative terms; but tempera, though varying in degree of transparency, is never as transparent as an oil glaze, nor as opaque as an impasto in oil, which is applied in thick lumps. Although, as in oil, the lights being mixed with white paint, are *comparatively* opaque and the shadows *comparatively* transparent, the difference in thickness of paint is hardly perceptible; for, as in all media except oil in one of its uses, the final surface is smooth.

Wood was the more frequent ground for tempera paintings; but linen and canvas were also used. Examples on linen are Bouts's *Entombment* [(664), Pl. 15] and Massys's *Virgin and Child with SS. Catherine and Barbara* (3664); on canvas, Mantegna's *Triumph of Scipio* (902) and *Madonna and Child with Saints* (274); Botticelli's *Birth of Venus* (Uffizi, Florence) was also painted in this method. It is not certain whether these works were carried out in egg tempera or size (i.e. thin glue). Their technique is similar to that of *gouache*. The *gesso* priming is thinner than in most tempera paintings on panel and the paint is applied in at most two layers. It is of an even consistency, without contrasts of opacity and transparency. In the Bouts the grain of the linen contributes to the atmospheric distance.

Tempera differs from other media and especially from oil in the speed with which the paint dries. Though, when painting on wood, the gesso foundation takes at least a day to dry, the various coats of tempera dry so quickly, that one can be painted over another, after waiting a few minutes only. Oil on the other hand takes weeks and sometimes months to dry. Quickness in drying has advantages and disadvantages. Once the gesso has dried, a tempera painting can progress in methodical stages without delay; but the fusion of different tones or colours, which in oil is easily effected by brushing one area of wet paint into another, is a most laborious matter.

The finely gradated skies in such pictures as Sassetta's *Charity of S. Francis* (4757) were built up gradually in a series of layers. Great care was taken to keep the lights opaque and the darks transparent. In the first layer the separate brush-strokes of dark and light were more visibly separated; but the final layer of paint produces an effect of almost perfect fusion. In smaller areas (e.g. in the modelling of flesh, at least before *c.* 1450) the fusion was less complete.

The labour involved in merging light into shadow makes the tempera painter primarily a draughtsman. He holds his brush like a pencil. The contours in his work are hard, or at least firm. He can render softness of atmosphere or texture only to the most limited extent. In the painting of flesh and drapery, where gradations of tone are needed to give the form relief, the shadows are dragged to meet the lights in separate pencil-like strokes which never completely fuse. These can be seen in the flesh and drapery of Botticelli's *Mars, Venus and Satyrs* [(915), Pls. 24 and 25].

Tempera has been described as a discipline, rather than a medium. The speed with which the paint dries and the impossibility of matching colours and tones direct from Nature, make it unsuitable for sketches, improvisations or even *impressions* of appearance, but highly suitable for the *re-creation* of forms either as idealized symbols of another existence or as explanatory statements of structural facts (see Chapter VII). The infra-red photograph of the detail from Tura's *Madonna and Child Enthroned* [(772), Pl. 22 A] shows how separate brush-strokes can be used to build up the form. Here their shape varies and is often curved. In Botticelli's *Mars, Venus and Satyrs* [(915), see Pl. 25] they are straighter, but vary in direction. In Baldovinetti's *Portrait of a Lady* [(758), Pl. 23] the shading is stippled, i.e. in dots, not lines.

In tempera painting subtle colours are produced by super-imposition, not mixture (see p. 118). In Uccello's *Rout of San Romano* [(583), Pls. 16 and 17] the *terre verte* (a greyish green) is clearly visible under the partly faded pinks of the flesh, and red under the grey of the hills.

These methods are in accordance with a law of appearance governing all media. A *lighter* tone painted over a *darker* tone looks comparatively *cool* colour; a *darker* tone painted over a *lighter* tone results in a comparatively *warm* colour. Super-imposition of layers of the same tone causes a muddy appearance and should be avoided. In Bosch's *Crowning with Thorns* (4744) the same moderately light and warm flesh tint of the tormentor's right hand on Christ's shoulder looks hot brown when painted over the white robe, and cold bluish pink where it covers the dark green robe. Here the result is accidental; but in many pictures (in tempera and oil) the warm colours are painted (somewhat transparently) over a lighter, and the cool colours semi-opaquely over a darker, foundation. In the latter case the effect is cloudy and opalescent.

In earlier pictures in tempera, the flesh was painted in three stages: first, dark brown or black for the outlines and for the shadows (which were indicated in hatched strokes, not flat planes); secondly, a smooth coat of terre verte (through which the brown was visible), followed sometimes by complete hatched shading in terre verte and white, as in Duccio's *Madonna* [(566), see Pl. 3]; and thirdly, a series of pinkish orange colours, transparent and warm in the darkest shadows, thin enough in the half-tones to let the under-painting show through as a cool colour, but thick enough to be fairly opaque in the highest lights. Every stage involved precision of drawing. The process was one of construction as though the painter were creating first the bones, then the flesh and then the skin. The terre verte is visible in Masaccio's *Madonna and Child* [(3046), Pl. 7] and many other examples. It even persists in Vermeer's much later oil painting of the *Lady Standing at the Virginals* [(1383), Pl. 64].

Towards the end of the fifteenth century painters began to omit the second or terre verte stage and to rely for the cool half-tones entirely on the painting of lighter over darker colour. In Piero della Francesca's *Baptism of Christ* [(665), Pl. 20], terre verte has been used, but not in his *Nativity* [(908), Pl. 21], where the first stage, the warm underpainting, is uncovered on the faces of the shepherds. In Michelangelo's *Madonna and Child with S. John and Angels* [(809), Pl. 30] the flat coats of terre verte can be seen on the unfinished figures; but in his *Entombment* [(790), Pl. 31] the second stage is omitted and the only underpainting is a warm brown: the greenish hue of the body of Christ, painted over the brown, intentionally gives it the pallor of a corpse.

Drapery was gradually built up in similar manner. The colour of the under-painting usually differed from that of the covering coat; grey was painted under crimson, cold green under warm green and so on. Often the tonal contrasts of the underpainting were stronger than those of the final phase; if Michelangelo's *Madonna and Child* [(809), Pl. 30] had been finished, the present black and white of the Virgin's cloak would have been covered with more delicate gradations of blue.

(v) GOLD-LEAF AND SILVER-LEAF

In most early pictures in tempera there are areas of gold-leaf: e.g. in haloes, ornaments and above all, backgrounds. The effect is unrealistic but adds to the richness of the pattern. The figures look as though they had been painted over a complete gold background, but this is not actually the case. A line was incised in the gesso where the gold area was to leave off and the area devoted to other colours was to begin. The red bolus preparation and then the gold-leaf over it were made to cover the whole of the future gold area and also a *part* of the future non-gold area *beyond the incised line*. Then the colour, say the blue of the Virgin's hood, was painted exactly up to the edge of the incised line, so that part of it covers the gold and the whole picture deceptively *appears* to be painted on a gold ground.

Especially in the haloes the gold-leaf was often punched with a tool, so that different parts of its surface might appear light or dark as the spectator altered his position. Silver-leaf was used less often because of its tendency to tarnish; but this has been successfully avoided in Pisanello's *SS. Anthony and George* (776) and in Uccello's *Rout of San Romano* [(583), Pls. 16 and 17] in which there are examples of red, blue and greyish brown over silver-leaf and red and black over gold-leaf. In Foppa's *Adoration of the Magi* [(729), Pl. 27] the bluish grey of the robe of the dark king has first been painted all over an area of gold-leaf and then scratched away to reveal gaps of the underlying gold, by a method known as *sgraffito*.

Gold patterns over another colour were usually painted in shell or powder gold, which never shines so brightly as gold-leaf, but has a soft charm of its own. It is used with great delicacy in Baldovinetti's *Portrait of a Lady* [(758), Pl. 23] and effectively contrasted with gold-leaf in Masaccio's *Madonna and Child* [(3046), Pl. 7].

(vi) RAISED GESSO

According to pure aesthetic theory, a picture ought not to break out piecemeal into rivalry with low-relief sculpture. Still less should the raised surfaces occur on the subordinate ornamentations of jewelry—collars, etc. In practice these excrescences are welcome, provided the aim of the picture is flat decoration rather than realistic representation. They are known as *pastiglia*, and are produced by adding lumps of liquid gesso with the brush to the original coat of smooth gesso. When the lumps have dried, their form can be finished with a tool. The method is frequent in the decoration of frames. Such raised ornaments are usually covered with gold-leaf, as in Pisanello's *Vision of S. Eustace* [(1436), see Pl. 8] and in Foppa's *Adoration of the Magi* [(729), Pl. 27]. In the left panel of the '*Wilton Diptych*' [(4451), Pl. 6] the jewels in the kings' crowns were once coloured, but are now white. It would be ungrateful to carp at such charming effects. It is only when the relief is too high, or when raised wood takes the place of raised gesso as in the mitre, brooch and keys of S. Peter in Crivelli's '*Demidoff Altarpiece*' (788) that the mixture between sculpture and painting becomes questionable (see p. 18).

(vii) TEMPERA AND OIL COMBINED

Towards the end of the fifteenth century, the Italians began to complete their tempera paintings with final glazes of oil. There are even tempera pictures of the first half of the century, now covered with such glazes, e.g. Andrea dal Castagno's *Crucifixion* [(1138), Pl. 13] but these glazes may have been added by a later hand. Filippino Lippi himself may have painted the glaze in the *Madonna and Child with SS. Jerome and Dominic* (293). Perugino's *Madonna adoring the Child* (288) and Piero di Cosimo's *Death of Procris* (698) were probably begun in tempera and finished in oil by the painters themselves.

Certainty as to media is not always possible. When the lights and shadows do not completely fuse, but are joined by interlacing brush-strokes, as in the *Madonna* (296) by a pupil of Verrocchio, the medium is tempera. But the fusion of shadows does not prove conversely the presence of oil. It is possible that Lorenzo di Credi's two *Madonna* pictures (593 and 648) are in egg tempera and that the tones have been fused by purging the yolk of all white of egg. Remarkable fusions occur in Giovanni Bellini's *Agony in the Garden* [(726), Pl. 19], which is nevertheless a tempera painting.

The presence of oil may be equally hard to detect. When the paint is of appreciable thickness in the lights, or when the shadows are very dark as well as transparent, or when the atmosphere or the textures are rendered with exceptional softness, then there can be little doubt that oil has been used. Three considerations make it difficult to pronounce on every case. Tempera pictures were finished in oil. Oil was used as though it were tempera. Painters could produce in tempera fusions almost as complete as in oil. When to these is added the fourth possibility of the two media having been mixed in a single emulsion, dogmatic assertion becomes impossible.

CHAPTER XXV

TECHNIQUE: OIL

FOR more than four centuries oil has been the painter's favourite binding medium. Turpentine is normally the diluent. Various vegetable oils are used, of which linseed oil is the most frequent. Oil is by far the freest and most flexible of media. The differences between the various ways of using it are as great as the differences between one medium and another. The surface of the painting in any other medium is always comparatively even and smooth; the surface of an oil painting may be smooth or rough, in degrees varying from the perfect evenness of a Van Eyck to the richly unequal finish of a Rembrandt, smooth in the shadows but embossed with thick lumps of *impasto* (i.e. thick opaque paint) in the lights.

When critics contrast 'painterly' and 'draughtsman-like' qualities, the medium implied is usually oil. The other media suit the draughtsman equally, in being more exclusively linear. It is possible to use oil in this restricted manner; but its peculiar expressiveness depends on its adaptability to a great variety of other treatments. In oil one can render atmosphere by blurred edges and broken contours, texture by quality, and substance (among other means) by thickness, of pigment.

Oil lends itself to direct sketching from Nature, since the final tone and colour can be applied at once. Within limits it also allows of change of mind. A mistake can be covered up with opaque paint, though sometimes later the surface becomes transparent and the *pentimenti*, intended to be hidden, show through, as in Titian's *Vendramin Family* [(4452), Pl. 44] and in De Hooch's *Interior of a Dutch House* [(834), Pl. 63]. This freedom has its dangers. Many experiments in oil have ended in muddles and messes; and oil is the medium of the great majority of pictures that are now cracked, faded or darkened wrecks. Its most permanent results are the outcome of method and discipline, as severe as those governing other media.

The slowness with which oil paint dries makes it possible completely to fuse one tone into another without visible brush-strokes. For this reason it is ideal for rendering effects of softness of atmosphere and texture. In no other medium could Renoir have expressed so well the changes of colour upon one surface, caused by reflection from another or Correggio have represented the varied softness of flesh, hair, garments and grass.

Yet the propensity to dry slowly is not wholly an advantage. While the paint remains really wet, one brush-stroke can still be worked into the next; but as soon as the paint has become 'tacky' (i.e. neither wholly wet nor wholly dry) the canvas cannot be touched without risk of cracks, discoloration, etc. The first stage of impetuous work must be followed by a stage of patiently waiting until the paint is dry through and through.

Oil is capable of greater extremes of transparency and opacity than tempera. An oil glaze can be as transparent as any water-colour wash; and oil paint, mixed with enough white, can be more opaque than the densest layer of gouache. This helps in combining two problems of representation. An opaque passage, by its mere body, can convey bulky proximity; and a glaze, by its transparency, distance and separation by air; for in any medium, if two areas be covered by paint of the same colour and tone, but applied in one case opaquely and in the other transparently, the opaque area will render a near, and the transparent area a distant, appearance.

Darker shadows are possible in oil than in any other medium. Provided the contrasts of tone are not forced (see Chapter XIX), this is an advantage from the standpoints both of realism and of design. Because of their transparency, the slightest differences of tone in the dark shadows of a Rembrandt perceptibly contribute to the effect of depth.

The finest tempera painting may be likened to music played by a string quartet, exquisitely subtle, but limited in *timbre*; the grandest oil painting to a symphony played by an orchestra, richer and more powerful in contrasts. This power entails some sacrifice; and certain *nuances* of cool colour and crisp pattern can more easily be achieved in tempera.

The full possibilities of oil were developed only by degrees. At first, except for taking advantage of its transparency and slowness in drying, painters did not use it very differently from tempera. By the middle of the sixteenth century all connexion with tempera technique had disappeared. I propose now to discuss oil painting (still somewhat broadly and arbitrarily) under twelve headings (partly chronological and partly technical):

(i) The Van Eyck Medium;   (vii) Brush-work;
(ii) Glazes;   (viii) Rubens's methods;
(iii) Oil on Canvas;   (ix) Palette-knife work;
(iv) Titian's Development;   (x) Turner's later oils;
(v) Scumbling and Impasto;   (xi) Pre-Raphaelite methods;
(vi) Rembrandt's methods;   (xii) Impressionist methods.

(i) THE VAN EYCK MEDIUM

The legend of the 'discovery of oil' by the Van Eycks is now exploded. A coarse kind of oil paint had already been used for centuries on church woodwork, but not, at least in medieval times, for pictures. The first pictures to be completed in glazes of oil seem to have been by the late fourteenth-century painters of Cologne, the predecessors of Stefan Lochner, whose *Three Saints* (705) wear garments more transparent in colour than tempera alone can produce. What the Van Eycks probably did was to systematize and purify the use of oil glazes. They may also have invented the use of oil (in the final stage of their painting) as the *sole diluent*; that is, they may at this stage have mixed oil and tempera in an emulsion, substituting oil not for tempera but for water. They probably continued to use tempera alone for the earlier stages of painting, where its speed in drying was an advantage. In Jan Van Eyck's unfinished *S. Barbara* at Antwerp, the separate hatched brush-strokes of the brown monochrome shading prove the presence of tempera or some similar medium soluble in water.

The Van Eycks began their pictures, like the tempera painters, by priming the wood with a smooth coat of white (usually gesso) and, when this was dry, drawing over it with the brush the monochrome outline and hatched shadow in tempera or size. In the next, i.e. the second stage, they may have mixed oil with the tempera; with this, without any hatching, they modelled the faces in *planes* of semi-transparent flesh colour and white and treated the rest of the picture with colours preparatory to the final colour. When the second stage was dry, the third and final stage was carried out, certainly in oil (whether or not egg was mixed with it) in glazes of colour of great transparency; here the lights and shadows fused completely and left no trace of brush-strokes (see the wall in Van Eyck's *Arnolfini* group [(186), Pls. 10 and 11]. The glow of colour in the early Flemish pictures, different from the semi-opaque translucency of tempera, is due to this final transparency.

In one respect the final stage of painting faces varied. Campin in his portraits of a *Man* and a *Woman* (653 A and 653 B) relied for the high lights on the light pinks of the second stage which he was careful *not* to cover by further colour when he applied the third stage. In fact, in the third stage he painted over every part of the face *except* the highest lights. Memling on the other hand in his 'Young Man at Prayer' (2594) painted the high lights of the flesh last of all in opaque paint of a thickness perceptible under the magnifying glass.

By the sixteenth century, several Flemish painters had begun to simplify and expand Van Eyckian practice. Bosch in portions of the *Crowning with Thorns* (4744) omitted the second stage, so that there is nothing between the white priming and the final transparent or semi-transparent colour. In Bruegel's *Adoration of the Magi* [(3556), Pl. 43] the brown monochrome foundation is often left uncovered (e.g. in the shadow of the farthest king's mauve-grey sleeve). Some of the reds (e.g. of the old king's over-robe) are painted directly over the white priming; others (e.g. the Virgin's under-robe) have a coat of grey paint under them. There is a constant alternation between meticulous detail and freedom of brushwork. Most of the white passages are smooth and consist of little more than the priming; but the white lights in the stooping soldier's armour have been applied quite thickly, last of all.

(ii) GLAZES

A glaze means that oil paint has been used transparently without mixing it with white. The degree of the transparency varies. A glaze may be as transparent as a varnish, but there is a distinction between them. A varnish is an addition to the painting, not part of it; it is the thin protective layer that covers the entire picture. It consists as often of resin as of linseed oil and should be colourless. A glaze covers only a restricted area of a picture with a particular colour. Glazes, like washes in water-colour, may be useful in unifying a group of details. Giovanni Bellini in the *Madonna of the Meadow* (599) floated a lighter glaze over the sunlit part of the meadow and a darker glaze over its nearer shadowed area, without disturbing the fine drawing of the stones and grasses underneath. By a similar method the Master of S. Giles brought the mullein, irises and other flowers together as one mass of greenery in *S. Giles and the Hind* (1419).

(iii) OIL ON CANVAS

Some follower of the Van Eycks taught the Van Eyck medium to Antonello da Messina, who in turn handed it on to various Venetians, notably to the brothers Gentile and Giovanni Bellini, the masters of Giorgione and Titian. During the sixteenth century Titian and his successors modified and extended the technique of oil painting, so as to become examples to succeeding generations.

Antonello was faithful to the tradition of Van Eyck. Nor did Giovanni Bellini depart from it much; in his later work his painting of textures was rather softer, and his rendering of atmosphere subtler, than Antonello's; but he preferred wood to canvas and put exactness before freedom.

The Venetians appear to have been the first to use canvas as a support for painting in oil. The soft textures (especially of the hair) in Gentile Bellini's portrait on canvas of a *Mathematician* (1213) (even softer now than when first painted) may be compared with the smooth, hard appearance of *Doge Loredano* (189) painted by Giovanni Bellini on wood.

Canvases were not so thickly primed as panels and the use of tempera in the earlier stages was gradually abandoned. The thinner priming led to the labour-saving device of a half-tone priming. In Gentile Bellini's *Adoration of the Magi* (3098) (on canvas) lighter accents have been painted over large passages of a dark colour. The distant figures on horseback, executed in this way, have almost disappeared. Painting light over dark always entails this risk, especially if the picture has to be relined.

Thirdly, the use of canvas led to the use of larger brushes and to more emphatic *impasto*. If accents of light over something darker are to last they must be painted fairly thickly; and the coarser the grain of the canvas is, the thicker they must be.

(iv) TITIAN'S DEVELOPMENT

The changes undergone by Venetian oil technique during the sixteenth century are apparent in three portraits: in Giovanni Bellini's *Doge Loredano* (189) of about 1500 the paint is smooth and the flesh represented as hard; in Titian's so-called 'Ariosto' (1944) of about 1510 the paint is also smooth, but the textures represented as soft; in Tintoretto's *Morosini* (4004) the uneven paint, thinnest in the half-tones and thickest in the lights, contributes to the effect both of the projecting form and of the textural contrasts.

Similar developments are traceable in Titian's works. *Bacchus and Ariadne* [(35), Pl. 36] of about 1520 still has a comparatively smooth surface due to the gradual superimposition of many thin layers of paint. The *Vendramin Family* [(4452), Pl. 44] of about 1545, though larger, evidently took less time to complete; the half-tones, e.g. in the sky and steps, are thin enough to show the canvas grain; the darks, glowing with varied transparent colour, are nearly as thin; but the lights, especially on the foreheads, are quite thick—a fact which contributes to their projection, just as the dry dragging of thick light into thin shadow contributes to the texture of the beards. In the *Mother and Child* (3948) of about 1570 the technique is more mysterious; in the dress, the thin warm brown shadows have been painted first and the cooler greyish lights floated semi-opaquely over them in a kind of scumble.

(v) SCUMBLING AND IMPASTO

Scumbling is a quality half-way between impasto and glazing. A principle governing oil painting may be expressed thus: *Shadows must be thin; lights may be thick.* For the sake of transparency, shadows must be painted thinly, whether they cover canvas coated with a slight priming, wood covered with a thick priming, or a layer of thick paint, light in tone. The darker the shadow is, the greater is the need for painting it thinly.

The thickness of an accent of light, on the other hand, is a matter of taste. Unless the accent is due to the white priming underneath—or in other words, provided it has been painted over a darker, even a slightly darker, ground—it will always have some thickness from the opaque nature of white paint; but the *degree* of its thickness will vary with the painter.

The glaze and impasto constitute the extremes in oil painting of thin transparency and thick opacity. A glaze is something darker painted transparently over something lighter; an impasto something lighter painted opaquely over something darker. A scumble is a sort of thin impasto. To obtain a dragged broken scumble, the brush is filled with a considerable amount both of opaque paint and of the diluent, so that when the scumble is loosely applied, particles of light opaque (and normally cool) colour remain on the upper threads of the canvas, leaving gaps between on the lower threads, where the transparent darker layer of underpainting remains visible. A scumble in oil often has the same opalescent quality as in tempera (see p. 136). In Crome's *Mousehold Heath* (689) a scumble of mauve pink, taken over the darker green fields towards the horizon gives the effect of the atmosphere hovering above the ground.

Impasto (see p. 17) can be one of the most pleasing qualities of paint, merely as paint. It can also be one of the chief means of individual expression. The various degrees of thickness, liquidity or viscosity of particular impasti are often compared with milk, butter, cream or cheese. The impasto in tempera paintings and in Memling's 'Young Man at Prayer' (2594) is like milk. In Van Goyen's *Windmill* (2578) and in many works by Cuyp, Guardi and Hogarth, it is like butter or thin cream, liquid enough to be worked about easily with the brush. The impasto of Rembrandt and of Chardin is usually stiffer and more solid, like clotted cream or cheese.

(vi) REMBRANDT'S METHODS

Rembrandt's shadows are not mere dramatic contrasts with the lights, but mysterious areas penetrated even at their darkest by light. Out of this gloom his forms emerge gradually into full light and full solidity. His method of putting whatever is most important in the strongest light (see p. 110), e.g. the head in his *Portrait of Himself when Old* [(221), see Pl. 61] gives it what may be called psychological proximity. The building up of the head must have been fairly gradual. Rembrandt's deliberate roughness of finish was compared by Sir Charles Holmes with a sculptor's display of the marks of the chisel. The shadows in the face have been painted over the impasto; and, though the half-tones are exquisitely transparent and cool, the darkest shadows under the eyes and nose and upper lip are less transparent than any in the background, which for this reason appears more distant.

(vii) BRUSH-WORK

In painting *par excellence* the quality of the paint and the shape of the brush-stroke play equally important parts. Great pictures exist in which the surface is perfectly even and the brush-strokes entirely hidden; but texture of paint and grace of brush-work can have their own expressiveness. Variety in the texture of paint belongs almost exclusively to oil painting. Brush-work can exist equally in other media. The danger of skilled brush-work lies in a temptation to repeat such graceful shapes as the brush produces most easily with too little reference to the shapes of the objects represented. In his late works like the *Baillie Family* (789) Gainsborough's brush-strokes are more graceful than truthful. Turner achieved the ideal in such sketches as *Treetops against the Sky* (T.G. 2309) where the foliage is recorded with ease, but with a searching eye for direction of growth. In the hair of *Mrs Collmann* (1775) by Alfred Stevens skill and truth are beautifully combined.

Sometimes spontaneity is more apparent than real. In Tintoretto's *S. George* [(16), Pl. 42] the brush outlines of the horse's belly and legs retain their grace, although the white and brown of his body above them and the green of the grass below them have been deliberately laid beside them later in thicker paint.

In other cases it may be hard to decide whether precision has degenerated into niggling or breadth into carelessness. Of all European painters Rubens most confidently and consistently avoided both pitfalls. Thus, in his *Peace and War* (46) the grapes, the vine leaves and the vine tendrils have a vitality, only possible when painting and drawing are one process. Each brush-stroke, however much it widens or narrows with the pressure, relaxation or turn of the hand, is controlled in direction along both its boundaries.

(viii) RUBENS'S METHODS

Rubens in all branches of design owed much to the Venetians, but in technique was faithful to the Flemish tradition. He revived the use of transparent colour over a white priming and used wood quite as often as canvas.

Rubens's technical practice was a brilliant adaptation of the methods of Van Eyck, for which Bruegel had partly paved the way. In the faces of his portraits, such as that of *A Lady* (lent by M. Gulbenkian) and the famous '*Chapeau de Paille*' (852), he covered the white priming of the panel with long grey brush-strokes, slanting down from right to left, and leaving gaps of white visible between them. The flesh was then painted in three stages. First, a fairly dark brown was used for the outlines, the darker shadows and even (applied less emphatically and with gaps between the strokes) the half-tones. Secondly, the flesh was completely covered with a light-toned pink tint, painted more thickly in the lights than in the shadows or half-tones. (The half-tones were cool because of the darker brown beneath; see p. 136.) Thirdly, the high lights were painted in opaque accents and the full shadows in dark transparent glazes.

To avoid long periods of waiting for each layer of paint to dry, he probably used some quickly drying emulsion, at least for the earlier stages of his pictures. He could also paint impasto over transparent passages and glazes over opaque passages to an almost indefinite extent, without letting the quality become tired. These alternations are particularly striking in the *Château de Steen* [(66), Pl. 54]. The cloud shadows, dragged horizontally into the lights on the distant fields, were glazed transparently over a light-toned foundation. Many of the lighter objects in the foreground were impasted over dark transparent paint.

(ix) PALETTE-KNIFE WORK

In the *Château de Steen* Rubens seems to have used a palette-knife for the high lights on the stream behind the tree stump. These two or three square inches of paint suggested to Constable a way of covering many square feet of canvas. In nearly all Constable's later pictures the sparkling high lights are produced in this way. Many of his most telling sketches, such as *Salisbury Cathedral* [(1814), Pl. 73], were painted mainly with the palette-knife, a speedier weapon than the brush (though less shapely in its results) for painting out of doors in opaque colours directly applied.

(x) TURNER'S LATER OILS

Turner worked in water-colour as a child and began oil painting only when he was of age. He then mastered impasto and used the grain of the canvas for atmosphere; but his instincts in favour of transparency reappeared in his later oils. In his final phase of absorption with colour and light (see pp. 104–5) he aimed at transparency for a further reason—as an additional means of attaining colourful luminosity. His later oils were painted in transparent colours over a white priming, as if they were water-colours and the priming were white paper. Unfortunately he used fugitive pigments and applied the glazes before the priming was thoroughly dry, with the result that many of these works are discoloured, cracked or uneven in surface and have lost their intended colour and tone; and it is seldom possible to do more than guess at their original beauty from his contemporary water-colours which, if protected from the sun, are still a delight to the eye.

(xi) PRE-RAPHAELITE METHODS

To pass from a room of early nineteenth-century English portraits and genre pictures to one of Pre-Raphaelite works is to leave a world of gloomy browns for one of exciting, if not always soothing, colour. Bitumen, a dangerous pigment, beset and blighted English oil paintings from 1780 to 1850 and not even the landscape painters entirely avoided it. Even in France many works by Prud'hon and Delacroix suffered from it. The other cause of dullness in early nineteenth-century English pictures is the traditional use of a rather dark, warm priming. This is an admirable basis for varied *impasto*, but entails the risk that the surface colours may become transparent and the whole picture too brown.

The vogue for the brown priming was followed by the vogue for the white priming; and this appears not only in the late Turners, but also in Pre-Raphaelite paintings and is used with consummate skill in Ingres' *Madame Moitessier* [(4821), Pl. 75]. The disadvantage of a white priming is that the final surface lacks variety, since the grain of the canvas is hidden.

The Pre-Raphaelites, however, should be given credit for banishing bitumen. Millais and Holman Hunt after priming their canvases with white, covered any given area to be finished in a day with another thinner coat of white into which, while still wet, they worked their transparent colours. Lightness of tone was obtained in this way and, in so far as the paint was transparent, considerable brilliancy of saturated colour; also, in the case of Millais, great skill in controlling edge-values. Changes in such pictures as Millais' *Ophelia* (1506) are due to the particular pigment, not to the method of applying it. The chief disadvantage of the method was the necessity of finishing pictures piecemeal—one reason for the frequent Pre-Raphaelite failure in tonal unity.

(xii) IMPRESSIONIST METHODS

Among the realists and impressionists of nineteenth-century France, there have been almost as many aims as painters and quite as many methods as aims; and each aim has produced its own method. A few have been incidentally touched upon in Chapters VII and VIII and again in the three chapters on colour. Courbet, in order to give form actuality and substance, used a heavy *impasto*; Seurat, in order to render atmosphere and light, placed spots of vivid colour side by side; Cézanne, in order to explain the direction of planes, used straight, rather than curved, brush-strokes; and so on. But the French Impressionists and Post-Impressionists had one technical tendency in common, which most twentieth-century oil painters share with them: the use of colours made opaque by admixture with white paint. They abandoned the glaze and the gradual application of paint in layers. They also tended to use as little oil as possible, for fear of yellowing and darkening.

Manet, in his earlier works, restricted the oil by applying paint in single coats of the tone and colour required. Monet, Sisley and Pissarro went farther, using little or no oil as a diluent and working with spots of solid colour. Monet, though influenced by Turner's colour (see p. 105), borrowed nothing from Turner's handling of paint. His range of tones and colours was similar; but Turner's white shines *through* the colours and Monet's white is mixed *with* them.

Cézanne modified the methods, as well as the ideals, of impressionism. In his early days his impasto outdid Courbet's in 'cheesiness'; it was applied in continuous areas, not like Monet's in broken touches. Under Pissarro's influence, his paint became thinner and was more broken up into touches of separate colour; but concern with form always determined the direction of his brush-strokes. As time went on, his paint became increasingly thinner, so that his late oils, though he used no glazes, have technical, as well as atmospheric, qualities in common with his late water-colours; in oils, parts of the canvas, in water-colours areas of white paper, were left uncovered.

The opaque colour, prevalent in modern oils, has advantages for direct painting. On the other hand, when luminosity is the aim, the glaze has advantages too, though (in our present ignorance) it has drawbacks as regards permanence. So unless and until the secrets of Rubens are rediscovered, the opaque method may be the best. In that event it would be possible to combine his alternating super-impositions of opaque and transparent paint with an even fuller range of saturated colour.

CHAPTER XXVI

TWO PICTURES ANALYSED

In the foregoing chapters each aspect of painting, emotional, decorative or technical, is considered separately. In this chapter and the next, four pictures are described and analysed in as many aspects as possible.

The group of *Jan Arnolfini and his Wife* [(186), Pls. 10 and 11] has recently been catalogued (on evidence brought forward by M. Panofsky in the 'Burlington Magazine', 1934, pp. 117ff.) as *The Marriage of Giovanni Arnolfini and Giovanna Cenami*. The statuette of S. Margaret and the single candle are symbols proper to the nuptial chamber; and the position of the lady's left hand may also be a marriage symbol. The apparent massiveness of her figure is probably merely the result of the prevailing fashion of dress.

The picture is signed (in Gothic letters with flourishes) on the wall above the mirror: *Johannes de eyck fuit hic*, and dated below the signature (in arabic numerals, an innovation of the period): *1434* (see Pl. 11). The words 'Jan van Eyck was here' are thought to mean that he was a witness to the marriage.

The identity of the sitters, which is unquestionable (though it has been questioned), is derived from descriptions in inventories from 1516 onwards. Arnolfini, a merchant from Lucca, was living from 1430 in Bruges, where he was buried in 1470. His wife was the daughter of another Lucchese merchant.

The picture is inspired by the keenest observation and zeal for overcoming representational problems. The painting has been carried out in the objective spirit of the clearest prose.

The revelation of character is complete and quite unbiased. Giovanni Arnolfini looks certainly crafty and probably cruel. His gentle wife, Giovanna Cenami, attempting a deprecating smile, can have been no match for him. These impressions are derived from the *structure* only of the faces; for their *texture* is that of carved wood. The hands are also, in a more derogatory sense, wooden—not only hard, but lifeless.

A certain woodenness of texture belongs to most things in the picture, except the fur and the brass of the chandelier. The straight folds of the drapery may be unconscious imitations of the technique of wooden statuettes. Apart from the question of texture, the only other obvious lapse in realism is the failure to indicate the shape of the bodies under the clothes. In almost every other respect the verisimilitude is complete. Of the many attractive details (all an unfailing source of delight to the public) the most fascinating is the circular mirror, which reflects in little everything in the room, including two figures at the other end of it, one in blue and one in red, looking over his shoulder. The reflection omits the dog, but includes the orange on the window sill and the three oranges on the chest.

So many details would be tedious but for three reasons: the enjoyment with which they were painted; the plain areas, free from detail (such as the wall and Arnolfini's wine-coloured cloak) which gave the eye rest; and the broad truth of the relations of tone (see p. 25). The truth of tone, colour, edge values and gradations also contribute to the effect of recession.

The gradation on the wall from light below to dark above is masterly. Van Eyck, an observer not a theorist, understood aerial, better than linear, perspective. He made the patterned carpet lie flat (presumably by means of measuring points), but represented the lines of depth (see p. 83) by lines converging at three different vanishing points: the planks on the floor at a point below the mirror; the rafters and the top of the bed, above it; and the divisions of the windows, within the mirror itself.

These lines, however, lead the eye near enough to the mirror to concentrate attention upon it, as the real centre of interest. It is central in relation to the width of the picture and the two figures stand symmetrically on each side of it. This symmetrical tendency of the linear design is in contrast with the non-symmetry of the tonal design. Arnolfini makes a dark shape against a lighter background (though within it his hands and half his face are light); his wife's head and head-dress are light against the darker bed, and the rest of her half of the picture consists of contrasts of colour: green dress, blue sleeves, red curtains.

The colour scheme as a whole depends on repetition, on the restricted number of vivid colours, and on the recorded changes of colour, due to light. The transparent green of Giovanna's cloak is almost the complementary of the repeated red (most prominent in the bed behind her). The wine-colour of Arnolfini's cloak has no vivid complementary in the picture. The complementary of the light but opaque blue (in the bride's sleeves and under-robe) occurs in the oranges and (in a more subdued variety) in the different orange-browns. The blacks, whites, browns and greys, here tinged with orange, there with green, occupy more than half of the total area and contribute to the harmonious whole.

The advantages of the Van Eyck medium are apparent in the transparency of the colours, jewel-like in the half-tones and glowing even in the shadows. Just as the treatment of the drapery may come from wood carving, so this transparency may have been encouraged by rivalry with the Northern art of stained glass and the minuteness of the detail by the example of contemporary illumination.

The *Nativity* [(908), Pl. 21] by Piero della Francesca, in contrast with the Van Eyck, belongs to the realms of poetry.

It was probably painted later than the *Baptism of Christ* [(665), Pl. 20] and at least as late as 1470, though precise dating is impossible, since the evidence rests on stylistic grounds only. The brown underpainting of the flesh (uncovered in the faces of the shepherds) has taken the place of the terre verte underpainting of the earlier picture (see p. 136).

The event takes place in the cool of the morning. The quiet is gently broken by the voices and instruments of the angels, and more harshly (perhaps because it is earth, not Heaven) by the braying of the ass; the magpie, goldfinches and chaffinch are silent. The angels are unlike the angels of earlier Italian painting in having no wings and in not being the sexless creatures of tradition, but unmistakably women (cf. the angel in Pl. 9). Yet they are not neighbours, who have walked up from the valley. Though they stand firmly upon the ground, their feet are unsoiled. They have descended without effort in compact formation. They are heard by the eager Christ Child, but unseen by S. Joseph or the shepherds.

These supernatural suggestions are combined with realistic representation. Haloes, still retained by Piero in his *Baptism of Christ* [(665), Pl. 20], are here omitted. S. Joseph's right leg is a triumph of foreshortening, which is also attempted with less happy results in the ox. The finely drawn figures resemble marble in texture and immobility; but the aerial perspective goes far beyond the limitations of bas-relief. Objects as they recede become less distinct, less contrasted in tone, and cooler in colour, effects only slightly obscured by the fact that the greens of the landscape have darkened; the shadows cast on the stone wall of the stable vary in tone and sharpness of contour and keep their transparency throughout.

The design combines inspiration with studied proportions. Flowing curves are contrasted with the basic pattern of straight lines. Each detail of drapery has both a realistic and a decorative function. The distant river has many windings. The Virgin's cloak, obedient to the laws of gravity, opens like the petals of a flower. The curved folds of the angels' skirts emphasize the pose of their feet, one in advance of the other, a pose repeated with variations. There are also echoes in the position of the hands of the two foremost. A long inverted S-curve with gaps in it connects the magpie on the roof with the sweep of the path in the foreground, and another connects the shadow above the shepherd raising his arm with the half of the Virgin's cloak on the spectator's right.

This linear pattern is perfectly reconciled with the three-dimensional composition. Though the angels are represented as being of equal stature, only their chins (exactly on a level with the eye) come to the same height on the picture. The tops of the heads of the two nearest come slightly higher than that of the central angel, and hers slightly higher than those of the two behind her. The five angels fill a rectangular area; but the three-dimensional volume they occupy is not a solid rectangle. The ground space on which they stand is a quadrilateral of which the near and far sides are parallel to the picture plane, but the two remaining sides not at right angles to it.

Regarded three-dimensionally, the concentrated block of angels is surrounded by an unoccupied space; for, although on the picture the Child's hand and the Virgin's cloak touch one angel's feet, they are not represented as touching them. The space round the angels is itself surrounded by a series of figures with gaps between them (the Child, the Virgin, S. Joseph, the Shepherds, the ox and the ass) covering roughly a semicircle upon the ground. Beyond this is the stable, and on each side of the stable a vista ending in buildings or mountains.

The contrast of tones is balanced and emphatic, though restricted in range. In the darkest passages colour is preserved and black avoided. Apart from the darkest browns the colours are contrasted in the 'natural order of tone' (see p. 125). That is, the darkest example of blue is darker than the darkest example of red, and so on. The dominant colour (see p. 127) is blue, seen in a subdued variant in the Virgin's gown and in a lighter variant in the sky. The colours 'similar' to it are turquoise-blues (light and dark) and the purple-blue worn by the central angel. The complementaries to these occur in the various light orange-browns. A second contrast of complementaries is that between the dull greens and the reds, which are more vivid but less varied than the blues and occupy less space. The angels in red, by tactfully standing behind their companions in cooler-coloured robes, help to preserve the balance of colour.

In general the balance of strength and tenderness expressed by this subtly satisfying picture, is derived from the balance of deep thought and deep feeling that has gone to its making.

CHAPTER XXVII

TWO MORE PICTURES ANALYSED

THE descriptions that follow of two more pictures concern mainly their design and the painter's mood and aims. For fuller historical information the reader is referred (at the end of each description) to catalogues, etc.

The portrait of *Christina of Denmark* [(2475), Pl. 39] the child widow of Francesco Maria Sforza, Duke of Milan, was painted by Holbein in 1538 at the order of Henry VIII, who sought her hand in marriage. The Duchess, who was fifteen years old, wisely declined the honour, pointing out that she had only one head.

Christina, who (as her skirt shows) has entered the room a little from our right, stands facing us, holding her gloves loosely in front of her, completely self-possessed and rather enigmatic. The painter has given an unbiased impression of her charm, which is felt to be latent rather than displayed. The Duchess has great dignity of presence, evidently the result of a strong will and of habitual diplomatic reserve. One could guess that she would gain her own end, after pretending to consult the wishes of others.

Unfortunately there is some repainting on the face, especially above the left eye; but the drawing of Holbein himself is masterly in its structural precision, although the gentle lighting precludes any immediate illusion of three-dimensional solidity and there is no attempt at three-dimensional design.

At a casual glance the picture looks flat, because the strong contrasts of tone are entirely local, and the tonal pattern depends on these only. By means of the exactness in defining the contours and the boundaries (even the blurred boundaries of shadows) the structure of the exquisite hands is completely explained, so is that of the head, where it has not been repainted; so is the relation of the figure to the loosely fitting dress and to the ground. The indications of texture are due to drawing and not to the quality of the paint, which is even and monotonous.

The pattern of the portrait depends upon austere elimination of the irrelevant and the nice balance, proportion and placing of shapes upon the picture-area. The Duchess's head is seen exactly full face, but is considerably to the left of the centre of the design. This leftward tendency is compensated for: (i) by the greater projection of the cap and the greater fullness of the skirt on our right; (ii) by the slight turn of the figure, of which the left shoulder is nearer than the right shoulder; (iii) by the position and size of the descriptive label or *cartellino*, which is so essential to the design as to make it hard to believe that, as scholars assert, it was added by a later hand in the early seventeenth century. Symmetry is further avoided by the difference in attitude of the two hands, which also interrupt the long curves of the edges of the gown.

The scheme of tone and colour is both bold and subtle. There are three contrasted groups of tone: darks (occupying the largest area); lights; and half-tones. Within each group, slight differences of tone accompany marked differences of colour. The darks consist of the ungradated turquoise background and the three different blacks of the cap, dress and cloak; the lights, of the white collar and cuffs, subdued white label, the pale yellow gloves and the flesh in light and pale shadow; and the half-tones, of the brown fur, reddish brown floor, red sealing-wax on the label, gold ring and its red ruby. The minute accents of red make a pleasing contrast to the large area of the complementary turquoise background. The complementary to the brown and gold is implied by the black (see pp. 116 and 121).

[For a historical account see 'National Gallery Catalogue, British School', by Martin Davies, 1946.]

Venus and Cupid [(2057), Pl. 65] is the only existing painting by Velazquez of the female nude. In addition he is known to have painted two others now lost, of *Venus and Adonis* and *Cupid and Psyche* for Philip IV's palace, as well as a third mythological subject *Mercury and Argus* of about 1659, which is still in the Prado, Madrid. Our picture may be confidently identified with the 'Venus stretched out', mentioned in the inventory of the contents of Velazquez's house and was almost certainly also painted for Philip. It is close in style to the *Tapestry Weavers* (Prado) of about 1657 and must be one of his latest works, painted between his return from his second visit to Italy in 1651 and his death in 1660. It shows the influence of such works by Titian as the *Danaë* (Prado); but no Venetian would have used the austerely neutral grey drapery as a foil to the flesh.

Velazquez's imagination depended upon closely observing everyday events. He could not visualize the supernatural; and in his early paintings his angels are individuals with wings absurdly attached. Here the wings of Cupid seem really part of him, and the subject is treated in a way that must be termed poetic. The poetry, however, arises not from the ferment of imagery *within*, but from genius in selecting effects of the world *without*.

The picture has a mystery of its own. We are not allowed to behold the face of Venus; for the reflection in the mirror is darkened and blurred and leaves us guessing. (It was probably once even less distinct; for the present coarse features in the style of Murillo are due to a later hand than Velazquez's.) A clearer reflection would have destroyed both this mystery and the unity of the design, by introducing a second focus for attention.

The design, in fact, depends upon focus. The area within the focus includes Venus's head and shoulders and most of her body down to her knee. It is an approximate ellipse, of which the centre is to the right of the centre of the picture. Whatever is outside this ellipse—e.g. Venus's elbow and left foot and the whole of Cupid—is less defined in structure and less strongly contrasted in tone than what is within it. The fact of Cupid's face being in shadow also subordinates him to Venus. The frame of the mirror, though partly within the ellipse, has blurred edges and is out of focus.

The edge-values also help in the rendering of texture and atmosphere; and this is combined (since even the softest edges are controlled in direction) with a decisive description of structure. For structural drawing there is, but no emphasis upon it. There are no outlines, such as are used for structural emphasis by all the great Italians, except Correggio and Titian in their final phases. There is equally no exaggerated tonal contrast. Velazquez puts down no more than what he saw. Not seeing outlines, he left them out. Seeing delicate relations of tone, he recorded them within the restrictions of his medium (see Chapter XIX).

At the same time, no mere impressionist, concerned with appearance only, revealed what Velazquez revealed. Behind his softest effects there is knowledge. Years of study—beginning in his early hard modelling—were the foundation for these brilliant results. Without this discipline, he never could have explained, by a shadow so pale and so blurred, the nearness of Venus's shoulder-blade to the surface of the skin.

Instances of contours (soft or hard) that explain the texture of the form described and the atmosphere surrounding it, are: the sharp edge of the grey silk on which Venus lies, against the white linen below it; the slightly softened edge of the thigh against the white linen beyond it; and the much softer edge of the shoulder against the darker wall—a softness due to its texture and distance from a darker background.

By such means, Venus is illumined by daylight and surrounded by air. These effects depend also on tone. The range of tonal contrast is much restricted, so that contrasts of colour have nearly their full natural force (see p. 105) and the white drapery is lighter than the flesh without being too prominent. The gradated tones on the wall behind Venus, in addition to their atmospheric value, provide a background for the dark or light silhouettes of her hair, shoulders, arm and what little can be seen of her face. In general the tones are so distributed as to reconcile contrast with a quiet balance.

These structural, textural and atmospheric truths are accompanied by some distortion of proportions. In order to emphasize the relaxed recumbency of the figure, Velazquez has exaggerated the length of the back and left leg, notably ignoring the foreshortening of the thigh.

The colour-scheme is somewhat subdued. The more vivid colours are contrasted with less saturated complementaries; the rose-colour with the warm green-grey of the wall; Cupid's blue sling with Venus's flesh. The neutral grey drapery also acts as a complementary to all the other colours (see p. 116).

Tone and colour are recorded together. In Venus's body the lights are rather warm, the pale half-tones cool, and the darker shadows (e.g. under the thigh) very warm with reflected light. Her brown hair, the white linen and vivid green silk beyond her, the dark grey drapery beneath her, even the flesh of the Cupid (rosier than hers in itself and by reflection from the curtain) are all contrasted with the beauty of Venus's flesh.

Most of the above analyses prove Velazquez's independence of Italian tradition. The three-dimensional composition of the picture is simple. The forms are consistently spaced within the limited picture-volume. The eye is led obliquely inwards from Venus to Cupid. The linear pattern is more interesting. Though only one of the aspects of the design, it is clearly based on Italian methods and contributes positively to the coherent whole.

Except for the mirror the most conspicuous contours are curves; and even the mirror's angularity is broken by the curves of the ribbon. The curves of Venus's spine and torso are echoed (with differences): by A, the edge of the curtain; by B, the long fold of grey silk hanging from points below the inside of her right elbow and left foot. Curve B is echoed in reverse by the upper edge of Cupid's wing, which contrasts with curves A and B, and rounds off the corner of the picture. Contrasted with it is curve C, the upper and outer contour of Venus's leg, thigh and hip.

Horizontals and verticals are present mostly by implication. A steadying vertical appears in one fold of the grey silk on the right and is implied by the downward drag of the ribbon over the mirror.

One implied horizontal, L, runs from Cupid's left instep to Venus's right elbow, touching his right knee-cap and the highest point of her hip. It is emphasized by the repetition in the angle of his knee and her elbow. Another, M, begins at her left toe, passes along the lower edge of what is visible of her legs, and is approximately equidistant throughout its length from the curves B and C. In other words curves B and C are symmetrically related to the horizontal axis M (see p. 78).

Venus's left toe and right elbow are important points in the linear design. Horizontal M and curves B and C converge at her toe. At her elbow two implied straight lines converge: horizontal L and an oblique line running down from Cupid's shoulder and elbow and across her wrist.

A steadying vertical appears in one fold of the grey silk on the right and is implied by the downward drag of the ribbon over the mirror.

[For further history and analysis of the picture see 'The Rokeby Venus', by Neil MacLaren (Gallery Books, Number 1, published by Percy Lund Humphries and Co.).]

CHAPTER XXVIII

THE ETHICS OF PAINTING

IT takes more courage to state a platitude than to invent a paradox and more courage to preach a sermon than to utter a blasphemy; but in order to carry conviction familiar truths may sometimes need to be disguised, so that platitudes look like paradoxes. In what follows, the disguise is sometimes thin, sometimes non-existent.

To say that an artist ought to do this and ought not to do that is to preach. It is impossible in generalizing about art not to make use of moral terms. The greatest rebel against Ruskin's sermonizing cannot do without them.

In art, as in life, the dividing line between virtues and vices is almost imperceptible. Courage at its worst becomes bravado; and timidity at its best becomes sensibility.

Courage and humility are contrastable but compatible virtues. For courage means mastery of fear, not freedom from it; and humility involves recognizing difficulties, not shrinking from them. Both virtues involve a sense of responsibility. 'The task is great,' says the brave man, 'but I must not let it overcome me.' 'The task is almost beyond my powers,' says the humble man, 'but all the more worth attempting.'

In some painters courage, and in others humility, is more conspicuous; but in the greatest both virtues are present. There is a quality of assured skill that is saved from ostentatiousness by the painter's reverence for his theme. It might be called courage tempered by humility. It is present in the art of Veronese, of Rubens and (paradoxically) of Bruegel.

There is another quality that trembles on the verge of failure, but yet miraculously succeeds, upheld by the painter's zeal. It might be called humility re-enforced by courage. It appears in the mature work of El Greco, in the sketches of Constable and in the last paintings of Titian and Rembrandt.

These impressions are derived from the paintings themselves, not from reading biographies of the painters. Knowledge of an artist's life and character is an invaluable accompaniment to knowledge of his art, but a valueless substitute for it. Pictures often supply the only evidence of the emotions that inspired him. Biographical material may be lacking; or may prove only, as in Turner's case, that in his work alone the artist truly lived.

Biography may even mislead. Browning, by concentrating upon what he knew about Fra Filippo Lippi as a man, gave a false impression of his achievements as an artist. The greatest artists are often less likeable men than their inferiors. Greatness of mind is not always accompanied by moral virtues. Yet greatness does include a potentiality for moral good. The painter of genius shows in his art what his ideals are, even if he fails to carry out those ideals in other aspects of his life. Rembrandt was not only a greater artist than Hals, but also, whatever his actual life may have been, a man of finer moral fibre.

An artist need not consciously express his moral ideals; nor is the expression of these ideals the only purpose of art. Their conscious expression for propagandist purposes often leads to deplorable results (see p. 51). Nevertheless, a true work of art reveals not only the artist's emotional and intellectual bent, but also something of his ethical ideals.

The adjective 'good' varies in the degree of praise that it implies; but phrases such as 'good butter' and 'a good painter' prove that it is not synonymous with the word 'righteous'. Good in the widest and most positive sense, the goal that can satisfy the cravings of man, includes beauty and truth as well as righteousness. Most attempts to attain righteousness by distrusting beauty have failed. So have most attempts to follow righteousness while refusing to face truth. Morality needs emotional support from forces other than morality. Similarly the narrow pursuit of truth without aesthetic fervour or ethical purpose has negative, unproductive and even harmful results. And beauty also, like truth and righteousness, needs to draw sustenance from the other two aspects of good. Asceticism is as dangerous to aesthetics as to ethics.

Enough has been said in earlier chapters about the relation of beauty to truth. I propose now to discuss the relation of beauty to morality.

The morals of life are only one of the many possible subjects for art; but art itself is necessarily regulated by morals of its own. These include the already stated need for loyalty to emotion, to vision and to material conditions.

The spectator's duties are: first to find out what emotions the artist intends to express, secondly whether he has expressed them well and thirdly whether they are worth expressing (see p. 2). With this third problem, this chapter is specially concerned.

The three duties of the artist correspond with the three duties of the spectator. The first and second of these are sincerity and clarity. The artist's third duty is the choice of an emotion worthy of expression.

The value of the emotion depends upon something more than the artist's sincerity. The emotion ought to be capable of being shared (see pp. 3–4). It need not be immediately pleasurable in its effects; it may include painful feelings; but the feelings aroused should not be exclusively painful (see p. 49). There should be a balance between joy and sorrow (cf. p. 124).

In addition to sincerity and clarity, there is need for sanity, wide sympathies, humility, courage and the power to instil courage. Some of these qualities are both intellectual and moral. Wide sympathies are the cause of the active sanity that prompts the artist to express widely experienced emotions.

The emotion expressed in a work of art should be both intense and balanced, both subjective and objective. It must have been deeply felt by the artist, but not by the artist alone. El Greco was more subjective than objective, more visionary than visual. He expressed what he saw with passion, rather than what he calmly observed. Yet not only could he always rely on the sympathy of other ardent Catholics; but he could also, when he chose, record normally seen appearances.

De Hooch was more objective than subjective, more visual than visionary. He recorded soberly what others could have observed calmly. Yet the nicety of his design and the restrained emphasis of his colour show that, under his calm, he felt personally and deeply.

El Greco's sincerity is more evident than his sanity and De Hooch's sanity more evident than his sincerity; but both artists possessed both virtues. In an age in which we meet far too often with professed works of art that succeed in cleverness but fail in sincerity, we are apt to prize sincerity above sanity. Hence the cult of art by the insane. Madness is a guarantee of sincerity, though frequently not of clarity. Though it is reasonable to prefer the sincere work of a madman to the insincere work of a sane person, such an estimate does not close the subject; it is well to retrieve one's sense of proportion by studying the work of some great painter, like Rubens or Renoir, Poussin or Cézanne, whose sincerity is equalled by his sanity.

Occasionally, however, insanity is accompanied by an intensely emotional response to something which the sane person is capable of feeling, but has not yet felt. In such cases we must be grateful to the madman for enlarging our experience. Most of us never found touching and looking at the seed-case of a sunflower exciting until we saw Van Gogh's painting (T.G. 3863). His *Chair* (T.G. 3862) has similar qualities. But in these cases, though we infer that Van Gogh's insanity was connected with his susceptibility to certain emotions, the pictures prove not his insanity, but merely the intensity of his feelings. Moreover, highly subjective though the inspiration of these pictures is, it clearly springs from things concrete and objective. In contrast, his *Cypresses* (T.G. 3861), in which there is far less objective basis for the emotion, is more disturbed, but less moving.

But although Van Gogh's best flower-pieces, still-lifes and landscapes are immediately and even lastingly stimulating, there are other moods which only a more balanced and intellectual art can satisfy. The deepest emotions are reached only through the intellect. Cézanne is less easy to appreciate than Van Gogh; but his greater intellect and his capacity for a wider range of feelings makes his art no mere stimulant, but, when digested, a staple diet.

The spectator, like the artist, cannot always be objective. Some art with a partly abnormal flavour will always have its devotees. For instance I enjoy Gauguin's painting, though it expresses narrower and less normal emotions even than Van Gogh's and contains even more stimulant and less nourishment. But a person who dislikes Gauguin is missing less than one who dislikes Cézanne or Renoir.

The greatest artist gives forth that part of himself which eventually the widest public will cherish. His emotion is deep and its applicability wide. The qualities of awe and wonder that inspire the greatest art make it in the widest sense religious (see also p. 54).

Great art is also religious in that it leads into positive, not negative channels. Even the art which extols the physical joys of existence can become an act of praise. And art, if it be worthy of the name, when it deals with the blacker aspects of life, evokes courage, not despair, philosophical acceptance of inevitable griefs and active resistance of remediable evils. It is not merely the expression of painful emotions, but the expression of their mastery that has the power to achieve what Milton, translating Aristotle, calls the purging of the soul by pity and fear.

Great tragic art does not present despair as final and irrevocable. The hero of tragedy is noble, not merely pitiable. His likeness to ourselves evokes our sympathy with him and extends it to others. It enables us to see our own griefs in proportion to universal experience. Even the villain of great tragedy often has the attributes of a fallen angel. The Judas of Leonardo's *Last Supper* at Milan has retained his conscience.

Secondly, great tragic art is not measured by the loud ranting of the actors, nor great comic art by their gift for playing to the gallery. Both, but especially tragedy, require restraint in the means of expression. A voice louder and gestures more emphatic than the voice and gestures of ordinary life may be necessary to enable the audience to see and hear; but loudness, restlessness and violence, carried too far, insult the intelligence. In painting, we may be similarly insulted by over-violent contrasts of line, tone, colour or even pigment or too much movement, unrelieved by repose.

The recipient prefers some reticence in the expression of the artist's passion. Otherwise his sympathies are alienated and he suspects insincerity. Roger Fry suggests that every great classic artist is a repressed romantic. This implies the double need for the deep emotion itself and for the restraint with which the emotion is given utterance. Both are necessary. The spectator's emotions can never be aroused, unless the artist has genuinely experienced them, nor unless they have been expressed with some restraint (see also p. 2).

Restraint in style is strictly a means of expressing emotion and not therefore nominally a topic for these chapters, which are concerned with emotions themselves. But it is relevant to the present discussion, because the true artist, in expressing his emotions, instinctively and invariably exercises restraint. This applies even to Rubens, who so evidently believed that 'you cannot have too much of a good thing'. But vivacious, flowing and extravagant though his style is, it emphatically *is* a style, clear, selective and coherent, not an outpouring of emotions in mere disorder. Conversely restraint is more conspicuous than emotion in the later work of Nicolas Poussin; so imbued is it with moderation and reasoned balance; but it would be the height of superficiality to fail to detect the deep feeling inspiring such masterpieces as the *Landscape with the Woman of Megara* (Earl of Derby), some of the qualities of which can be seen in his *Landscape with Figures* [(40), Pl. 55].

In addition to sincerity and restraint, the artist must show courage, humility and understanding sympathy in his attitude towards his subject, his medium and his public. Pandering to the public, by appealing to emotions one despises, is not giving it sympathy.

The aim of art is to bring the emotions of spectator and artist into accord. When human beings are represented in a picture, their emotions are one of the means of achieving this. It is often necessary for brevity to speak as if the feelings of the artist and those of the characters in his picture were identical. Although this is an over-simplification of the facts, the artist must at least sympathize with the feeling of his characters.

CHAPTER XXIX

VIRTUES AND VICES

THE topic of the two remaining chapters is mainly the quality of the emotion expressed, but this often leads to a discussion about methods of expression. In this chapter, four praiseworthy qualities are discussed and each of them compared with a blameworthy quality superficially resembling it.

The eight virtues and vices are grouped in pairs:

    (i) Sensibility and Sentimentality;
    (ii) The Dramatic and the Theatrical;
    (iii) Idealism and Escapism;
    (iv) Popularity, good and bad.

Neither the virtues nor the vices are, of course, mutually exclusive.

(i) SENSIBILITY AND SENTIMENTALITY

I mean by sensibility the capacity to respond emotionally to experience, and, in the case of the artist, the power of expressing this response. This capacity is a primary condition for all artistic creation. Without it the other seven virtues under discussion here and in Chapter XXX cannot exist. There is no necessity for a picture to be dramatic, idealistic, popular, erotic, humorous, naïve or dependent upon tradition; whereas every picture must show sensibility.

For this reason, the first vice under consideration, sentimentality, i.e. sensibility misapplied or insincerely professed, is treated more fully than the other seven vices.

The word 'sentimentality' is used in a great variety of senses. Often it merely implies lack of sympathy with the sentiment expressed. This is unfair. The twentieth-century fear of sentimentality may be as great a foible as the nineteenth-century indulgence in it.

Yet the term can imply justifiable repugnance. The cause of this is often insincerity. Most of Millais' pictures of children express neither sympathy with the children nor even his own feelings about them, but merely what he expects the spectator to feel. In contrast there is genuine pathos in Velazquez's children (see p. 62) because of his wholehearted sympathy with them. The child in Renoir's

Les Parapluies [(3268), Pl. 80], may be less deeply understood but expresses at least the artist's own response to her charm.

Another type of sentimentality consists in pretending one emotion when actuated by another. Thus Greuze's professed admiration for youthful simplicity is merely a cloak for a crudely erotic impulse. His characters, such as the *Inconsolable Widow* (Wallace, 454), are frequently as gross hypocrites as he is himself.

Other painters, without being manifestly insincere, are justly called sentimental because of their own, and their characters' lack of restraint. The self-command of the Virgin in Francia's *Pietà* (180) arouses more sympathy than her lack of it in Correggio's *Christ taking Leave of His Mother* (4255) or *'Ecce Homo'* (15). Correggio is undoubtedly Francia's superior in *power* of expression, but in this case his inferior, both in the *quality* of the emotion expressed and in the *manner* of expressing it. His greatest masterpieces illustrate happy themes (see Pl. 40) in which the need for restraint is less than in treating the tragic.

El Greco's *Agony in the Garden* [(3476), Pl. 50] might seem at first to be a tragic theme expressed without restraint, but though the contrasts are violent, elements of restraint are supplied by the rigidly controlled geometrical design and the rigidly expectant immobility of Christ.

El Greco seemed merely neurotic to our grandparents. Murillo, whom they loved, often seems sentimental to us. Murillo was at his best as an objective observer, as in a *Spanish Peasant Boy* (74), and at his worst in such attempts at the visionary as the *Holy Family* (13). The fault of the latter is partly the portrayal of a weak gentleness and partly its visual equivalent—a softness of all kinds, textural and atmospheric. Sentimentality indeed implies understatement as often as overstatement.

As applied to modes of human behaviour, sentimentality often means indulging in emotions with insufficient cause. This implies not exactly insincerity, but certainly self-deception. Artists, as well as visitors to galleries, may be guilty of it. It often takes the form of that ignoble, if genuine and powerful emotion, self-pity. This in turn leads to a kind of spurious sympathy, the practice, not of entering into the feelings of others, but of pretending that they are identical with one's own.

On the other hand, the form of self-deception described and condemned by Ruskin as the 'pathetic fallacy', the pretence that the mood of Man's natural surroundings reflect his own mood, is not merely defensible, but necessary to some branches of art. The tormented writhing clouds and dark hills in Andrea dal

Castagno's *Crucifixion* [(1138), Pl. 13] are as necessary to the completeness of the vision as the sunrise in Giovanni Bellini's *Agony in the Garden* [(726), Pl. 19; see also p. 56)]. .

(ii) THE DRAMATIC AND THE THEATRICAL

Both these words mean literally 'like what occurs on the stage'; but 'dramatic' implies merit and 'theatrical' blame. It is not the business of one art to imitate another. Only a few masterpieces of painting can be described as dramatic; and even in these cases the analogy applies only to certain aspects of the two arts.

Yet some generalizations are applicable to both. The business of both arts is to be loyal to the medium as well as true to Nature, not merely to imitate life, but to comment upon it by means of the special capabilities of the art in question. We may accept many conventions on the stage that are not 'true to life'; and it is only when their violence or awkwardness hurt us that we call them unnatural. Ballets and operas are allowed even more licence; and in painting there are analogous conventions, dramatic rather than technical. The poses of the figures in Rubens's *Rape of the Sabine Women* [(38), Pl. 53] bear the same kind of relation to real life as the movements of the dancers in a ballet. This is also true (allowing for their immobility) of the figures in Van Dyck's *Villiers Brothers* (3605) and in Veronese's allegories [(1318, 1324–6), see Pl. 49]. In these cases there is no distortion of proportions and no one is in an attitude impossible to adopt, however improbable it may be. The skilful use of a frankly artificial pose is accepted as natural; whereas an awkward pretence of naturalness, as in Zoffany's conversation pieces, is at once condemned as artificial.

Veronese, however, is the last painter who could be described as dramatic. The word usually refers to crises in which individual characters react on each other.

Other great painters, such as Raphael, had their dramatic moments, but were not in the main dramatic. In contrast, Titian and Rembrandt, though capable of quieter moods, were powerful illustrators of human crises. This is apparent in three of the four works by Titian reproduced here and in Rembrandt's *Woman taken in Adultery* [(45), Pl. 58].

The representation of movement or potential movement is essential to a dramatic painting. In Andrea dal Castagno's *Crucifixion* [(1138), Pl. 13] the figures are represented as momentarily still, but as having the power to move. In Antonello da Messina's *Crucifixion* (1166) they are permanently quiescent from choice.

Reasons for the rarity of good dramatic pictures are the difficulty of representing movement and the difficulty of expressing the dramatic, especially the tragically dramatic, with sincerity and restraint. Thus the actor's emotions in the best illustrations of the *Entombment*, such as Bouts's [(664), Pl. 15] and Michelangelo's [(790), Pl. 31], are expressed with more restraint than Titian's *Noli Me Tangere* [(270), Pl. 33], which illustrates a happy theme.

Good examples of one branch of dramatic painting, the horrific or *macabre*, are rarer still. This may be partly because taste in these matters changes from age to age, almost as much as taste in humour.

A satisfactory expression in painting of the emotion of fear has seldom been achieved. Goya stands out as a master of the *macabre*, but even he sometimes failed in this vein. Of his horrific works, his larger oil paintings are often less convincing as visions than his disturbing etchings or the superb *Bewitched Man* [(1472), Pl. 69]. Blake was also a past-master in making the flesh creep. His *Pity* (T.G. 5062) and *Hecate* (T.G. 5056) are striking examples; but others inspired by these aims (such as *Nebuchadnezzar* of the same group) come dangerously near to the ridiculous.

The epithets 'dramatic' and 'theatrical' can reasonably be extended from figure compositions to 'sublime' landscapes (see p. 64). In a few quieter, more restrained instances, such as Wilson's *Cader Idris* (5596) or Turner's *Ship Aground* [(T.G. 2065), of about 1829] the 'sublime' mood produced a masterpiece; but more often attempts to express it failed by insincerity or loudness of utterance. Of seventeenth-century examples, three by Elsheimer in the National Gallery just escape being theatrical by being small; but Salvator Rosa's *Mercury and the Woodman* (84) is crudely unrestrained; Ruisdael's *Waterfalls* (628 and 737) and Bakhuisen's stormier seascapes (see 819) are too literal in detail and too forced in tone to communicate the exultation intended.

So-called romanticism, as it appears in paintings from *c.* 1780 to 1850, often implies in practice a willingness to sacrifice formal values of design to the associations aroused by the subject; but the romantics failed in sincerity of vision quite as often by forcing their turbulent groups into conventionally balanced compositions. This is what is wrong with most of the oil paintings of their forerunner Fuseli and with Delacroix's *Liberty Guiding the People* (Louvre). But the great romantics had their great moments. In the *Free Races at Rouen* (Rouen) Géricault, in restrained language, expressed excitement, strength and speed; and few nightmares in painting are more convincing than Delacroix's sketch of the *Shipwreck of*

Don Juan (V. and A.) in which the compact group in and around the boat is surrounded by a dark infinity of sky and sea.

(iii) IDEALISM AND ESCAPISM

Most critics of to-day are as severe as any Victorian in condemning 'escapism', i.e. taking refuge from hard present-day realities in agreeable dreams of the imagination. This tendency certainly led in the nineteenth century to repulsive results: the languishing ladies of late Rossetti; the tired, timid larger canvases of Burne-Jones; and worse, the many shallow masquerades, not even now quite extinct, in the costume of Arabia or the Middle Ages. In such instances 'the idiot who praises with enthusiastic tone every century but this and every country but his own' certainly deserves condemnation; but the weakness of such examples of escapist art does not prove that the literal description of the most unpleasant contemporary facts is the only legitimate field for the artist. Those who condemn Victorian escapism evidently do not think so, when they uphold abstract art and surrealism.

In fact it is not easy to distinguish between escapism and what I am calling here 'idealism'. By this I mean that dissatisfaction with things as they are, that yearning for a better existence, which has inspired poets, musicians and painters since the arts began. The dream has taken various forms: the golden age; paradise; Utopia. From the ethical standpoint such dreams are good, when they are for the betterment of the world, and bad when they produce despair or the shutting of the eyes to the existence of evil.

Art, however, cannot be so simply judged. Sincerity and clarity in the expression of *any* emotion are the first criteria of good art, but not the only criteria. The purpose of art is not directly to stimulate the recipient to action, but rather to provide him with refreshment, emotional, intellectual and spiritual. A picture, therefore, must have *some* merit if it expresses genuine escapist emotions in terms of a clear vision; but if the emotions contain some positive message for man as a whole, its merit increased.

When, however, particular works of art come to be examined, the dividing line between idealism and escapism cannot easily be drawn. What about the work of Gauguin for instance? He escaped from civilization and sought a golden-age existence in Tahiti; but his art, steeped though it is in abnormal flavours, is too vital a stimulant, too dependent on real experience to be called escapist in the worst sense.

Or again to take a very different case, what about Fra Angelico? His very saintliness often involved timidity. He shirked the fact of human wickedness. His villains look feeble or sorry for what they are doing, or else are represented symbolically by a head or hand only, as in the impressive *Mockery of Christ* (San Marco, Florence). He could never have achieved the grand tragic realism of Giotto's *Mockery* at Padua, an epitome of varied individual passions, good and bad. Yet Angelico was not merely the mild recluse that sentimental admirers and anti-sentimental disparagers would make him. His *Transfiguration* (San Marco) expresses, in addition to his usual sweetness, a generous strength.

In medieval times poets and painters expressed their dreams of ideal happiness by visions of Heaven. With the development of the Renaissance they tended more to dream of a golden age upon earth. The art of Botticelli is transitional in alternating between these two dreams, his Christian subjects being inspired by a hunger and thirst after righteousness and his Pagan subjects by a yearning for perfect beauty. In both the passion, if vague, is too intense to be justly termed escapist. An underlying strength of intellect, latent in his Madonna tondos, becomes apparent in his powerful *S. Augustine* (Ognissanti, Florence); and again the superficial estimate of the *Birth of Venus* (Uffizi) as merely languorous may be corrected by a study of the *Calumny of Apelles* (Uffizi), a vision, bitter in inspiration and harsh in expression.

At first sight such pictures as the *Concert Champêtre* in the Louvre by either Giorgione or Titian might seem to express nothing but the desire for an irresponsible existence of endless leisure; but when this famous masterpiece was first painted the contemporary clothes of the men brought it into closer contact with real life.

Most of Watteau's work may make a similar first impression, subsequently to be corrected by a study of his brilliantly remembered poses. Watteau drew his inspiration from contemporary court dresses and court manners, idealizing what he saw and infusing into it his own spirit of melancholy sweetness. A century and a half later the colder temperament of Manet in his *Déjeuner sur l'herbe* (Louvre) hardly succeeded as well as Watteau, in recapturing the poetry of the first of the *Concerts Champêtres*.

(iv) POPULARITY, GOOD AND BAD

The word 'popular' as applied to art tends increasingly to be used disparagingly. The popular artist and the man 'who plays to the gallery' are identified. It is certainly easier to point to examples of popular art in the bad, than in the good, sense. Yet good popular art, like good light music, exists. The fact that a picture has an immediate appeal does not of itself prove anything about its lasting appeal.

The crux of the question is the painter's attitude towards his potential public. If he sincerely believes in what he has to express, his art may be popular in the good sense. It is bad if he panders to a mood that he despises.

Much depends upon what kind of public is implied by the word 'popular'. The uninstructed public of seventeenth-century Holland had many tastes in common with that of twentieth-century England. The painter who achieves a justifiable popular appeal tactfully leads such a public. Jan Steen's *Skittle Alley* (2560) will first be liked for the anecdotal interest, the action and the details, then for the truth of the lighting, and last for the completeness and unity of the design. Or again one may be led by the gay colour of De Hooch's *Interior of a Dutch House* [(834), Pl. 63] to study its lighting and composition or by the prettiness of the girls in Renoir's *Les Parapluies* [(3268), Pl. 80] to appreciate the colour, atmosphere, brush-work and pattern.

Other painters, often greater (Piero della Francesca, Poussin and Cézanne are among them), provide this uninstructed public with no such pleasant introductions. Appreciation of their work demands patience in understanding what is at first obscure, alien or even repugnant.

The popular picture in the bad sense appeals to first impressions only. No one, experienced or inexperienced, can want to look at it frequently for long. The bad kind of popularity is even harder to define than sentimentality. It usually implies insensitiveness, lack of true feeling, and in art is usually the result of conceit. Conceit being a false estimate of one's abilities, or an overestimate of those that are least important, is both a moral and an intellectual failing. The bad popular painter is disrespectful to his public (condescending or flattering or both)— and equally disrespectful to his chosen subject—so that true vision is impossible. In seeking to arrest the spectator's immediate attention, he sacrifices everything else to some single effect, a loud contrast or display of technical skill.

The painter who thus caters solely for an immediate response can never satisfy posterity. He must inevitably propitiate passing fashions. His art is bound to be superficial. He may not be a conscious hypocrite; but he will pay disproportionate attention to externals and neglect fundamentals.

The wrong sort of popularity consists as often of flattering the dress circle as of playing to the gallery. In early art it is relatively rare. It becomes apparent first among the many non-Italian painters of the late fifteenth century, who imitated the grandeurs and graces of Italian art without understanding them. Since then, pretentiousness among painters similar in spirit, but varying in its outward guise, has become increasingly common. Such art is inevitably encouraged by increasing commercial competition.

In the first decades of this century, this often took the form of a show of rapid execution, not unlike that of G. B. Tiepolo's *Madonna and Child with Saints* (2513). Laborious smoothness can be as ostentatious as careless freedom. In Van der Werff's *Repose in Egypt* (3909) this is combined with startling, insensitive colour and a forced cult of elegance; in J. Van Os's *Fruit Flowers and Dead Birds* (1015) with a display of shining objects, displayed for the plutocrat's pride.

A picture with a lasting appeal can be appreciated for many qualities and from many standpoints. One that aims exclusively at gaining an immediate response necessarily usually depends on one characteristic. The shock of discovery that what looks like a fly on the head-dress of the *Lady* (722) by a German artist is only cleverly applied paint is an experience not to be repeated. The startling greens of J. F. Lewis's *Siesta* (3594) prevent any pleasure in returning to it.

CHAPTER XXX

MORE VIRTUES AND VICES

FOUR more virtues and four more vices superficially like them may now be considered:

      (i) Eroticism, good and bad;
     (ii) Humour and Facetiousness;
   (iii) *Naïveté*, genuine and spurious;
   (iv) The Traditional and the Derivative.

(i) EROTICISM, GOOD AND BAD

Many would applaud one picture and condemn another for apparently the same reason, the erotic impulse behind its creation. Only when the nature of the impulse and the manner of its expression have been analysed, can a just conclusion be reached.

The causes of the erotic emotion and its effects upon life are outside the scope of this book. I can only begin the discussion with platitudes: the erotic emotion is complex; the subconscious mind plays a large part in it; and its character varies with each individual and even with each of his moods. As expressed by the painter, it may vary from a purely physical passion to a yearning so spiritualized as to seem almost devoid of anything bodily. Between these extremes occurs an infinite series of emotions, in which the physical and spiritual are mixed in varying proportions. The ideal in art is an approximate balance between these two aspects of the emotion.

As with other emotions, the value of the erotic impulse that inspires any given picture depends largely upon the painter's sincerity, courage and humility. Humility implies restraint in that it involves a certain reverence and wonder, which prevents the artist from over-particularizing his emotions. One reason why Velazquez's *Venus and Cupid* [(2057), Pl. 65] is so moving is the reticence shown in emphasizing the general characteristics of young womanhood, rather than the individual traits of a particular young woman.

Bad erotic art arises from failure to feel deeply or justly in matters erotic. Many such failures are closely interconnected. Thus it is not uncommon to find combined insincerity, cowardice (especially disguised as bravado) and an arrogant lack of humility.

Painters guilty of insincerity in this connexion are of two kinds: those who pretend that their emotion is not erotic, when it really is; and those who pretend that it is erotic, when it really is not. There is a third kind of pretence: in his *Head of a Girl* (206) Greuze professed an unreal tenderness, when inspired by a real sensuality. Boucher satisfies present-day taste much better by his exclusively and undisguisedly physical inspiration.

The second form of pretence, the profession of a non-existent erotic impulse, is commoner than the first and quite as offensive. It mars many contemporary paintings of the nude. Pictures of nudes are not obliged to express erotic emotions. It is only when an erotic purpose is intended that one complains of its absence. Sometimes it may have moved the painter before he began to paint, but if all evidence of it has vanished from the completed work our feelings must remain cold. No picture in the National Gallery suffers from this fault at its worst; but Bronzino's *Venus, Cupid, Folly and Time* (651) for all its decorative merits, lacks warmth of inspiration.

Lack of courage in this connexion takes two forms: (i) timidity, pure and simple; (ii) bravado. Those of the first type usually aim at expressing the spiritual and those of the second type the physical, aspect. Burne-Jones, as in the *Car of Love* (V. and A.), is an example of the first type.

Bravado has equally displeasing results. Some painters express erotic emotions forcedly, betraying by their very lack of restraint that they are half-ashamed of them. This attitude is almost as common to-day and as objectionable as the profession of non-existent erotic feelings. The exhibitionist spirit is all the more revolting because the artist is a coward about confessing his own cowardice.

Some of Rembrandt's works might at first sight seem open to the same charge. Rembrandt had none of Rubens's straightforward and unabashed power of expressing the erotic. His deeply moving *Hendrickje Stoffels in Bed* (Edinburgh) and even his beautiful *Woman Bathing* [(54), Pl. 59] prove the intensity of what he felt but also an attitude of guilt towards it—a guilt which he is no coward in confessing. The emotion is bound up with awe and reverence, and, while unmistakably involving strong physical desires, involves also even greater tenderness.

Lack of humility is usually combined with exhibitionism and often with over-emphasis upon the individual model. This is undesirable, when a strongly physical element has entered into his sitter's attraction for him. In portraits in which the attraction has been mainly of the spirit, more emphasis upon individuality is allowable; though even in this case (see pp. 61–2) the portraits most expressive of feminine charm emphasize something shared by many women.

A tendency of some erotic painting is that of making the actors of the drama self-conscious. Absurd and childish examples of this occur in most nudes by Lucas Cranach, such as *Charity* (2925). In Goya's *Maja Ignuda* (Prado, Madrid), a far more sophisticated conception, the self-consciousness has dignity and pathos. On the other hand Correggio's *Venus, Mercury and Cupid* [(10), Pl. 40] loses in dignity what it gains in charm from the actors' consciousness of the audience (see p. 59).

As to erotic inspiration at its best, each masterpiece, according to the painter's temperament and mood, has its own particular flavour. Velazquez in *Venus and Cupid* [(2057), Pl. 65] combined deep, but comparatively calm feeling with a perfect balance between the physical and the spiritual. Titian, in his prime, in *Bacchus and Ariadne* [(35), Pl. 36] imparted drama to an equally perfect balance; and in his old age, in *Medor and Angelica* (Vienna) still maintained this balance, though his mood had changed to contemplative brooding.

Other great painters tended to stress the physical more than the spiritual or vice versa. At one extreme such painters as Boucher in *Venus, Mars and Vulcan* (Wallace, 238) and Fragonard in the *Swing* (Wallace, 430) narrowed their appeal, but increased its immediate force by concentrating solely on the physical. At the other extreme Gainsborough, by expressing an almost exclusively spiritual response to feminine charm, achieved an unsubstantial sweetness incompatible with much strength.

Rubens, without entirely ignoring the spiritual, laid great stress upon the physical. In this respect Renoir resembled Rubens, though he expressed himself with French grace rather than Flemish vigour. Watteau, technically like Rubens, was emotionally nearer to Gainsborough; but his perception of the body's movements made his work more solid.

Other examples, each with a different and indefinable flavour, might be multiplied, only to prove once more the impossibility of translating the visual into the verbal.

(ii) HUMOUR AND FACETIOUSNESS

Humour has never been satisfactorily defined. It is a fundamental emotion and one of the emotions expressible by the arts. Attempts to define humour are inevitably humourless. Here, therefore, I only suggest some of its causes and some of its results.

Humour involves pleasure in noting the incongruous. Contrast can exist without humour, but not humour without contrast. When we call something absurd, we are commenting on the unsuitability of one thing in relation to another, and usually of one human being in relation to his surroundings. For humour is confined to things human or what reminds us of things human.

Humour is apt to be topical. It is well known that the humour of one century or nationality usually fails to appeal to another. Its ephemeral appeal may be one reason why it plays so small a part in painting as compared with literature. Books are to be read from time to time, when the mood demands them; illustrations to books may serve a similar purpose; but pictures, hanging permanently on the walls of buildings, need to appeal to a greater variety of moods; and those most valued by posterity are usually inspired by emotions other than the humorous.

In distinguishing humour from wit, it is convenient to define humour as mainly an emotion and wit as mainly a mode of expression, humour as an attitude towards experience and wit as a manner of expressing an experience. Wit in its primary sense is an attribute of something verbal, a special felicity in the choice of words. Strictly speaking therefore a picture can express humour, but cannot be painted wittily. On the other hand, if analogies be allowed between the two arts, there are more successfully witty, than successfully humorous, pictures. Much French painting has qualities analogous to the French command of verbal wit. Degas' *La Plage* [(T.G. 3247), Pl. 76] might be described as both witty and humorous, the wit being shown in the skilled juxtaposition of unexpected shapes and the humour in the insight into individual characters.

Humour, however, is no more indispensable to a great painter than to a great poet. Painters deeply inspired by respect for the dignity of man are often entirely without it. If Veronese had had any sense of humour, he could not have painted *Happy Union* (1326) or its three companion pictures (see Pl. 49). If Rubens had had any sense of humour, he could not have painted the *Apotheosis of the Duke of Buckingham* (?) (187).

Italian painting, which has kept up a higher continuous standard than the painting of any other European country, has been almost totally devoid of deliberately humorous intention. Even the rare exceptions, such as Carpaccio's *S. Jerome introducing his Lion into the Monastery* (San Giorgio dei Schiavoni, Venice) are of the most childlike order. Unintentional humour, as in Uccello's *Rout of San Romano* [(583), Pl. 16] is often met with in Italian art; and gaiety of the playful sort, both naïve and sophisticated, is more frequent still; but of humour, such as abounds in English literature, there is nothing. No one misses it; its absence is infinitely preferable to the forced introduction of jokes into pictures.

Now certain painters, without introducing anything specifically humorous into their works, give the impression of a latent humorous capacity. This impression is given by Chardin's *The Lesson* [(4077), Pl. 67] and Rembrandt's *Woman taken in Adultery* [(45), Pl. 58] and *Adoration of the Shepherds* (47).

Facetiousness in conversation, the forced effort to be funny, has an analogy with the dragging in of a joke into a picture, made irritatingly obvious by a smiling or gesticulating character, such as the lady in Maes's *Idle Servant* (207). The same artist shows much more true humour in the *Cook-Maid* (159) in which both the woman and the child are entirely serious. A jest that no one can miss quickly palls. It is greatly preferable to come upon the joke by degrees as in Steen's *Music Master* (856), or even not to be quite sure how far humour is intended, as in his *Terrace Scene with Figures* (1421) or Terborch's *Guitar Lesson* (864).

A smile, if introduced at all, needs to be a masterpiece of spontaneous observation, like that of the old man half leaning on the table in Teniers's *Players at Tric Trac* (242).

The above examples are all by Dutch and Flemish artists of the seventeenth century; humour was already latent in fifteenth-century Dutch and Flemish art and had reached a climax in the 1560's in the work of Pieter Bruegel [see his *Adoration of the Magi* (3556), Pl. 43]. Bruegel, indeed, combined spontaneous humour with visionary inspiration in a manner rare among European painters. In the seventeenth century, the artist who most nearly approached him was Adriaen Brouwer (see p. 68); but Brouwer had less creative invention; and Steen, though gifted with a similar geniality, was not so invariably spontaneous.

True humour is distinguishable from gaiety on the one hand and the more bitter sort of satire on the other. In portraiture it is possible to be humorous without being satirical, as Reynolds was in his portrait of *Dr Johnson* (887) or Hogarth in his *Servants* (1374). The portrait of Johnson is a rare example of humour made compatible with dignity. Of satire in painting too bitter strictly to be humorous, the most striking European exponents were Goya and Daumier. Hogarth's satire and also his humour were sometimes forced; but in *Calais Gate* [(1464), Pl. 68] he achieved a happy blend of both, combined with more than a hint of a sentiment perfectly compatible with humour, namely pathos.

(iii) *NAÏVETÉ*, GENUINE AND SPURIOUS

A genuinely childlike simplicity of outlook on the part of a painter is an added attraction to his work; but such simplicity, under modern conditions, becomes increasingly rare; and the pretence of possessing it is an affectation. A few temperaments may successfully recapture the emotions of their childhood; but conscious attempts are usually insincere. For the consciousness of the aim destroys the *naïveté* of the result.

Naïveté may be shown in the artist's attitude towards life or in his lack of realistic or decorative skill. Antoine Le Nain's *Portrait Group* (1425) combines all these qualities, but though genuine, is hardly a masterpiece.

On the other hand a childlike attitude towards life may accompany consummate skill in the art of expression. There is a *naïveté* of mood but not of method about Stubbs's *Phaeton and Pair* (3529). That simplicity of feeling and subtlety of invention are compatible is evident in the work of Rembrandt. An example is the little boy who brings his large dog to worship in the *Adoration of the Shepherds* (47) some of whose *naïveté* is shared by the artist. In other cases too Rembrandt's illustrations of the Bible have a childlike literalness and his self-portraits, while they reveal the complexity of his intellect, also bring to light his unselfconscious simplicity. Cézanne is an even more extreme example of searching brains and singleness of soul.

Veronese and Van Dyck both admired good manners, and were both skilled in imparting to their sitters a studied elegance of pose; but, whereas Van Dyck was sophisticated through and through, Veronese's admiration was essentially naïve.

Sophistication is by no means in itself a vice. Often, as in Titian's case, it accompanies the rarest wealth of invention. An understanding expression of complex problems may add to a picture's lasting powers. Nor does complex emotional content necessarily involve complex expression.

There is, however, a type of sophistication that is *ipso facto* vicious, that of the artist who has nothing to express, but knows all the tricks of the trade. Impatience with this is responsible for the present vogue of the naïve. But *naïveté* is not to be had for the asking. An artist who is asked to be simple, ceases to be simple. Henri Rousseau's works have great charm, partly because he did not know that he was naïve.

Primitive art, whether ancient or modern, is often to be admired, because of the artist's instinctive genius for creating design out of the limitations of his material. In archaic art this quality may even be helped by lack of realism. But archaistic art, the deliberate revival of the archaic, has no such pleasing results. After a period of sophisticated skill, even when skill (an inspiration at first) has ultimately deadened inspiration, it is impossible consciously to return to an earlier outlook.

Henri Rousseau's work is the result of an instinctive bias, not of a deliberate aim; and naïve though he was, he was also supremely skilled in the gift that mattered to him, the invention of pattern.

Conscious imitators of Rousseau are never so convincing; yet there are ways in which painters can consciously learn from primitive art. Matisse, whom no one would accuse of *naïveté*, uses certain external traits of primitive art and turns them to his own highly sophisticated purposes.

Even genuine *naïveté* may be overvalued. So far as it goes, that of Margaritone contributes to the vivacious execution of his *Scenes in the Lives of Saints* surrounding his *Madonna and Child* (564); but there are works by Giotto and even Duccio, one degree less naïve in mood and many degrees richer in design and vision.

(iv) THE TRADITIONAL AND THE DERIVATIVE

The scorn often poured on derivative art can be misleading. Every artist inevitably derives some of his ideas from others. His merit cannot be judged by the fact of his indebtedness, but only by what he makes of his borrowings. Derivative artists in the bad sense copy the letter and miss the spirit. Originality consists, not in independence of tradition, but in the power to develop a tradition and expand it.

In any case, originality is not attainable as a conscious aim. Many would-be artists have not got it in them to be original; while the originality of others is evident however much they borrow and even the more they borrow (see p. 9). Almost every great painter has had feeble followers unable to strike out on lines of their own. Too exclusive and unintelligent a dependence upon a single artist leads to feeble results; but an equally unintelligent dependence on many artists leads to nothing better.

Yet there is a type of painter whose originality grows by degrees out of his powers of imitation. Raphael began by absorbing the style of one painter after another, until suddenly he combined them all in what has the air of a complete novelty, the *School of Philosophers* [(Vatican, Pl. 35)]. Poussin's genius was of a similar kind; but even his most obvious plagiarisms have a flavour utterly different from their source; in his *Cephalus and Aurora* (65) the turn of Cephalus's neck and torso comes directly from the pose of Bacchus in *Bacchus and Ariadne* [(35), Pl. 36]; but the lover's emotion, though tense, is expressed with restraint and has none of the abandonment of Titian's figure.

Every sensitive artist is indebted both to other men's works and to Nature. 'Study Nature attentively', wrote Reynolds in his Sixth Discourse, 'but always with those masters in your company': a wise supplement to his persistent advice to study other painters. The greatest examples prove its soundness. The debt of Raphael and Poussin to Nature, especially in their later works, is as great as their more obvious debt to other painters. On the other hand Constable's work at first appears a transcript of what he saw, independent of tradition, and his own remarks about 'seeing no handling in Nature' encourage this impression; but investigation proves his respect for traditional technique and his indebtedness to Girtin, Gainsborough and Rubens.

The claim to be 'natural' and 'realistic' often goes with the boast made by Caravaggio and Courbet, of owing nothing to tradition. But Caravaggio towers above almost all his non-Italian imitators partly because of the linear tradition he had unconsciously inherited; and the best work of Courbet (the most unequal of great painters) repeatedly proves how much he owed to the seventeenth-century Spaniards.

The view that genius is a capacity for taking infinite pains, though not the whole of the truth, constitutes a great part of it. Inborn enthusiasm, also a requisite of genius, can never bear fruit, unless supported by infinite pains; and part of these pains must be applied to studying other masters. The rich creative variety of the works of Titian, Rembrandt, Velazquez and Turner owes much to their power of discovering, transforming and re-combining the methods of their predecessors— even sometimes of their most insignificant predecessors. This is what makes the minor instructors of great men, the Lastmans and Thomas Maltons, more interesting than the great man's pupils, such as Dou or Mazo; for, though the little man learns little from the great man, the great man learns wonders from the little man. The mere imitator misses the meaning of what he imitates; the genius gives it new meaning.

Every artist, except the first prehistoric inventor of outline, has always owed something to his predecessors. Bruegel owed less than most; but Bosch's example first put him on his path. El Greco, an apparent freak in European art, depended imaginatively on Byzantine, and technically upon Venetian, traditions.

It is not always his immediate predecessors upon whom a painter depends. He may react from them and turn to artists of the remote past or of a remote nationality. Revolutions are sometimes necessary in painting as in politics. A prevailing tradition may have become stale or unusable. When a painter carries out certain aims to perfection, his very perfection may paralyse his successors. They need to strike out on fresh lines. But this freshness can never be complete newness. Their work must in some respects resemble what has existed before. Thus, when Cavallini and Giotto rejected the prevailing and long-standing Byzantine tradition of symbolic flat pattern, they turned for inspiration not only to Nature, but also to ancient Roman sculpture. So in this century, those who have broken away from the long tradition of representational realism have derived at least *some* of their ideas from traditions, ancient or Oriental, that accepted something other than realism as their main aim.

Conservatism for its own sake has its dangers. Respect for tradition is not enough. The tradition needs to be supplemented by something else. Even Reynolds's reasonable advice to combine those qualities for which the greatest artists were most remarkable, has often led to the tepidly academic. Painters cannot afford to broaden their tastes as much as art critics. Or, if their admiration be wide, they must reject the influence of much that they admire. But a revolution for its own sake is more dangerous still. The humility that partly depends upon others is a surer foundation for excellence than the pride that strives to stand alone. Humility inspired Duccio's tenderly human *Madonna and Child* [(566), see Pl. 3]; and such humility has always belonged to those painters who best fulfil the most practical function of art, the refreshment, uplifting and strengthening of the spirit, which is as necessary to its life as food is to the life of the body.

PLATES

1. DUCCIO. *Christ Healing the Blind Man*, 1308–11

2. SCHOOL OF PISA? *Madonna and Child, c. 1230–50*

3. DUCCIO. Detail of *Madonna and Child, c.* 1290

4. AMBROGIO LORENZETTI. *Heads of Four Nuns, c.* 1330?

5. SPINELLO ARETINO. *Two Apostles, c.* 1380

6. FRENCH SCHOOL? *Wilton Diptych* (right half), *c.* 1395?

7. MASACCIO. *Madonna and Child*, 1426

8. PISANELLO. Detail of *Vision of S. Eustace, c.* 1430

9. FRA FILIPPO LIPPI. *Annunciation, c. 1450?*

10. JAN VAN EYCK. *Jan Arnolfini and his Wife*, 1434

11. JAN VAN EYCK. Detail of *Jan Arnolfini and his Wife*, 1434

13. ANDREA DAL CASTAGNO. *Crucifixion, c. 1445?*

14. SASSETTA. *Stigmatization of S. Francis*, 1437–44

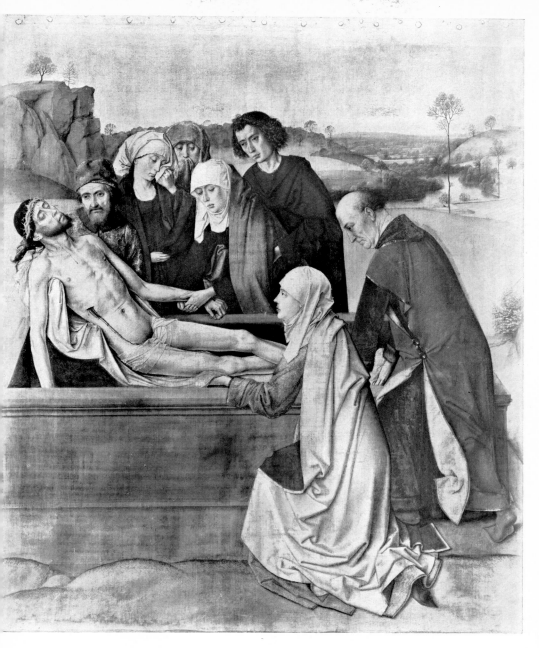

15. DIERIC BOUTS. *Entombment, c.* 1445?

16.   UCELLO.   *Rout of San Romano*, c. 1454–7

17. UCELLO. Detail of *Rout of San Romano, c.* 1454–7

19. GIOVANNI BELLINI. *Agony in the Garden, c.* 1460

20.　PIERO DELLA FRANCESCA.　*Baptism of Christ, c.* 1450?

21. PIERO DELLA FRANCESCA. *Nativity, c.* 1470

22b. COSIMO TURA. Detail of *Madonna and Child*
Enthroned, 1474–80?

22a. COSIMO TURA. Detail of *Madonna and Child*
Enthroned (infra-red photograph)

23. BALDOVINETTI. *Portrait of a Lady, c.* 1460

24. BOTTICELLI. *Mars, Venus and Satyrs, c.* 1475–80?

25. BOTTICELLI. Detail of *Mars, Venus and Satyrs, c.* 1475–80?

26.   GEERTGEN TOT SINT JANS.   *Nativity, c. 1480?*

27. FOPPA. *Adoration of the Magi, c.* 1490

28. BOTTICELLI. *Nativity*, 1500

29. LEONARDO DA VINCI. *Virgin of the Rocks*, after 1483, and 1506–8

30. MICHELANGELO. *Madonna and Child with S. John and Angels, c. 1495–1500?*

31. MICHELANGELO. *Entombment, c. 1512–16?*

32. RAPHAEL. *Ansidei Madonna*, 1506

33.   TITIAN.   *Noli Me Tangere, c.* 1514–15

34. Perugino. *Christ giving Keys to Peter* (Sistine Chapel, Vatican), 1482–3

35.   RAPHAEL.   *School of Philosophers* (Stanza della Segnatura, Vatican), 1509–11

36. TITIAN. *Bacchus and Ariadne, c.* 1516–20

37. TITIAN. *Venus and Adonis, c.* 1554

38. DÜRER. *The Painter's Father*, 1497

39. HOLBEIN. *Christina of Denmark, Duchess of Milan, 1538*

40. CORREGGIO. *Venus, Mercury and Cupid, c.* 1525

41.   CORREGGIO.   Detail of *Venus, Mercury and Cupid, c.* 1525

42. TINTORETTO. *S. George and the Dragon, c. 1555-60?*

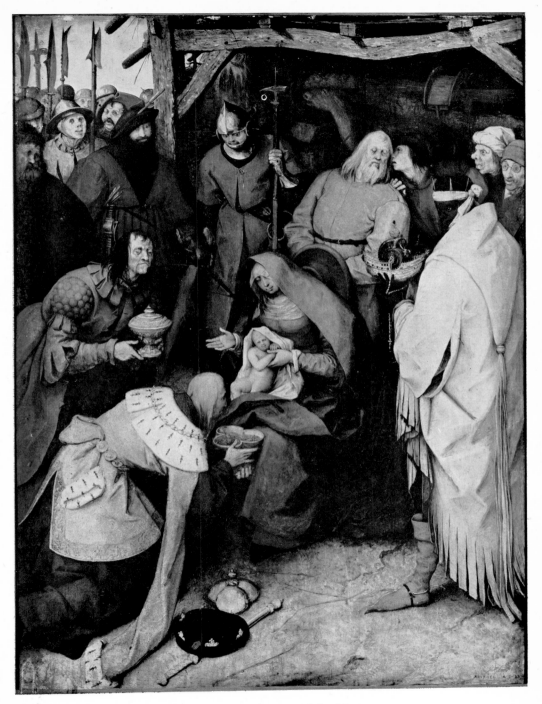

43. BRUEGEL. *Adoration of the Magi*, 1564

44. TITIAN. *Vendramin Family, c. 1545–50*

45. PAOLO VERONESE. *Family of Darius before Alexander, c. 1570?*

46. PAOLO VERONESE. Detail of Child from *Family of Darius before Alexander, c.* 1570?

47. PAOLO VERONESE. Detail of Alexander from *Family of Darius before Alexander*, *c.* 1570?

48.   TINTORETTO.   *Origin of the Milky Way, c. 1570?*

49. PAOLO VERONESE. *Unfaithfulness, c.* 1570?

51.   EL GRECO.   *Purification of the Temple, c. 1595–1600?*

52. CARAVAGGIO *Christ at Emmaus* c. 1595–1600

53. RUBENS. *Rape of the Sabine Women*, c. 1635

54. RUBENS. *Autumn: the Château de Steen,* 1636

55. NICOLAS POUSSIN. *Landscape with Figures, c.* 1650

56. CLAUDE. Detail of *Embarkation of S. Ursula*, 1641

57. ZURBARAN. *S. Francis*, 1639

58. REMBRANDT. *Woman taken in Adultery*, 1644

59. REMBRANDT. *Woman Bathing*, 1654

60. REMBRANDT. *Portrait of Himself at 34, 1640*

61. REMBRANDT. Detail of *Portrait of Himself when Old, c.* 1665–7

62. PIETER DE HOOCH. *Courtyard of a Dutch House, c.* 1655–60

63. PIETER DE HOOCH. *Interior of a Dutch House, c. 1655–60*

64. VERMEER. *Lady Standing at the Virginals*, after 1660

65. VELAZQUEZ. *Venus and Cupid, c. 1656—9*

66 WATTEAU La Gamme d'Amour c. 1710

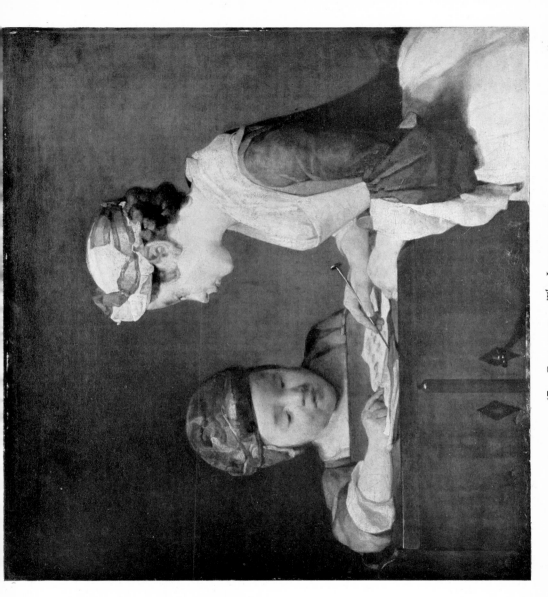

67. CHARDIN.   *The Lesson, c. 1740*

68 HOGARTH *Calais Gate* 1748

69. GOYA. *The Bewitched Man, c.* 1797–8

70. TURNER. *Calais Pier*, 1802

71. CROME. *Moonrise on the Marshes of the Yare, c. 1808*

72. TURNER. *Frosty Morning*, exhibited 1813

73. CONSTABLE. *Salisbury Cathedral, c.* 1831

74. FRITH. Detail of *Derby Day*, 1858

75. INGRES. *Madame Moitessier,* completed 1856

76. DEGAS. *La Plage, c. 1880?*

77. MANET. *Bar of the Folies Bergères* (Courtauld Institute), 1882

79. SEURAT. *La Baignade,* c. 1885–6

80. RENOIR. *Les Parapluies, 1879–83*

INDEX

[Names of painters are printed in large and small capitals and names of pictures in italics]